Between Gaia and Ground

BETWEEN

Four Axioms of Existence and the
Ancestral Catastrophe of Late Liberalism

AND

GAIA

Elizabeth A. Povinelli

GROUND

Duke University Press
Durham and London 2021

Project Editor: Lisl Hampton
Designed by Aimee C. Harrison
Typeset in Portrait Text and Antique Olive
by Copperline Book Services

Library of Congress Cataloging-in-Publication Data
Names: Povinelli, Elizabeth A., author.
Title: Between Gaia and ground : four axioms of existence and the
ancestral catastrophe of late liberalism / Elizabeth A. Povinelli.
Description: Durham : Duke University Press, 2021. | Includes
bibliographical references and index.
Identifiers: LCCN 2020051109 (print)
LCCN 2020051110 (ebook)
ISBN 9781478013648 (hardcover)
ISBN 9781478014577 (paperback)
ISBN 9781478021872 (ebook)
Subjects: LCSH: Ontology. | Biopolitics. | Ecology—Philosophy. |
Postcolonialism. | Liberalism. | Power (Philosophy) | Human
ecology. | Critical theory.
Classification: LCC BD311.P68 2021 (print) | LCC BD311 (ebook) |
DDC 111—dc23
LC record available at https://lccn.loc.gov/2020051109
LC ebook record available at https://lccn.loc.gov/2020051110

To my Karrabing family
Especially to my beloved Kaingmerrhe
My amazing first great-granddaughter

Run, run, run, run,
We run under the sun . . .

However entangled the petroleum's arteries may be,
however the layers may change their silent site
and move their sovereignty amid the earth's bowels,
when the fountain gushes its paraffin foliage,
Standard Oil arrived beforehand
with its checks and its guns,
with its governments and its prisoners.
—PABLO NERUDA, "Standard Oil Co.," 1940

CONTENTS

PREFACE

THE FINAL DRAFT OF THIS BOOK was completed during the beginning of the COVID-19 pandemic and in the midst of the Black Lives Matter protests against the murders of George Floyd, Breonna Taylor, Ahmaud Arbery, and countless other Black Americans. Some prefatory remarks seem important in light of these events and for guiding readers through this work.

First, although the chapters were conceived and written prior to the pandemic, the different discourses about COVID-19 and the starkly different impact of the virus on Black, brown, and Indigenous communities haunted my final edits, as they no doubt haunt the following pages. I make a few explicit references to the devastating landscapes of COVID-19, but I chose not to overly knead this immediate crisis into the discussion. Unfortunately, I don't think this crisis changes the fundamental point of this book, that the axioms on which a segment of critical common sense is now built—especially claims that existence is entangled—have no political content in and of themselves but can only derive their politics from the ongoing effects of the ancestral catastrophe of colonialism and slavery. In other words, structural racism and colonialism and their devastating effects on the health of Black, brown, and Indigenous bodies and their environments existed long before COVID-19. The catastrophe of climate change, toxic exposure, and viral pandemics are not *à venir*—they are not on the horizon coming toward those staring at it. These are the ancestral catastrophes that began with the brutal dispossession of human and more-than-human worlds and a vicious extraction of human and more-than-human labor. These dispossessions and extractions gave birth to liberalism and capitalism, and alongside them, a massive machinery that disavowed their structural violence.

This book takes these historical violences as its starting point, arguing that every theory of existence—whether positing an ontological entanglement of existence or some form of ontological object (hyper-, hypo-, or micro-)—must begin with and have as its ultimate goal the dismantling of this rolling ancestral catastrophe. Any discussion that shifts attention from the uneven social and physical terrain of the ongoingness of this catastrophe or begins with a general theory of the human and nonhuman world contributes to the reinforcement of late liberal capitalism's disavowal of its toxic machinery. The title of this book, *Between Gaia and Ground*, means to pull critical analysis from the abstractions of the planetary and the human to the dynamic unfolding forms of late liberal violence—the ways the colonial catastrophe knotted and continues to knot together a multiplicity of worlds even as it concentrates wealth and well-being in some places and bodies and destitution and toxicity in others.

Second, when I am working on a new book, I imagine myself elaborating a point made in a previous work. This book was intended to provide a fuller account of a set of critical discourses coming into view as the presuppositional nature of geontopower cracked. **Geontopower** refers to the governance of human and more-than-human existence through the divisions and hierarchies of Life and Nonlife and the toxicity of existence this division has left in its wake. Since writing *Geontologies*, I had become particularly interested in a set of critical theoretical statements about the nature of existence and eventfulness emerging in the wake of geontopower. I began calling these the four axioms of existence, and I wanted to understand not just what they meant but what various approaches to them were doing. *Geontologies* also introduced a set of figures that I claimed were displacing the four figures of biopower. I asserted that critical theory had been so entranced by the image of power working through life that we'd failed to notice the emerging problems, figures, strategies, and concepts that together suggested another formation of late liberal power had been fundamental to but hidden by the concept of biopower. The three figures of geontopower are the desert, the animist, and the virus. Each figure was meant to be diagnostic and symptomatic signs of the ways geontopower has long been openly governing in settler colonialism and was now seen as a threat to those who had benefited from this governance.

Even when thinking of the virus as figure, I tried to forestall the celebration of it as a radical exit from geontopower. I argued that to be the virus was to be subject to intense abjection and attack and to live in the vicinity of the virus was to dwell in an existential crisis. With COVID-19, this becomes terrifyingly clear. Perhaps more controversially, I also argued that although the rhetoric and practices of war accumulate around it, the virus is neither a friend nor an enemy; it is agnostic about what it is called.[1] The virus is an emergent or residual form of a previous human–more-than-human arrangement. It operates to create a new dwelling, along the way diagnosing the structures and contours of power. How terribly true this seems at the moment. COVID-19 emerged from extractive capitalism and was disseminated by transportation capitalism. It devastates the poor, Indigenous communities, and communities of color because these communities embody the long arm of the ancestral catastrophe of racism and colonialism. Rather than seeing COVID-19 as a horrifying analytic of power's embodiment, as a devastating critique of late liberal capitalism—rather than understanding late liberal capitalism as the source of this horror we are experiencing—we are told to view the virus as our enemy. In other words, COVID-19 now operates in the framework of what, in *Empire of Love*, I called **ghoul health**. Certainly, COVID-19 is not our friend. But neither is it our enemy. It is a manifestation of the ancestral catastrophes of colonialism and slavery and of the continual destruction and dispossession of existence by the massive extraction and recombination machine of late liberal capitalism.

Third, this book, as with all my work, comes from the ways my thinking and acting in the world have been shaped by my long intimate life with the ancestors and current members of Karrabing. Karrabing is not a clan, language, or nation. It is an Emmiyangel word referring to the moment when the vast saltwater tides that define the coastal region of the northwest territories of what is now known as Australia reach their lowest point and are about to turn to shore. It is a group of mutually aiding kin, most of whose countries lie along the coastal region of Anson Bay, Northern Territory. It is a concept, aspiration, and endeavor to mobilize film, song, and art as a means of maintaining Indigenous worlds by blocking the extractive powers of late liberalism and its political, social, and economic dimensions and keeping open a space for an otherwise in the current configuration of settler power. The Karrabing is the model of my understanding of a *social project*.

Fourth, this book sinks its feet into numerous debates and scholarly areas in which others have far more expertise. I do not pretend to know these debates as fully and with the nuance that they do. Instead, I try to point to these debates in the text and notes. I see my effort here primarily as lending energy and focus to a much broader field of anticolonial, decolonizing, and late liberal critique.

Finally, over the years, I have created a pile of somewhat specialized terms for describing late liberal processes and dynamics. I lean on many of these terms in the following chapters. Rather than pause and define each as they arise, I present them in **bold italics** (as with the above use of *geontopower*, *ghoul health*, and *social project*) and provide a glossary at the end of the manuscript that includes other key concepts. There readers will find a definition of the term and a guide to how they fit within some of my previous writings. The idea is to map a deeper and more meaningful understanding of a concept's journey and authors who have provided the rich vocabularies within which these concepts make their way.

ACKNOWLEDGMENTS

MY THOUGHT IS UTTERLY DEPENDENT on the generosity of interlocutors who push me beyond the limits of my thinking. While many of the following people have commented on part of the manuscript, many others have decisively shaped my thinking in a more general way; they may be surprised to see their names here. Thinking is weird in that way, as is life—so much of what is decisive is not on point. Alongside the incredibly perceptive comments of the anonymous reviewers of this manuscript, I thank Nadia Abu El-Haj, David Barker, Sheridan Bartlett, Thomas Bartlett, Gavin Bianamu, Sheree Bianamu, Trevor Bianamu, Katrina Lewis, Kelvin Bigfoot, Marcia Lewis, Natasha Bigfoot Lewis, Filipa César, Rex Edmunds, Natasha Ginwala, Patsy-Anne Jorrock, Patrick Jorrock, Lorraine Lane, Robyn Lane, Tess Lea, Angelina Lewis, Cecilia Lewis, Natasa Petresin, Roberta Raffaetà, Benedict Scambary, Stefanie Schulte Strathaus, David Scott, Sheila Sheikh, Aiden Sing, Kieran Sing, Miriam Ticktin, Daphne Yarrowin, Linda Yarrowin, Sandra Yarrowin, Gary Wilder, Susanne Winterling, and Vivian Ziherl. Many of the arguments found in these pages were enlivened by students in my graduate course on political concepts in the wake of geontopower, Mohammed Alshamsi, Joanna Evans, Sophia Jeon, Hanwen Lei, Connor Martini, Andrea Montemayor, Stephanie Ratte, Jennifer Roy, Bruno Seraphin, Rishav Thakur, Fern Thompsett, and Nick Welna. Susan Edmunds has put up with my ravings for over three decades. Of course, I once again thank my editor, Ken Wissoker, for his steadfast support and shepherding of not only this book but so many others into existence.

Introduction

THIS BOOK EXAMINES FOUR AXIOMS of existence that have emerged in recent years across a significant section of critical theory. They are: the entanglement of existence, the unequal distribution of power to affect the local
and transversal terrains of this entanglement, the multiplicity and collapse
of the event as the sine qua non of political thought, and the racial and colonial history that informed liberal Western ontologies and epistemologies and
the concept of the West. Beyond the axioms, I am interested in the broader
anticolonial struggles from which these axioms emerged and a reactionary
formation, late liberalism, that has attempted to remold, blunt, and redirect
these struggles. Although I treat these axioms as distinct theoretical statements, they are part of a much broader discursive surface of political thought
and action arising in the wake of *geontopower*. Paying attention to how they
operate is crucial if we are to avoid them being co-opted into late liberal and
illiberal capitalism. The current rise of illiberal xenophobic liberalism, zero-
interest capitalism, and ecofascism concurrent with the collapse of a uni-
polar US power may be signaling a new reorganization of liberalism.[1] If so,
then the stakes of how or from where and when we construct concepts—with
concepts understood as action in the world—in this wobbling of late liberal
power are crucial.

At the center of this book is an inquiry into the *social tense* of these
axioms—a discussion about how the order and arrangement of these axioms
create different imaginaries of social time and eventfulness and, thus, different

accounts of social and environmental justice. On the one hand, I am interested in a syntagmatic tendency in some quarters of critical theory—mimicked in how I just introduced the axioms—to begin (and sometimes end) with an ontological claim and then (sometimes) to scale up or slide over to the social, political, and historical ramifications of the claim. This book demonstrates how a seemingly casual syntactic arrangement of these axioms effects our ability to break the stranglehold of what Sylvia Wynter has called the overrepresentation of a specific history of Man.[2] It asks what thoughts and actions become visible when we begin with the colonial history of the Western entanglement of the world and with the differential powers unleashed on various regions and modes of existence—on the human and the more-than-human world—rather than with questions about first conditions. Put another way, what kinds of questions become unavoidable when we begin within the force of history rather than with a claim about ontology?

The answer *Between Gaia and Ground* proposes does not merely reverse the order of the four axioms; it attempts something stronger, namely, to show that the first axiom has no political relevance in and of itself, indeed, that it may well function as an antipolitical diversion if we begin our approach to social power with it. I will argue that the political relevance of any claim about existence emerges from the ways colonial power entangled existence, spawning capitalism and its long-standing governmental partner, liberalism, and in the process leaving the earth potted by the materially differentiated force of their toxic activities. In short, the first condition is a racial and colonial condition, not an ontological one.

One of the first things we see when we pay attention to how we order these axioms is the effect they have on our understanding of contemporary climatic, environmental, and social collapse—whether we understand them to be a coming catastrophe (*l'catastrophe à venir*) or an ancestral one (*l'catastrophe ancestral/histoire*). When figured as coming or arriving, climatic and environmental catastrophe is often read as specific sort of event, a future event that will constitute a new and dramatic beginning, a radical death and a radical rebirth. They are represented as the potential end of one kind of human and natural history. In geontopower, this imaginary of the event is a key feature of the **carbon imaginary**—a propositional hinge that joins the natural and critical sciences and creates the differences between them by laminating the concepts of birth, growth and reproduction, and death onto the concepts of event, conatus/affectus, and finitude. The coming climatic catastrophe builds on, intensifies, and collapses into these concepts of birth and death, event, and finitude. The ancestral catastrophe does not.

The ancestral catastrophe is not the same kind of thing-event as the coming catastrophe, nor does it operate with the same temporality. When we begin with the catastrophe of colonialism and enslavement, the location of contemporary climatic, environmental, and social collapse rotates and mutates into something else entirely. Ancestral catastrophes are past and present; they keep arriving out of the ground of colonialism and racism rather than emerging over the horizon of liberal progress. Ancestral catastrophes ground environmental damage in the colonial sphere rather than in the biosphere; in the not-conquered earth rather than in the whole earth; in errancies rather than in ends; in waywardness rather than in war; in maneuvers, *endurance*, and stubbornness rather than in domination or resistance, despair, or hope.

A second thing we see when we pay attention to how we order these axioms is a very different approach to truth, power, and history. I think we catch a glimpse of this when we place the US pragmatists Charles Sanders Peirce and William James in conversation with the French philosopher and psychiatrist Gilles Deleuze and Félix Guattari and Martinique poet, philosopher, and critic Édouard Glissant.

In three foundational essays, "A New List of Categories," "How to Make Our Ideas Clear," and "The Fixation of Belief," Peirce argued that truth was not derivable from formal abstractions or general states of affairs but was a habit of thought situated within, stretched between, and responsive to the dynamics of changes in habits of mind and habits of existence. The strangeness of this way of thinking about truth should not be underestimated. A pragmatic approach to truth does not locate its source in the mind or in a finished world, or in the relay between the conditions of mind and the conditions of a stable world. But neither is truth considered to be relative in a culturalist or multiperspectival sense. Neither relative nor universally given, truth is, instead, a habit that regions of existence (human and otherwise) get into. Somewhere gravity got to be a habit of object relations. This habit spread until it seemed to be a universal law.

For human minds, truth inhabits us through dynamic loops of belief and doubt. Belief is a current habit of mind built out of a series of encounters with regions of existence, while doubt is the embodied register of the difference between this history of belief and ongoing encounters with the world, itself undergoing change due to our habituated treatment of it and its own modes of responsiveness. Doubt is a kind of grit that registers the difference between the part of the world that has constituted my habits of belief and other regions of the world within my world but invisible to me.[3] Doubt is a pesky sense that something just isn't correct between my habits of mind and the given or changing existence of the world. Together, doubt and belief are the embodied mental surfaces of the intentional and chance variations in a region of existence; they are the differential between calm (belief) and irritation (doubt), which registers the difference between a given arrangement of truth and the existence in which that truth operates including the subject herself. Thus, truth is not a thing but an evolution of habitations moving from within itself but outside any law that determines it. As Brian Massumi has written, the radical empiricism of Peircean pragmatism "will have to generate its world from a coming-to-be behind which there is nothing determinate— *but emphatically not nothing*."[4] Massumi continues: "If there is nothing 'behind,' no being, no what, no a priori, then the presentness of immediate consciousness is not in the mind any more than it is in the classically empirical world of already-given material substance. It is not 'in' anything. It is outside. Outside, coming in. Suddenly, and in the event, unrecognizably."[5]

It was Peirce's colleague William James, more than Peirce himself, who made the social implications of this approach to truth explicit. Like Peirce, James insisted that truth—and pragmatism as a method/concept—was irreducibly immanent to one's location in these entangled regions of existence and thus irreducibly informed by the forces and powers that kept it in place or could be mobilized to displace it. For James, however, a theory of force and power was crucial to understanding why, if the relationships among truth, belief, and doubt were open and dynamic, certain beliefs were experienced as hardened truth, able to keep doubt at bay. Why, for instance, have US patients struggling to breathe from a diagnosed COVID-19 infection insisted that they must have lung cancer since COVID-19 is not dangerous?[6] Or why did it take the murder of George Floyd to convince some white Americans that Black Americans have been subject to violent treatment in ways white Americans have not been, despite centuries of news coverage demonstrating racist vigilante and police violence? How can white American habits of truth statements survive, let alone dominate institutions of power? What James sought to show was how the powers of belief and doubt are determined by the complex energetics of social fields and relations. Indeed, for James, power as such can be measured by the ability of one region to seize hold of habituated practices across regions, forestalling other possibilities that are in existence from taking hold and extending themselves.

In an attempt to find a passage between Humean empiricism and the Kantian a priori, in *The Principles of Psychology* James critiques those for whom "the higher faculties of the mind are pure products of 'experience;' and experience is supposed to be of something simply given." Instead, "experience is what I agree" to or am forced "to attend to."[7] To discern is not, however, a transitive power operating over a world of preexisting subjects and objects. The effort of attention produces an arrangement, and these arrangements become true "in so far as they help us get into a satisfactory relation with other parts of our experience."[8] Because concept formation, like other mental practices, demands an effort, those who are constantly exhausted by the extractive machinery of capital are given a double task. On the one hand, they must carve effort from their world even as others are sucking as much energy from it as they can to enrich themselves. On the other hand, they must focus their effort on social analysis. It is a Herculean task because the power to form counterconcepts is in the same power attempting to drain the affective force of those who live and feel these countertruths.

Even as James argued that there is no place that doesn't feel the effect of other places, he insisted that the open resonating world always sits within and outside of the determining world.[9] Those bourgeois philosophers sitting in their chairs of contemplation are not simply engaged in a reflection but are actively cramping the energy of the poor; still, the poor "who live and feel" the regions of existence sucked dry of value "know truth" as an actuality. They are always, even if immanently, opposing the dominant (if ultimately sterile) ideas of bourgeois philosophers and statesmen. For James, radical empiricism meant to create a "fully armed and militant" philosophy whose purpose was to work to create "power-bringing" words (concepts) "as a program for more work" on the "superabundance" of existence, not to discover the underlying unity of existence nor even (per Peirce) develop a consistent logic of existence.[10]

The implication of this reorientation of philosophy to militant action was certainly a characteristic that drew Deleuze and Guattari to James's work. David Lapoujade, in particular, has pointed to what is gained when James is read from the perspective of Deleuze and Guattari and vice versa. He, Brian Massumi, and Isabelle Stengers have effectively wrenched the thought of Peirce and James away from Richard Rorty's and Jürgen Habermas's liberal neutralization of pragmatism and redeemed it from the simplistic denunciations of Max Horkheimer who, as Lapoujade notes, saw US pragmatism "as a sort of capitalist ready-made."[11] Perhaps the clearest example of the richness of the exchange and divergence of focus between James and Deleuze and Guattari can be seen in the text *What Is Philosophy?*

In *What Is Philosophy?* Deleuze and Guattari situate their reflections on the concept, the concept of the concept, in a language of proper domains—what philosophy, the sciences and logic, and the arts produce as proper to their mode of practice; namely, philosophy produces concepts, science and logic produce propositions, and art percepts and affects. To be sure, a political vision subtends this disciplinary work. Deleuze and Guattari believe that philosophical work is more or less dangerously deranged when liberal capitalism, democratic communicative reason, and the commercial arts lay claim to the task of concept formation. They write, "The more philosophy comes up against shameless and inane rivals and encounters them at its very core, the more it feels driven to fulfill the task of creating concepts that are aerolites rather than commercial products."[12] The resonances between James and Deleuze and Guattari are apparent—for Deleuze and Guattari, concepts do not come out of the mental interior of philosophical subjects any more than they did for James; nor do concepts refer to states of affairs in the world. Concepts emerge from and create new neighborhoods in and across an existence that is always in motion—including the concepts of subject and object and their possible interiorities, relations, and modalities. Concepts knot and create habits in the fields of immanence, they have ramifications in these fields, and they are strained by other regions. Thus, no concept explains the world. And no concept is *the* concept that everyone everywhere needs or wants.

A paradox emerges—which Deleuze and Guattari point to in *A Thousand Plateaus*—around the conceptual status of transcendental empiricism. This form of radical immanence is meant to dislodge the problem of essence to make way for eventfulness. Then again, transcendental empiricism could be seen as a new claim about the essence of existence. Consider James's point that the question is not what is true in a metaphysical sense but what is true in a political sense. "What difference would it practically make to anyone if this notion rather than that notion were true?"[13] The point is not to produce an idea that meets the criteria of absolute intensive consistency but to produce an idea that matters to some part of the world—that helps that part of the world matter forth. The ethical question is to which part of the world does one wish to lend their efforts of attention?

In *What Is Philosophy?* what needs to be understood—and thus what matters—is the distinct "vicinities" and "neighborhoods" among philosophy, science, and the arts. What does Glissant think needs to be asked for something to be done? In other words, what happens when we place conceptual work in the texts of Glissant, say, in the difference between how Deleuze and Guattari begin *What Is Philosophy?* and how Glissant begins *Poetics of Relation*? Glissant does not open *Poetics of Relations* with a disciplinary question. He opens in a boat in the middle of the Atlantic Ocean in the midst of the radical exploitation and dispossession of the West African men, women, and children "who lived through the experience of deportation to the Americas."[14] Three abysses unfurl on this turbulent sea: the abyss of the belly of the boat, the abyss of the depths of the sea, and the abyss of all that has been severed and left behind. From these gaping abysses, Glissant sees new concepts emerging: relation; écho-monde, tout-monde, and chaos-monde; arrowlike and circular nomadism. The stakes of what existence is—essence or event—shrink to a vanishing point relative to, on the one hand, how the world became entangled in these sadistic practices and, on the other, how the relation that opened in this specific scene continues to entangle existence. By anchoring his concept building in the horror of the slave boat, Glissant does not merely seek, like "every great philosopher," to "lay out a new plane of immanence, introduce a new substance of being and draw up a new image of thought."[15] Nor does he seek only to initiate and provide a new course for old affects and discourses. He does these things, yes; but he also does something else, something slightly errant to the obsession of Deleuze and Guattari—he asks whether any concept matters outside the world from which it comes and toward which it intends to do work. What do we ultimately care about: the ontological status of existence, or the modes of being and substance that a specific commercial engorgement of humans and lands produced and continues to produce? Glissant makes this question impossible not to ask. Do Deleuze and Guattari?

I do not pretend that the inversion and reordering of the four axioms that I am suggesting are inconsequential or uncontroversial from a philosophical point of view. Indeed, they might appear as incoherent claims from such a perspective. I could be read as asserting, for instance, that before these histories of colonization existence was not entangled. Or I could be called out for opposing ontological claims even as this book seeks to lend energy to various Indigenous and subaltern claims about non-Western ontologies. I address this latter point in most detail in chapter 4. For now, let me simply note, in relation to both worries, that both criticisms are correct even as they miss the point. If I were interested in existence as such or ontology as such then a massive incoherence would subtend this exercise. But I am not interested in either of these *as such*, that is, as if they could be abstracted out and said to exist outside of existence. Where is existence other than in existence? Where is being other than in being? More crucially who can believe without the slightest irritation of doubt that the figuring of existence as some sort of abstract something somehow neutralizes the specific historical contours of Black and Indigenous lives? Who can act as if this should be the first and final concern?

To show what is at stake in how one reads the relationship between the various axioms, the following chapters examine a set of alternative theoretical and activist perspectives on several atomic and environmental events. Examples stretch from the launch of Sputnik during the height of the nuclear Cold War in the 1950s to various ecological concepts emerging in the 1960s and 1970s to the concept of anthropocentric climate collapse in the 1990s and to the contemporary COVID-19 pandemic. Each example is used as a setting for putting a variety of political concepts in dialogue—the concept of the whole earth with those struggling against a conquered earth, the concept of the biosphere with those struggling against the colonial sphere, the liberal affects of empathy and hope against Indigenous affects of survivance and obdurate refusal.

I begin in the 1950s for a specific reason. I want to track a parallel relationship between tendencies and tensions in critical thought and the emergence of *late liberalism*. The glossary at the end of the book provides readers with more detail, but let me briefly summarize what I mean by *late liberalism* so as to suggest the correlational (if not causal) dynamics between critical thought and social power. As I have written elsewhere, late liberalism refers to a period stretching from the 1950s into the loosely defined present during which liberal nationalisms and their publics reacted to a set of extraordinarily powerful anticolonial, anticapitalist, and new social movements by superficially acknowledging the racist and paternalist foundations of its colonial and imperial practices and instituting explicit or implicit policies of liberal multicultural recognition.[16] The *cunning of late liberal recognition* was to treat radical critiques of liberal colonial capitalism as if they were a desire by the dominated to be recognized by the dominant state and its normative publics—as if what was being sought was inclusion into the liberal polis of the worthy.

Kyoto Prize recipient Charles Taylor exemplifies how this political sleight of hand was mirrored in critical thought in his much-cited essay "The Politics of Recognition." Taylor begins his essay by anchoring an understanding of Indigenous and ethnic minority struggles in classical philosophical approaches to recognition. From there, he argues that anticolonial and minority struggles should be understood as a demand for cultural recognition (that "different cultures" be recognized as having equal value and worth) in which "we not only let them survive, but acknowledge their worth."[17] In other words, what the oppressed want more than survival is the recognition of the oppressor because their sociocultural survival is dependent on the oppressor's recognition of their worth. Taylor thanks Frantz Fanon for this insight into the desire of the colonized for acceptance by the master! But to align his political program with Fanon's, Taylor must first strip from Fanon one of his most essential points, that liberation from colonialism demands a form of violence that matches "the original violence of the alien imposition."[18] It is not only Fanon's critical theory of violence that must be neutered. Taylor argues that any thought that centers the dynamics of recognition in the history of power must be rejected, especially "half-baked . . . neo-Nietzschean theories" drawing "frequently from Foucault or Derrida" that "claim all judgments of worth are based on standard[s] that are ultimately imposed by and further entrench structures of power."[19]

While Taylor was developing his theory of liberal recognition, settler colonial jurisprudence was likewise stripping anticolonial struggles of their power to transform the foundations of settler law. For example, consider the 1992 Australian High Court's judgment in *Mabo v. the State of Queensland*, which overturned the justification of Australian settlement in the concept of terra nullius.[20] Even as the justices acknowledged the racist underpinnings of terra nullius, they reaffirmed the supreme power of the settler state to determine the just and the good. Recognizing native title did not and would never touch "the skeleton of principle which gives the body of our law its shape and internal consistency."[21] This is because late liberal recognition was never intended to alter the substance or hierarchy of colonial power nor to provide substantive self-determination to Indigenous and First Nation peoples. Late liberal recognition was just the latest mode in a long history of pressure on all forms of existence to be amenable to capitalist extraction. Indeed, as Benedict Scambary, Glen Coulthard, and others have shown, late liberal recognition has facilitated extractive capitalism in settler societies like Australia and Canada.[22]

Between Gaia and Ground presents a critical genealogy of how a number of critical theoretical approaches to environmental catastrophe have absorbed and decentered anticolonial struggles. As I said, I begin in the 1950s and move forward across a series of critical debates culminating in current discussions about entangled existence. I juxtapose the notion of the whole earth to that of the conquered earth; the biosphere to the colonial sphere; liberal empathy and hope and Indigenous survivance and refusal. I use specific critical and political thinkers to create a discourse space for exploring the alternative worlds of action each of these concepts implies. For instance, even as they acknowledge the centrality of colonial and imperial history, how do theorists such as Hannah Arendt, Aimé Césaire, Gregory Bateson, Gilles Deleuze, Félix Guattari, Édouard Glissant, and Sylvia Wynter differently position the practice of critical thought in colonial and racial history? What kinds of political imaginaries and practices emerge when we begin with questions of ontology and existence rather than in the middle ocean of racial and colonial history?

The following chapters attempt to unpack the *social tense* of critical thought. They are split into two broad sections. The first section examines the social tense of the four axioms of existence in light of ancestral and coming catastrophes. It is primarily a conceptual discussion. The first chapter presses readers to consider the political stakes of starting from an ontological claim (existence is entangled) or a historical claim (Western ontologies and epistemologies and the West were crucially recalibrated during the history of colonialism). The chapter ends with a reflection on how political instincts and statements around hydraulic citizenship, to use a phrase of Nikhil Anand, would look if we examined it from a historical perspective rather than an ontological one.[23]

With this discussion in mind, chapter 2 turns to the meaning of toxic liberalism and late liberalism if we consider climatic and environmental collapse as a coming or ancestral catastrophe. It begins with a discussion of the meaning of toxicity when applied to climate and turns to the question of what describing late liberalism as toxic might do. That is, is this a metaphorical claim, a claim that implicates the nature of late liberalism as such, or is it a claim about the deadly conjunction between liberalism and capitalism? To unpack these options, the chapter examines the function of the frontier and the horizon in exempting and indemnifying liberalism from the violence it inflicts on others, including climate collapse.

Section II presents three case studies that demonstrate the difference between conceptual struggles seeking to maintain a form of existence in the context of the ancestral and ongoing onslaught of colonialism and conceptual innovations that arise from Western theorists looking to the horizon of a coming catastrophe. Chapters draw on the conceptual arguments outlined in section I but animate them in more concrete discussions of scholars and their historical contexts. Chapter 3 is situated in the mid- to late 1950s and early 1960s. It pivots between Hannah Arendt's use of the threat of atomic annihilation to frame the necessity of returning to the classical Greek understandings of plural agonistic politics and Aimé Césaire and other Black Atlantic theorists' use of colonialism as a frame for proposing a new form of transhumanism. The work of Kathryn Gines and Fred Moten is important here and crucial to understanding Arendt's atomic warning in the context of nuclear testing in Australian Indigenous lands. As opposed to how we might read Arendt today, the chapter situates her discussion of a coming atomic catastrophe next to the actual nuclear harms being done to Wongi, Pitjantjatjara, Anangu, and Ngaanyatarra peoples in the 1950s.

Chapter 4 is set in the 1960s and 1970s under the shadow of *Earthrise*, the 1968 photograph astronaut William Anders snapped of the blue-green earth rising above the horizon of the moon, and *Silent Spring*, Rachel Carson's environmental blockbuster. Once again, we find discourses of a coming and ancestral catastrophe, this time environmental, playing out at the same time. Using various theories of a more-than-human mind as a pivot, the chapter begins with First Nation Dene resisting the creation of the Mackenzie Valley oil and gas pipelines across their lands. It then discusses the difference between Australian Indigenous understandings of their relations to each other and land and state-based land rights legislation that emerged from the 1971 Aboriginal Land Rights Commission, established after the failed attempt of the Yolngu people to stop the Nabalco bauxite mine from digging in their lands. Understood from the perspective of the historical and ongoing nature of settler attempts to dispossess Native and Indigenous analytics of existence, these refusals are compared to Gregory Bateson's claim that only a biospheric understanding of mind and nature would forestall an environmental collapse. This chapter is loosely situated in the late 1960s and first part of the 1970s when late liberalism was emerging as a new strategy of governing difference and markets.

Chapter 5 is situated in the more recent present. I begin with a set of political concepts (precarity, solidarity, grievability, and autonomy) in order to juxtapose them to another set (tailings, embankments, and strainings). The idea is not to substitute one set for the other but to suggest the kind of odd ideas that might be necessary if we take seriously the four axioms of existence, the coming and ancestral catastrophe, and the shaking of *geontopower*. I use contemporary arguments for the recognition of ecological formations—rivers, mountains, nature—as legal persons to flesh out the juridical innovations of capitalism and the state in the face of threat.

The postscript reflects on the question raised in chapter 1: how we might think of the relationship between toxicity and late liberalism, liberalism, and capitalism. I use a postscript rather than a conclusion to signal my ongoing rhetorical and theoretical refusal to conclude. Thoughts—and books as entextualized forms of thought—do not conclude for me. They ram into a problematic and set the stage for other potential movements and possible directions.

SECTION I

The Four Axioms
of Existence

Beneath and across a large segment of critical thought and artistic practice can be found four recurrent strains—a set of discursive phrases that could be considered so widespread and authoritative as to constitute something like four axioms of existence. Nothing about the way I paraphrase these four axioms should surprise readers, given how deeply they lie in the habits of critical thought. Indeed, I am hoping that for many readers this list simply appears as self-evidently true—or minimally, as an accurate if overly mannered characterization of a tenor of contemporary critical thought:

- the entanglement of existence;
- the distribution of the effects of power and the power to affect a given terrain of existence;
- the multiplicity and collapse of forms of the event; and
- the violent roots of Western liberal epistemologies and ontologies, or, what I have called *geontopower*, in the history of colonialism and slavery.

This chapter opens this book's interrogation of how the syntax of critical thinking—the narration of theory that begins with an ontological claim and then moves logically into a historical outcome—recapitulates a form of colonial reason even though it seeks to confront and unravel it. It emerges from a simple question: what are we caring for and about when theoretical statements are placed in one or another order, one or another *social tense*?

My method for answering this question begins by following the above order of these axioms, conjuring them as if they were a short story with separate nested theoretical parts. I then turn against this narrative order by demonstrating how each statement reappears when we begin with the fourth axiom. In other words, I begin by acting as if what is most important is the problem of being—what is true in the sense of what we think is the state of existence as such—only to insist that all theories of existence matter only insofar as they direct our energy toward altering the *ancestral present* of colonial power. I hope to show why the syntagmatic reason of these axiomatic orders is crucial if critical thought is to avoid the repetition compulsion of *late liberalism*, whereby the different toxic accumulations of racial and colonial catastrophes are refigured as a coming catastrophe for humanity that can be solved only by returning to a set of first conditions—to ontology. To begin with an ontological claim purges Western thought of its colonial history, namely, the historical conditions that gave rise to such thought's modern methodological and epistemological maneuvers.[1] In other words, the purpose of first moving one way across these axioms and then turning and moving across them in the opposite direction is to dramatize the political and ethical stakes of how we relate each of these axioms to the others; how we narrate them, why we are attracted to one or another of them, what is foregrounded or occluded. Simply put, what are the political consequences of reading these axioms as a set of logical and semantic hierarchies that begin with axiom one and culminate in axiom four rather than as the shape of thought in the wake of geontopower? How do we see these consequences playing out in the contemporary politics of "hydraulic citizenship"?[2]

AS IF THE PROBLEM WERE THE ONTOLOGY OF EXISTENCE

Something has given way in a contemporary style and approach to critical theory. Since around 2000, practices that long defined cultural and critical studies have shifted from hermeneutic and deconstructive methods of reading to a set of maneuvers and tactics of knowledge production informed by mathematically inspired philosophy and the natural sciences. For some, the broad name for this current is the ontological turn, others call it new materialism, and others yet refer to it as posthumanism. But a common thread can be identified. Many scholars are trying to imagine a form of political solidarity grounded in the entangled nature of human and more-than-human existence. Physical and metaphysical questions about chaos, spooky action at a distance, pluri- and multiverses, and quantum entanglements are offered as grounds for rethinking political and social cause and event, effort and affect, intention and its extensions, politics and solidarity in the shadow of climate collapse. These efforts provide the common if sundry substance of the first axiom.

The status of this axiom varies, as we would expect, across specific disciplines and intellectual projects. Axiom one is not a singular discourse that scholars sign on to as if they were delegates to a climate conference. Rather, it is a shared and divergent space of intellectual maneuvering and dispute. Not surprisingly, the exact vocabulary, meaning, and dynamics of the claim that existence is entangled depend on whom you are reading. Some scholars approach axiom one as if it were true in the sense that it provides a better fit for what reality is and how it works than older theories that viewed the world as consisting of discrete subjects and objects acting in a cause-and-effect relation. Others scholars go further and argue that axiom one (and three) is true in a stronger sense—that it captures how existence works in relation to itself. For them, axiom one is not simply a better account; it is a true reflection of the nature of reality.

Many of our best thinkers about entangled existence move their arguments through the natural sciences—in quantum physics, evolutionary biology, or mathematics. For instance, Karen Barad's engagement with quantum physics exemplifies the careful reading of science subtending claims about entangled existence. She shows how quantum physics grounds the argument that "to be entangled is not simply to be intertwined with another, as in the joining of separate entities, but to lack an independent, self-contained existence."[3] Neither objects nor subjects are discrete things that are then tied together. Instead, subjects and objects are the more or less dense regions created by intersecting and materializing forces that knot matter together such that everything is at once inside and outside itself, here-ish or there-ish, now-ish or then-ish. Before Barad was Donna Haraway, whose long engagement with the biological sciences has helped us unpack and advance critical theories of extimate existence through multiple figures and concepts such as the cyborg, symbiogenesis, oddkin, companion species, and the Chthulucene. Such thinkers have long proposed that, in the words of Haraway, the "ordinary is a multipartner mud dance issuing from and in entangled species."[4] Haraway intends this symbiogenetic kinship to be the basis of an anticapitalist, antiracist, and posthuman feminist perspective in the Western academy.

The second axiom is often narrated as if it were the logical result of the first axiom. Because existence is entangled, we see a differential power to affect the entanglement regionally or globally. The first axiom provides the ontological setting, and the second axiom elaborates and situates it in actual social worlds. This way of moving is key to much of Judith Butler's work. For instance, her philosophical claim that no identity is proper is then situated in a social world that decides the stakes of which improper identity can kill you. We see a similar method in her argument that all humans share an ontologically grounded vulnerability, but this shared condition is differentiated in social worlds of grievability. In other words, the general claim holds everywhere, is universally true. How it is actualized in the social world is specifically true. The second axiom qualifies the first by reminding us that while in general axiom one is true, not every region of entanglement has the same power to reach out and disturb other regions or keep at bay those trying to reach in and disturb them. What appears to be an equivalence from a semantic perspective ("all existence is entangled") is not one from a material perspective. The confrontation between Standing Rock Sioux equipped with horses and makeshift gear trying to protect an embankment of water and the police equipped with "more than $600,000 worth of body armor, tactical equipment and crowd control devices" is not played out within equivalent forces or powers.[5] Residents of Flint, Michigan, do not have the power to roll into the white suburbs of Detroit to reroute their clean water supply. It is only when we pull the abstractions of axiom one into the differential dynamics of axiom two that the full implications of axiom one's politics come into view. But when we qualify the first axiom by the second, we see that no social content exists in axiom one. Axiom two lends axiom one its social import. So why do we need axiom one to understand hydraulic capitalization and citizenship? What historical forces motivated the necessity to think of existence as entangled?

The syntagmatic relationship between the third axiom—the multiplicity and collapse of forms of the political event—and the first two increase doubts about what axiom one is doing, why it attracts so much critical attention. If the second axiom lends a social weight to axiom one, the third axiom lends it political import. Axiom three seems to imply that because existence is entangled and because social worlds constituted out of this entanglement have different powers to affect the way they are entangled, then the nature of the political event has to be rethought.

The importance of the imaginary of the event to political theory would be hard to overestimate. As political theorist Iain MacKenzie notes, the central task of political theory, "to debate the meaning of political events," is always preceded by a need to provide "an account of political events qua events."[6] The accounts of and disputes over what constitutes a political event have been numerous and fierce. Political theory has defined the political event as that which structurally transforms a given arrangement of existence with potentially universal reach. Some see these elements—structural transformation and universal reach—as animated by the historical and global unfurling of recognition; others see them as the dialectical movement of the contradictions of capital or the vicious ongoing movement of colonization. In all these cases, political events must have a universal reach even as they are addressed to specific individuals. Alain Badiou roots these strange conditions in the militant thought of Saint Paul. He argues that the liberal political subject, understood as universal and particular, emerged from Paul's understanding of Christ as addressed simultaneously to all of humanity and yet as dependent on an individual's acceptance of Christ as savior. For Badiou, as for the Christian faith, the political event depends on an act of individual militant fidelity and pure conviction to the truth of a universal event (Christ event, political event) (believer, citizen).[7] I believe that 1968 was a political event for all. This approach finds an equal and opposite approach in Deleuze and Guattari's figuration of the political in A Thousand Plateaus. There the political event erupts in an act of radical infidelity to the current political territory. Put on a bridle; make yourself into a horsehumanwhip.[8] Approach every militant claim of fidelity with a wild perfidiousness. Yet as with Badiou's militant fidelity, so with Deleuze and Guattari's militant infidelity; the reach of the political event is universal, the address is to every individual equally, and the goal is the total transformation of sense and sociality.[9]

It would be a fool's errand to try to quickly summarize recent Western theories of the political event—not just Badiou and Deleuze but Jacques Rancière, Michel Foucault, Maurizio Lazzarato, Giorgio Agamben, Roberto Esposito, Silvia Federici, and so on. But whatever the range, disagreement, and maneuvering going on, the field itself has been disrupted by thinking about new dimensions and modalities of political eventfulness. Alongside these older accounts that emphasize the universal and structural nature of the political event are newer ones that stress the quasi, micro-, and slow nature of political power.[10] Because existence is entangled and those entangled in it have different powers to affect the flow of forces through it, the nature of an event in one region of the entanglement looks very different in another region. Theorists increasingly point to the political import of microenvironmental events on poor, brown, Black, and Indigenous bodies rather than singular transformative acts of resistance and revolution. Microevents rumble through microinhabitations. Their sensory effects barely break the surface of human perception. They are the crackling one hears just below the ambient sound of everyday life in rural and urban slums. They are the winds that carry toxic particles from massive geologically terraforming mines, belching factories, and rancid megalopolis dumps. These subsensory poisons have a specific direction of force and power—away from the rich and toward the poor. These small tectonic deformations of environment, psyche, and body pave the way for the big collapse. In other words, it is not the big wave, or even the last wave, that decides the matter but all the smaller ones secreted into what seems to be arriving on the horizon but has long been lapping over colonialized grounds.

This material sedimentation of colonial power is one reason capitalism seems so resilient and the rich so immune to revolution—those who have the resources can wall off their bodies and environments from cracks by controlling the direction and force of slow violence across various entangled regions and can rebuild more rapidly after the big event.[11] The COVID-19 pandemic makes this clear: politics is defined by all these forms of the event—the ruptures of social time and space; felicitous or infelicitous allegiance to an event; the reorganization of the senses; the micro- and molecular agencies providing the conditions or impediments to events; the discursive and affective dimensions of the event; the virtual, pure, divine, and intermittent event. These forms are crucial to understanding how the modes of distributing the effects of power and the power to affect a particular terrain of existence are maintained, navigated, and interrupted.

The third axiom, however, argues that the form of the event has been multiplied and that the event as such has collapsed. The collapse of the event does not mean that nothing ever happens. It is not an attitude of *plus ça change, plus c'est la même chose*. Rather, in the shadow of the first and second axioms, the third notes that political events occur locally and universally and that events as such are displaced by unevenly distributed and dispersed intensities. The concept of political intensity is usually attributed to Deleuze. Intensities may rise to the level of a threshold event—the moment when intensity creates a "phase transition." But most intensities that radiate from an "encounter" (or a shifting in a given extimate formation) are so small, occur at such a low level, or are so slow that no such transition occurs. They are the strainings of the current entanglement of bodies, psyches, and environments that have not yet—or will never—resulted in an event even as they are forces that must be constantly faced.

The nature of politically noneventful intensities fails the test of classic political theories of the event. They are not universal or structurally transformational. But what theorists of the *quasi event* and political intensities without an event are arguing is that no such thing as a universal or structurally transformational event exists. There is no one moment, decision, or event because there is no *at any given time*.[12] Political time is always off and elsewhere. Some might turn to Arendt's understanding of action to describe the kind of actions without events I am referring to: "These consequences [of action] are boundless, because action, though it may proceed from nowhere, so to speak, acts into a medium where every reaction becomes a chain reaction and where every process is the cause of new processes. . . . The smallest act in the most limited circumstances bears the seed of the same boundlessness, because one deed, and sometimes one word, suffices to change every constellation."[13] Counterintuitively, nothing happens, no phase transition occurs, because of the constant boundless and unpredictable nature of action across the multiple ways regions of existence are entangled. The event takes on the shape of entangled existence and its spooky action at a distance—events are only ever here-ish.

WHEN WE BEGIN WITHIN THE ANCESTRAL PRESENT (AXIOM FOUR)

In *Scenes of Subjection*, Saidiya Hartman situates her interest in a "politics in a lower frequency" in the conditions of African enslavement. Hartman notes that because the forms of resistance among enslaved Africans were "excluded from the locus of the 'political proper,'" the agencies of the enslaved Africans must be reconceptualized from the perspective of "the nonautonomy of the field of action; provisional ways of operating within the dominant spaces; local, multiple, and dispersed sites of resilience that have not been strategically codified or integrated; and the nonautonomy and pained constitution of the slave as person."[14] Likewise, Fanon described a form of political violence that lurked in small, everyday events of social reference and addressivity—"Look, a Negro!" or "He talks like a white man" or "You speak French so well"—accumulate until they burst forward and outward as well as inward.[15] These everyday interactional events crackle across the surface of social and political space, soundless to some, all too clear to others, *sonos* and *logos* simultaneously.

These politics at a lower frequency would seem to fit nicely into the politics of axioms one through three, making devastatingly clear why it is so necessary to understand the social conditions of entangled existence. How are we to forge a new mode of political historiography unless we understand that the way social worlds are entangled directly alters the modes in which political resistance and resilience are expressed? Yet is axiom four of a different order of argument than the first three (or at least one and three)? Axioms one through three seem to care first and foremost about the relationships among ontology, sociology and politics, whereas axiom four cares first and foremost about the historical roots of Western liberal epistemologies and ontologies, Western geontopower, in the history of colonialism and African enslavement.

So let me begin again, this time noting two ways that axiom four sits uneasily in the framework of the first three. First, axiom four is an irreducibly historical claim. The first and third axioms make no reference to time or space; they seek to make a claim about existence or the nature of one aspect of existence, such as the nature of the political event. The second axiom comes closest to axiom four, and if it could be liberated from one and three, it could easily be seen as its close cousin. Second, and relatedly, axiom four opens up a possible contradiction between what it is doing and what axioms one and three are doing. For instance, how do we reconcile axiom four's insistence that the violent history of colonial racism, as Denise Ferreira da Silva has argued, did not merely inform and qualify modern Western ontologies and epistemologies but formed and defined their key terms and maneuvers?[16] From this perspective, quantum physics, biology, and the univocal multiplicity of Deleuze and Guattari's metaphysical calculus are not simply ways of thinking about existence but a governance of existence that is irreducibly informed by power.

Several options present themselves for reconciling axioms one and four. One would be to provincialize Western ontologies and epistemologies. We see this, for instance, in the work of Isabelle Stengers, where she unpacks how the professionalization of scientists in the early nineteenth century impeded "the challenge of developing a collective awareness of the particularity and selective character of their own thought-style."[17] Another option would be to locate the history of Western mathematical and scientific thought outside the West—for example, the emergence of various theories of numbers, algebra, and geometry in northern Africa. The grounds of these sciences could be shown to have a common origin or multiple origins. Western thought would no longer be able to claim to unfold relative to itself but would be shown to have emerged across, into, and out of other traditions. Rather than asking what the Western sciences are and how they differ from other traditions, we would ask how Western thought extracts its essence by erasing its grounds within various other non-Western sources. Or, if not extracted, we might consider how Western thought was mediated by its encounter with other thought, as Barbara Glowczewski has shown in her account of the formative affect that Indigenous Australian modes of belonging to each other and the more-than-human world had on the development of Guattari's concept of ecosophy.[18] This genealogical approach to knowledge would tie Haraway's reading of Lynn Margulis's science of symbiogenesis to Octavia Butler's concept of xenogenesis, with a result that what looks like a purely biological question from one perspective becomes a story about the ancestral and ongoing needs of Black Americans and others to adapt and survive in hostile environments.[19]

Any of these strategic options seem viable to me if and only if they do not just invert the axioms but make irrelevant and inoperable all ontological questions that do not begin and end in the history of power. A soft way of putting this is: what do we really care about? Do we care first and foremost about an abstract claim, an abstract place none of us will ever be? Or do we care first and foremost about the concrete dispersed stitchings and sedimentations that arise from and keep sinking into the groundwater of existence as an effect of colonial power? A stronger way of stating this is: all ontological claims are and must be dependent on one's historical and social analysis of power. Readers might object that most of the scholars who promote the claim that existence is entangled do so exactly in order to intervene in current forms of injustice. So, let me reiterate something I stated at the start of this chapter— I am trying to understand how beginning with an ontological claim and then moving to the social, political, and historical implications of that claim recapitulates a form of colonial reason even as it seeks to confront and unravel it. To suggest why, let me return to a conversation I touched on in the introduction of this book: the different approach to concept building. Instead of Glissant's *Poetics of Relation* and Deleuze and Guattari's *What Is Philosophy?* let us look at their work on rhizomatic power.

The long intellectual friendship among Glissant, Deleuze, and Guattari is, of course, well known. Glissant first met Guattari in the 1980s and then, through him, Deleuze.[20] The "time-marking words such as *influence* and *antecedent*," as Neal A. Allar notes, continually impose an intellectual hierarchy on what was a reciprocal relationship.[21] Nick Nesbitt argues that although Guattari and Deleuze certainly "profoundly" influenced his thinking, Glissant was "as much of an inventor of concepts" as they were and had already developed his general critical framework.[22] This much is certain: the conceptual convergences and divergences among these men centered around, among other things, the concepts of relation (Glissant) and rhizome (Deleuze and Guattari), circular and arrowlike nomadism (Glissant) and nomadism (Deleuze and Guattari), the three worlds (Glissant's tout-monde, écho-monde, and chaos-monde) and territorialization (Deleuze and Guattari), and the open (Glissant) and univocal multiplicity (Deleuze and Guattari).

For instance, consider the well-known differences between discussions of the political possibilities of rhizomatic movement in the work of Deleuze and Guattari and of Glissant. For Barad, the form and dynamic of Deleuze and Guattari's concept of a rhizome nicely fit a quantum understanding of political and ethical entanglement.[23] The rhizomatic frontier is organic, mechanic, and quantum—a hunk of ginger and swarming ants; the internet; the "now you see it, now you don't" nature of Schrödinger's cat. The root can be broken, the nest scattered, data routes closed, objects disturbed by quantum logics. But each will start again—the root now has two separate surfaces through which it can reconstitute and expand itself; the ants set off in search of new crevices; the hacker opens portals; the cat grins. The rhizome does not mind moving across lattices because they provide the condition for its spatial unfolding. Put anything in its way, and the rhizome simply alters its shape. It absorbs its surroundings and becomes something else without remorse, without guilt or shame, because it is the multiplicity of its potential becomings. Some believe that this becoming makes the rhizomatic frontier a space of radical motion. In stark contrast to the sovereign and its frontier, the motion of the rhizome is "an acentered, nonhierarchical, nonsignifying system without a General and without an organizing memory or central automaton, defined solely by a circulation of states."[24]

Glissant takes a somewhat different approach to rhizomatic rooting, examining it from the viewpoint of two sorts of nomadism—circular nomadism and arrowlike or invading nomadism. Glissant argues that, prior to colonization, Arawak communities practiced a form of circular nomadism. They navigated from island to island in the Caribbean, moving from one place to another in order to return to the first. Arawak and other Indigenous communities were not the only ones to practice circular nomadism. So did hired laborers in their pilgrimage from farm to farm and circus people in their peregrinations from village to village. For Glissant this form of movement is driven by a specific need, daring or aggression playing no part. Each time a portion of the territory is exhausted, the group moves to another place, leaving the abandoned territory time to replenish itself so that the group can return to it. The movement's function ensures the survival of the group by means of revitalizing the area in its absence.[25] Arrowlike nomadism is a very different sort of rhizomatic movement. "The Huns, for example, or the Conquistadors" perfected an "invading nomadism" whose goal was to "conquer lands by exterminating their occupants."[26] Like advanced runners of a spreading plague from which they believe themselves to be immune, "conquerors are the moving, transient root of their people."[27] They are agnostic about what lattice they climb.

When nomadism is seen in its multiple modalities, we can no longer rush quickly past the rhizomatic amnesia of arrowlike nomadism—the fact that it does not remember where it started or where it is going. It also goes even if, as Glissant notes, it ultimately roots down, fences off, and absolutely depletes everything it touches. This motion without memory or remorse ultimately suffocates what it encounters. Thus in 1492, a Protestant rhizome, cleaved from a fibrous, unfolding Christian European bulb, floated to the Americas in an arrowlike nomadism as the beginning of the process of its reterritorialized rooting. This settler rhizome happily threw off its previous form and declared its new becoming, a liberation from anything before, a new Jerusalem, a mode of sociality that was relentlessly everywhere and anywhere, without remorse. It dug in and changed the nature of the ecology. Like invasive ants, it took advantage of scraps of food offered or left behind. Newtonian physics did not phase it. Every event of opposition provided an opportunity for swarming. It surrounded what impeded it and declared the new form to be of its own making. Nothing in this form of the rhizome takes side. It is instead engaged in an endless game of *espionage* and counterespionage, insurgency and counterinsurgency. Hackers happily hitch a ride on mom-and-pop businesses, international corporations, or state agencies. The US National Security Agency turns to hackers to hack a terrorist's phone. The frontier is wherever an opportunity for movement is afforded.

Thus rather than engaging in a debate about who influenced whom, we should focus on the sociohistorical contexts in which these men situated their discussion of concepts and what the concepts were meant to create or reinforce. What is crucial about Glissant's understanding of the multiple nomadic forms of the rhizome is not found in the distinction itself, but in how the distinction illuminates the political irreducibility of conceptual thinking that makes certain ways of thinking about axioms one, two, and three irrelevant if not inoperable. As An Yountae argues, if we stop seeing theory as something emanating from Europe into other worlds, then the conceptual work of thinkers like Glissant might alter our understanding not only of the multiple trajectories and grounds of theory but also what theory is attempting to do.[28] The purpose of fashioning an ontology is not for existence in the abstract but for cultivating a "strong sense of ethical responsibility and accountability to the haunting memory, historical trauma, and the reality of death surrounding the colonial subject."[29] This is crucial to our understanding of why Glissant begins *Poetics of Relation* on the open boat and within his three worlds (tout-monde, écho-monde, and chaos-monde).[30] Instead of listening to a discussion about whether or how this boat and these worlds apply or extend Deleuze's understanding of univocal multiplicity, we can listen to how Glissant roots his theory in neither the circular nomadism of the pre-colonial Arawak nor the war nomadism of European invasion but in a specific situation, the open boat, or what Christina Sharpe has called being in the wake.[31]

> The first dark shadow was cast by being wrenched from their everyday, familiar land, away from protecting gods and a tutelary community. But that is nothing yet. Exile can be borne, even when it comes as a bolt from the blue. The second dark of night fell as tortures and the deterioration of person, the result of so many incredible Gehennas. Imagine two hundred human beings crammed into a space barely capable of containing a third of them. Imagine vomit, naked flesh, swarming lice, the dead slumped, the dying crouched. Imagine, if you can, the swirling red of mounting to the deck, the ramp they climbed, the black sun on the horizon, vertigo, this dizzying sky plastered to the waves. Over the course of more than two centuries, twenty, thirty million people deported. Worn down, in a debasement more eternal than apocalypse. But that is nothing yet.[32]

On this boat, three abysses radically opened: the abyss of the belly of the boat, the abyss of the depths of the sea, and the abyss of a crossing without the arrogance of the self-proclaimed chosen ones. ("Peoples who have been to the abyss do not brag of being Chosen. They do not believe they are giving birth to any modern force. They live Relation and clear the way for it, to the extent that the oblivion of the abyss comes to them and that, consequently, their memory intensifies."[33]) In these three abysses, enslaved Africans experienced the chaos-monde—the radical multiplicity of relation that "dissolves you, precipitates you into a nonworld from which you cry out."[34]

Glissant not only puts the concept of relation to political and historical use but also signals that all concepts are precipitates from and for locations in the differential spaces of the entanglement of existence wrought by colonialism. As a result, the questions are always from the beginning: what concepts emerge from the differential spaces; who and what bear the mark of these experiences; and what forms and practices can intrude on the arrangement of these entanglements? Allar points to exactly this when he discusses the source of Glissant's notion of Relation as arising "from the severing of genealogies and the absence of what he calls *un arrière-pays culturel* ('a cultural hinterland') that could anchor a project of cultural recuperation in the post-slavery Antilles; Relation describes the process of entanglement and inter-mixing that results from this irretrievability."[35]

Does it matter if Glissant's concept of relation is not true for everyone everywhere in the same way and before anything ever happened? Is the ir-reducible historical nature of the relation emerging from the abysses of this boat any less true, less decisive in how we begin our conceptual work? My answer is no. We do not need to make the relation that emerged from these three abysses ontological to understand that they created a social and politi-cal entanglement still gripping the world today. Glissant allows us to see the four axioms of existence as a battle over how we rank the things we care for and about—the sedimentations of historical injustice or the being of being. After all, axiom one has no political or social import. It becomes social and political only when qualified by axiom two. Axiom two is explained by axiom three insofar as the multiple forms and collapse of political events keep some regions of existence drained of the energy to sever and rearrange the differen-tial forces. All these axioms emerge from the actual specific histories of slav-ery and colonialism (and thus the prehistories of liberalism and capitalism) that created the current arrangement of existence based on a specific kind of Man and his refusal to eat only his fair share.

AXIOMATIC REFLEXES

I now turn to how the narrative logic of these axioms alters our political in-stincts and reflexes by engaging the scholarship on what Nikhil Anand calls "hydraulic citizenship," the simple but powerfully revelatory unequal distri-bution of potable water as a reflection of the ancestral catastrophe of colo-nialism.[36] How might our response to water justice appear if we began in and never left the ground of axiom four? The politics of water is especially per-tinent to the narrative force of these axioms given, Anand notes, the rights to the infrastructures of water should not be considered "ontologically prior to politics nor are they merely effects of social organization."[37] Water is in-stead part of the *geontological* history of differential materialization and *en-durance*—water citizenship is a *manifestation* of the present reach of the colo-nial catastrophe. The COVID-19 crisis in Detroit makes this point terrifying clear, as Nadia Gaber has shown.[38] Those who bear the corporeal reality of the ancestral catastrophe of colonialism and slavery are more exposed to the virus's damage and left especially vulnerable by the lack of comparable water infrastructures in predominantly white suburbs.

While Anand focuses his ethnographic study on Mumbai's water infrastructure, he concludes by turning to the water crisis in Flint in order to remind readers that "Mumbai's leaky infrastructures, bursting as they are at the seams in environments of disrepair, are not metonymic of cities in the Global South." He warns that by "marking cities of the South as places that are typified by dysfunctional and differentiated infrastructure, we risk overlooking the ways in which such infrastructures also divide and differentiate publics in the Global North."[39] These divisions are usually marked by race and class, settler and Indigenous. Tess Lea and Kirsty Howey, for instance, have mapped protected freshwater supplies in the Northern Territory of Australia, which demonstrates the tight correlation between settler colonial occupation and potable water supplies (figure 1.1). But as Achille Mbembe notes, what the West tests in colonized spaces eventually makes its way home. So it is with water rights. Although the capitalization of water infrastructures began in the Global South, Andrea Muehlebach has documented how these neoliberal infrastructures of water have now reached the heart of Europe, inspiring antiprivatization revolts in Ireland and Italy.[40]

In the United States, the most recent public example of hydraulic citizenship is found in the predominantly African American city of Flint.[41] The history of the crisis has been narrated many times.[42] Flint had been placed under emergency management from 2002 to 2004, and then again starting in 2011, brewing what Catherine Fennell calls an intense "collision of segregation, racism, and austerity demands"; austerity for some, that is, and not for others.[43] Overpaid and underexperienced city managers had the power to "overrule local elected officials, dictate decisions about finances and public safety, terminate or modify contracts and sell off public assets."[44] On April 6, 2013, looking to cut costs, the city's new emergency manager, Ed Kurtz, informed the state treasurer, Andy Dillon, that Flint was leaving the Detroit Water and Sewerage Department and would build its own pipeline to connect to the Karegnondi Water Authority. Until the pipeline was built, the city would rely on water from the Flint River, widely known to be highly polluted. Instead of immediately treating the water before pumping it into homes, officials decided to take a "wait-and-see" approach. (The head of the state's health department and four other officials were later charged with involuntary manslaughter.[45]) Residents immediately complained. Officials told residents to boil the water, effectively holding individuals responsible for purifying their water supply. It then pumped increased levels of chlorine into the water system, levels so corrosive that General Motors stopped using Flint water because of the damage it did to metal parts. Before the racialized

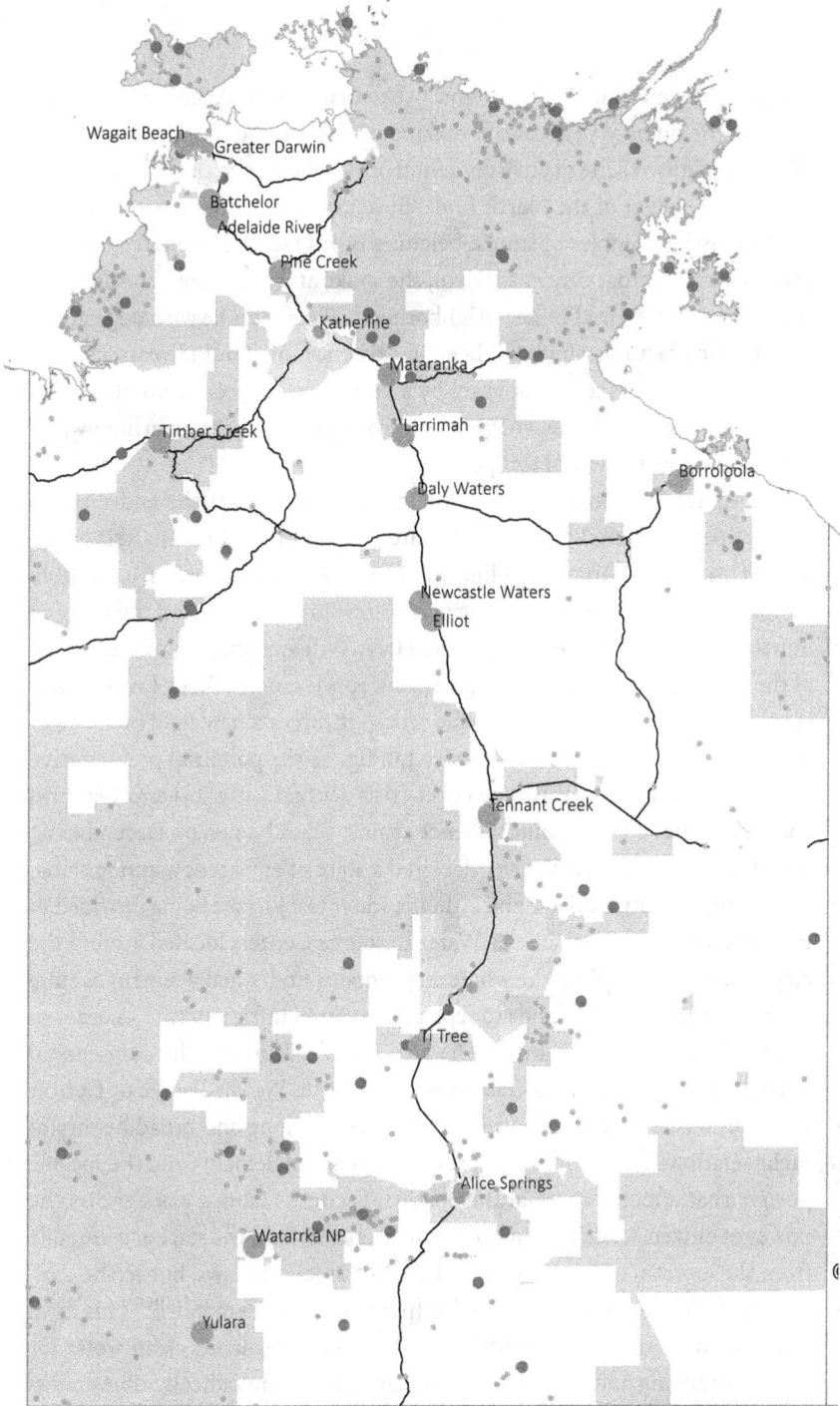

austerity of water flowed into Flint, other toxins wafted their way in. In a news report on fifty years of the making of the water crisis, the *Los Angeles Times* highlighted a life of environmental protest by Ailene Butler, an African American resident of the North End. "Butler owned a funeral parlor not far from a massive complex of smoke-belching Buick factories operated by General Motors. A throat cancer survivor, she spoke at length about the dreadful conditions that existed in her neighborhood. 'There is a heavy smog caused by the Buick factory, which has been in existence for about 18 years. . . . The houses in this district are eaten up by a very heavy deposit, something like rust. . . . You can imagine what we go through down there breathing when this exists on just material things.'"[46]

Even after Michigan pediatrician Dr. Mona Hanna-Attisha and Virginia Tech professor of civil engineering Marc Edwards sent their analysis of the level of lead and pollutants in Flint water to network news outlets, it arguably took the vibrant force and analytics of Black Lives Matter for the story to puncture the mainstream news cycle. Here, William James's understanding of the social location and energetics of concepts is crucial. Black Lives Matter is a concept in this rich sense of the term—it forces a new field of arrangement and emits all sorts of discursive tailings as the potential prefigurative signs for new concepts. With the water crisis denounced as just another form and case of the state's ongoing violence against Black bodies, on December 14, 2015, Flint mayor Karen Weaver declared a state of emergency, announcing, "Water filters, bottled water and at-home water test kits are being provided to Flint residents free of charge at Water Resource Centers located around the city."[47] As of this writing, the whole city remains under management as state officials struggle to find funds to replace the rotted infrastructure in order to return the city to a clean future ("return . . . to . . . future"; this nonsensical twist is intentional). Nadia Gaber's work with the We the People of Detroit Community Research Collective shows, first, the long and broad history of racial relations that created the specific water entanglements and the specific powers that affected these arrangements. Second, Gaber's work shows the power of citizen science to empower "residents to hold the state accountable from the 'bottom up'—not only to the letter of its own laws, but to the ethical standard that the human right to [potable] water demands."[48] This form of activism is crucial as COVID-19 simultaneously demands clean water for social distancing and personal cleaning and shows the radically uneven distribution of water across race in the United States.[49]

At this moment, we begin to understand the troubling implications of the liberal responses to the water contamination crisis in Flint and elsewhere.

The call to remove toxins, replace the spoiled area with clean material, and restore residents to shared infrastructure points not to a belief in a common future but a stubborn present refusal. Those who have long benefited from an entangled arrangement refuse to become strained or dissipated by a new arrangement. The three steps of remove, replace, and restore shift attention from the fact that certain areas are free of pollution because that pollution has been dumped elsewhere. And it shifts attention from the fact that to restore a place depends on the gutting of some other place. Rather than a common and differentiated present, the liberal response to its distributed toxicity is symptomatic and diagnostic of its blocked and disavowed networks, namely, that some regions are built up and sustained by ripping and disemboweling other regions while leaving behind the chemicals needed to separate metals and ores, the fungi that thrive in machine-friendly fields, and the winds and waters that flow differently when the trees have been uprooted.

The answer from the white heteronormative households when (once again) forced to acknowledge that there is nothing ghostly at all about the circuits and transpositions connecting the "common" body in one part of the world to another is that adequate infrastructure should be built for those who have none. In other words, the common body is still not acknowledged to be common. The rich cities and suburbs dig their psyches deeper into disavowal. They refuse to acknowledge that new infrastructure would need to be built from materials found far away from their own neighborhoods, ripped from someone else's land, manufactured in such a way that still another set of lands and peoples are contaminated. What they will never do is allow others to move into their suburbs or agree that some of the shiny lead-free pipes be ripped up and exchanged with others. This is also true of nation-states signing climate change treaties. The very action of signing, or not, disavows that they could not be what they are without the surface and subterranean passages ravaging one area for the benefit of another. As Césaire, Arendt, and Mbembe all argue, the sewers will start overflowing at some point, and then there will be nothing left to consume but one's own spoiled self. Someone has to eat the outcome. Would it be ethically sensible for those who produced and benefited from the distribution of commodities and waste to be the first in line to begin spooning it up?

The water crisis was, in other words, part of a series of small and large events, intensities and intensifications, that kept in place a specific entangled terrain of wealth and power. For some bodies to remain in a purified form, other bodies must drink the effluvia—money must be deducted from someone so that it can be added elsewhere; materials to build the infrastructures of health must be pulled out of somewhere. As Myra Hird has written quite powerfully on the myth of recycling, recycling has not meant repurposing waste into new products but rather moving waste from affluent areas to the Global South or far Indigenous north.[50] Those who benefit from the way materials move globally demonstrate little obligation to the ravaged spaces on which they depend. They pretend that events in one place are related to them only by some spectral connection, by spooky action at a distance. They disavow their relationship to devastation at a distance, to the linkages among their healthy food, clean water, and fresh air and the toxic dumps elsewhere.

If Michelle Murphy's work on restoration projects in the Great Lakes is our model, this trial call to remove contaminates, replace what was removed with clean versions of the same, and thus return (or restore) the area to its original condition characterizes the built-in structures of disavowal of late liberalism when it comes to its own toxic productions. This disavowal takes the form of the proposal that the best way forward is to create the infrastructures through which everyone can return to a life where food and water are presumed to be healthy and safe to consume. Certainly, late liberals acknowledge that trust also has to be restored. But once racism is shown to be operative, the only problem is saying "no" to the racism and finding the money to uproot the rot and extend the foundation. Nothing in such proposals mentions what is being restored to what or returned to when. Are Native American lands being restored to their precolonial conditions? Or returned to Native Americans? Surely, we should be wary if the conceptual spread of the four axioms of existence has presented ethical and political action with nothing more surprising than a call for those who have suffered from the ravages of extractive capital to be given what those who have benefited from it have—with apologies for the delay as funds are raised.

How might reversing the narrative order of the four axioms of existence change the form of late liberal responses to hydraulic citizenship? For one thing, the ontological question would collapse into axiom four—would not be needed. Certainly political affects and responses can no longer be lodged in the abstractions of "I-you-we-here-now," "that-they-there-then," and "mine-yours-theirs-then-here-now," even as they must be grounded in an "I-ish-you-ish–it-ish–now-ish" and so on. In *Economies of Abandonment* I used Ursula Le Guin's 1973 story "The One Who Walked Away from Omelas" to make a related point. Le Guin's story imagines a city where the happiness and well-being of its inhabitants depend on one small child being constrained and abused forever in a small dark closet. I read Le Guin as rejecting an ethics of liberal empathy. Instead, the ethical imperative is to know that your good life is already in—obligated to—the child's constraint and abuse, and as a result, you must either relinquish your perfect health and happiness (and the idea that the health and happiness you experience is yours) or recommit to the current organization and distribution of powers and affects. At the end of the story, some people walk away from Omelas and its paradox. The residents of Omelas can walk as far as they would like, but they do not leave Omelas until the city itself is dismantled, or they allow themselves to be less perfect by giving pieces of their perfect lives to the girl in the closet.

But I think there is more at stake than merely noting that we are all only here-ish. I think, for instance, that Glissant's poetics of relation is staging a different beginning to politics. The politics of relation that opened on Atlantic slave ships neither calls for the sharp divisions of I and you, us and them, nor for the affect of empathy. But neither does it begin with a university gesture of us-ish, here-ish, we-ish. A globalizing entangled difference—a differentiating—opened in the movement of these death ships, in which the good bodies and societies of some would be built out of the casual and sadistic destruction of others. One does not have to place oneself in the boat empathetically; we are all already there, but we are there differently. Glissant thus punctures two liberal fantasies. The first is that those who have benefited from the extimacy of existence can simply walk away from its unjust differentials. The other is that the remedy for the wretched of the earth is to understand the extimacy of existence as either revealing what is happening to all of us or fixing it in a way that doesn't affect all of us. We see these elements of the second fantasy playing out in the Flint crisis. One outcome of the crisis was the publicity of a general crisis in the national infrastructure. Other communities suddenly wondered if toxins resided in their water, land, and air, giving rise to a new movement called "citizen technoscience."[51] In other words, the systematic differential of toxicity was made a general problematic. The pernicious response to Black Lives Matter was that All Lives Matter, twisting intentionally (or not) the point—which is that Black and brown bodies are actually treated as if they did not matter, and this deadly neglect or outright murder is woven through and extimate to the existence of other bodies and their infrastructures.

Here we remember the caution of axiom two, namely, not to take a semantic equivalence ("everyone's existence is distributed across everyone else's existence") as a material equivalence. Nothing and no one may be a sealed subject, but simply repeating this fact makes no political headway. Politics emerges when we add the additional step—that no one and nothing are unsealed and quasi-sealed in the same way. The argument that certain kinds of things (say, white people) are able to pull themselves up by their bootstraps and thus everyone (say, Black and brown people) should be able to fails the conditions of the second axiom. But so does the multicultural politics of allowance—the state allowing Indigenous, brown, Black, and queer people to solve their own problems. The suffix -*ish* interrupts this liberal double step even we must be wary not to treat it as a new universal condition. As the Black Lives Matter movement argues, the violence against Black persons is not merely visible when police kill African Americans (largely with impunity) more than other US citizens but when white Americans refuse to acknowledge how their intact bodies are internally tied to what Sharpe calls zones of Black killability.[52] And these Black American refusals to be killable are allied with the refusals of Indigenous peoples, such as the Oceti Šakowin Sioux of Standing Rock, to cede their ways of relating to the more-than-human-world.

The demand that those who have benefited from the creation and sequestration of poisons in other organic or inorganic zones rebalance this history by taking on the toxic load would seem to assume a closed system. A zero-sum game would assume that if one removes toxins and replaces the material with decontaminated versions of the same, then an equal and opposite result would occur elsewhere. But axiom one insists that excess exists in every system, and that this excess is the unending well of an *otherwise*, a world that exists in the potentiality of articulating this excess into an actuality. All those trails and tailings ground in, cast off, or newly created by the continual sacking of existence—couldn't these be captured by a more progressive vision and techne in such a way that they built a new, better world? What happened to the unpredictability and unknowability of cascading action? The answer is that nothing happened to them. Quite the contrary, it is exactly the cascading effects of actions, tailings, and strainings they produce that must be highlighted, as those who benefited from liberal capitalism refuse to relinquish their benefits.

Perhaps the new sciences of waste management that dream of transforming steaming toxic landfills into new forms of materials and energy will decompose the decomposition without having to be composed.[53] In the meantime, the *towhere* and thus *whichwhom* the removed contamination will be put, the *fromwhere* and thus *whichwhom* the replacements will be taken, and the *fromwhere* and thus *whichwhom* tailings will accumulate and strainings exerted are bracketed, ghosted. Ken Saro-Wiwa and other activists from the South are formally and informally executed for highlighting the multinational networks of financial engorgement that flowed out of the vicious pollution of Ogoni lands. Sorted and recycled waste from middle-class lives in the North is dumped in China and in Indigenous lands.[54] The integrated industries of material extraction, commodity manufacturing, global shipping, and all the machine-mediated intellectual labor surrounding these activities vomit pollutants and stowaway invasive creatures, and they demand more energy to keep the cold fact of their existence sealed away from anything touched by the vast majority of the middle class and wealthy.

The materials used as embankments between asbestos and soil, lead and water, and toxic oils and aquifers provide different temporalities, materialities, and eventualities of tailings and strainings than the materialities that compose a line of people protesting the extension of a pipeline through their sacred lands, on one side, and fire- and baton-wielding people, on the other. Here we can move from the embankment of various forms and bodies (police, the Sioux and their allies, rock, dirt, and signs) to their power to affect others and constrain their affects. If we think via tailings, embankments, and strainings, we see with Standing Rock not Life or Nonlife but the extimacies among water, person, place, ground. We see this as an effort to embank in lines of humans, ridges of ancestors, forces of pumping and tunneling. At the straining, extimate interface, new forms are coming. The question is what efforts and energies are directed toward which regions of our entangled existence that do not need the deep Western philosophy of Geist-soul-spirit or the fact of capitalism. It can begin, as Glen Coulthard suggests, with the Dene proclamation or with Glissant's poetics of the Middle Passage. It has begun again and again with such poetics and proclamations—and without need to exit into abstractions like ontology.

Toxic
Late Liberalism

THE LATE LIBERAL PHARMAKON

It's hot and it's getting hotter. As the machinery of capital extraction, industrialism, and consumption refuses to relinquish its grip, temperatures continue to rise, meteorological systems change, colossal fires and sandstorms rage, and entire islands and their modes of existence sink in saltwater graves. But the overheating we are feeling is not merely meteorological. Atmospheric changes are just one element of an accelerating spread of the long-standing toxicity of *late liberalism*.

My characterization of late liberalism as toxic may at first seem simply metaphorical. *Toxicity* technically refers to those substances that are biologically noxious or poisonous—those things that have the capacity to disrupt biological function. The relationship between toxic and nontoxic things is not a line so much as matter of degree. All substances have the capacity to become toxic; all substances can move from medicine to poison, hero to scapegoat.[1] Even the purest water can be toxic to humans if ingested in sufficiently large amounts. Thus, medical discussions of toxicity typically emphasize the means by which toxins enter the body and the amount a body can safely process before becoming overwhelmed. Climatic overheating, while technically external to the body, can disrupt internal biological functions as profoundly as any toxin. High temperatures don't literally boil the blood, but they put cardiac functions under serious stress even in the healthiest individual as they raise the level of ozone and other pollutants (pollen and other allergens), which can dramatically affect preexisting cardiovascular and respiratory diseases. In this way, the heat index of rising temperatures and humidity are a part of a more general expansion of uninhabitable zones. What surprise, then, that the advice of some policy experts for mitigating the effects of climate change sounds eerily like older advice for interacting with chemical toxins: don't let them in (seal yourself off with air-conditioning and air purifiers) or remove yourself from the contaminated area (join the great climate migration). The eerie similarities to the mitigation and containment strategies of the COVID-19 pandemic are hard to miss. As Andrea Bagnato notes, with "the establishment of new networks of free circulation" and "permanent urban spaces" also came "unwelcome matter like viruses and bacteria," revealing "the misguided nature of Western aspirations to bring order and civilization to the rest of the world."[2]

The assertion that late liberalism or previous forms of liberalism are toxic depends on three different ways of interpreting this claim: as a metaphor for liberalism, as a quality of liberalism, and as an effect when liberalism is aligned with capitalism. Since I do not mean the phrase to be a mere metaphorical flourish, how might toxicity characterize something in the internal dynamics of late liberalism? Could these dynamics be altered in such a way that it is no longer toxic while remaining liberal?

In light of the goals of this book, this chapter is divided into two broad sections. First, I examine the toxicity of late liberal governance from the perspective of a dynamic between its frontiers and horizons, its facts and norms, and its unintended outcomes and promised redemptions, arguing that these dynamics allow the ongoing harms of liberalism to be disavowed, thus separating liberalism from the history of its toxic excrement. Then I examine how these dynamics of disavowal work in capitalist extraction and its geontological underpinnings, powering a perpetual extraction machine and unequally distributing its toxic harvests. The second section examines these dynamics from the perspective of the ancestral catastrophe of settler colonialism in which the toxicity of late liberal capitalism collapse norms into facts, horizons into frontiers, and intentions into outcomes. In other words, I read liberalism from axiom four rather than from various attempts to say what liberalism is in the abstract.

THE COMING CATASTROPHE

If you are sitting in certain places in Europe, the United States, and Australia, you will see a multitude of the middle class and affluent staring at the horizon. Numerous climate scientists have told them that a massive toxic and climatic storm is heading their way. It is now likely that the overall temperature of the planet will rise by as much as 4°C. In such a scenario, multiple cascading disasters will swamp the current configuration of existence—rising ocean levels and acidity, increasing desertification, collapsing ecological diversity, melting and crumbling polar ice shelves, massive firestorms and cyclones, and so on. Already the effects are all around them, made worse by the refusal of local and global governments and corporations to take any meaningful action. Yet still they stare at the horizon as if they will see the coming catastrophe or a savior standing there. Part of the current disorientation of liberal subjects is that the horizon has suddenly taken on a "dark" aspect, when for so long it was brightly lit with possibilities for those now staring at it in horror. What if the only thing on the horizon is not just one but a series of ever more colossal storms—first climate collapse, then COVID-19, then a massive environmental shift? How do they right themselves when they have long been told that the horizon is where the truth, goodness, and justice of liberalism reside as opposed to the frontiers of harm where liberalism implements its unsavory policies? To account for the intensity of anxiety captured in their knitted brows, it helps to remember the function of the horizon and frontier in liberalism as a mechanism of disavowal.

Political theorists of radical democracy, deliberative democracy, and liberal exceptionalism point to and try to exploit the seemingly unclosable difference between the horizon of liberalism's promised justice and the frontiers of its actual harms. The difference between the liberal horizon and its frontiers is captured and expressed in various theoretical registers—norm and fact, universal human recognition and actual human treatment, general inclusion and specific exclusions. As Adrian Little has noted, for scholars of radical democracy, such as Ernesto Laclau, Chantal Mouffe, and Wendy Brown, the goal is "to found a politics focused on the exclusions and inequalities that characterise liberal democratic regimes."[3] The search is for a common norm, dynamic, or principle that can function as the ground of universal inclusion or general constant self-correction. For instance, Judith Butler anchors the reinvigoration of liberal democracy in *Frames of War* not in the radical openness of subjectivity suggested in her early work but in what she sees as the ontologically shared human quality of vulnerability and thus grievability.[4] Others, such as Martha Nussbaum, ground liberal political legitimacy in how it collectively provides for the capacitation of all persons, not just for those for whom a liberal world has been built. For Nussbaum, the legitimacy of a liberal world should be judged from its frontier—those who land in or are placed at the frontier of a specific social organization of capacity.[5] The horizon of a full inclusion offers an imaginary ideal and normative point toward which liberalism should be oriented and against which it should measure its state of affairs. Against such fixed norms, Jürgen Habermas understands facts and norms (actual practices and horizontal orientations) as shifting substances. When deliberative publics realize that their facts were wrong, their account of and orientation to the good and just must also have been wrong. In other words, norms are not Platonic forms; they are as revisable as facts. Both measure and adjust the truth of the other. Habermas writes, "Horizons are open, and they shift; we enter into them and they in turn move with us."[6] We saw a version of this double movement in the Australian High Court case *Mabo v. the State of Queensland (No. 2)*, which I mentioned in the introduction. The High Court acknowledged that the factual basis of Australian sovereignty in the concept of terra nullius was wrong, and indeed, was racist in its characterization of Indigenous peoples as lacking the social structure to have evolved a form of land ownership. As a result, the norms of ownership had to be reconsidered.

This model of an open and shifting domain of facts and horizons doesn't characterize all liberal political theory, of course. Some post-Hegelian political philosophers continue to believe there is some fixed spirit of liberalism struggling to actualize itself. In this model, the violence of the past is nothing but the unfortunate spasms of the birth of the recognition of universal freedom. As G. W. F. Hegel so nicely put it, "the cunning of reason," or Geist, "sets the passions to work in its service, as a result of which the agents by which it gives itself existence must pay the penalty and suffer the loss."[7] As G. H. R. Parkinson reminds us, the cunning of reason operates across the two levels in Hegelian historical dialectics. At the "universal level are such seemingly metaphysical entities as 'the spirit of a nation' and 'the spirit of the world'; at the particular level, there are the human passions."[8] Within this circle of thinkers, we hear now and again that history has finally established whatever *nomos* they believe has been struggling to actualize itself. For instance, Carl Schmitt claimed that 1492 marked the moment Europe became the world; Hegel marked Napoleon's 1806 siege of Jena as the advent of universalization of Geist; Alexandre Kojève marked 1945 as the last world war; and Francis Fukuyama marked the Soviet Union's 1989 collapse as the end of history. There is always a sigh of relief, however, when these ends of history are proven wrong. The relief reveals a certain truth—the horizon is not where European Man is hoping to land.

The distinction between a universal good unfolding itself through a series of violent rebirths could well be seen as the genealogical source of the

Oops!

- -

2.1 The meandering horizons of liberal perfectibility. Horizon 1 will inevitably be the wrong direction for the progress of truth and justice, but the correction toward horizon 2 will suffer the same fate in time.

disavowal function of the liberal horizon. In Hegelian and non-Hegelian versions of the difference between the actuality of liberal harm and the promissory note of its coming good, the focus is on the drama of the negative as it struggles with its inner and outer global frontiers, on what theory might align what liberalism says it is and what it is actually doing, and on the skyline where a pure light rises. The horizon is liberalism's governmental imaginary, its means of bracketing all forms of violence as merely unintended, accidental, and unfortunate consequences of liberal democratic unfolding.[9] How quickly do we see any announcement of an actual end of history excitedly announced to have been a mirage?[10] Why? Because the Spirit lives on only insofar as it continues to violently unfold against its inner or outer horizon. If the Man embodying this Spirit actually arrived at his horizon, he would become no different than any other form of existence, no longer exceptional to himself. The violence he does will be violence, nothing more, nothing less. In being the same as all others, he will experience himself as having lost something—his own distinction.

Liberal disavowal does not simply emerge from the dynamic between norm and fact. When necessary, it relies on a more straightforward approach—the apology. Liberals are quite forgiving to liberals who engage in self-reflection and self-correction. Indeed, the discourse of the apology is a key discursive feature of liberalism. As Michel-Rolph Trouillot long ago noted, the apology can be issued in an explicit and formal register, such as when a head of state stands before a legislature and, as the representative of the state, apologizes for historical acts of injustice, as did the prime ministers of Canada and Australia for harms against Indigenous people, the US president for the Tuskegee experiments on African Americans, and the chancellor of Germany for the Jewish Holocaust.[11] The apology can also be more covert, informal, and observational. The idea of apologies can be stretched to include comments in court judgments, such as the observation in *Mabo v. the State of Queensland (No. 2)* that the doctrine of terra nullius on which Australian settler colonialism was grounded was based on "the theory that the indigenous inhabitants of a 'settled' colony had no proprietary interest in the land" and thus "depended on a discriminatory denigration of indigenous inhabitants, their social organization and customs."[12] Lest readers mistake this and other such court decisions as an indictment of liberal sovereignty—that the liberal order is overthrown by acknowledging the radical injustice of dispossessing people and their a mode of existing with other beings—the court reaffirms settler sovereignty by readjusting its grounds and thus its horizons. In *Mabo*, the High Court adjusted the grounds on which settler sovereignty rested;

it did not dispute that such ground existed and had precedence over Native title.

Mabo provides a stark example of a common maneuver in late liberalism—the court corrects the past wrong of liberal history and in so doing reestablishes its dominance as the ruling sovereign condition.[13] The facts were wrong because the horizonal norms were incorrect. The regret—the *regreter*, the bewailing of the dead—expressed is not intended to bring the murdered back to life. But the facts and norms will always have been wrong, according to Habermas, or will be wrong until the end of historical time, according to Hegel. This is why, as Trouillot argued, apologies are permanent "abortive rituals" of liberal self-reflection. They are discursive actions that cannot end injustice "because their very conditions of emergence deny the possibility of a transformation."[14] The problem is not self-reflection or self-correction. The problem is that self-reflection and correction are the precise tactics that foreclose the possibility of liberalism fatally wounding itself. "Just apologize," we hear people tell politicians who spout grossly racist comments, companies whose profit incentives lead to massive ecological catastrophes, and so on. Just apologize and then you can move on—the system can continue.

What would it take to puncture the fantasy of the horizon, for a violent liberal action to cease being merely a measure of the distance liberalism must travel to embody its shifting ideals and instead become a death sentence for liberalism itself? Is there some point, some example, or some instance that liberalism cannot redeem by pointing to the horizon of liberal justice? Are the endless slow or explosive deaths in chemical and industrial manufacturing plants enough? Are the bodies of Chilean men and women excreting copper from their pores sufficient to say something is wrong with the form and not just the dynamic of liberalism?[15] What amount of harm might be enough to overflow the defenses of late liberalism as a form of governance? Certainly, corporate or state actors may garner a prison sentence for having grossly ignored even the veneer of a normative orientation to humanity. They can be charged with acting with intentional brutality, disregarding collective liberal norms and laws. But most are let off more lightly when they express sincere regret for not understanding the consequences of their actions or for not having been fully aware of a change in community norms.

The insistence on the difference between frontier and horizon, fact and norm, and vicious cunnings of reason and its coming universal goodness allows violence to be normalized vis-à-vis these forms of disavowal. It naturalizes systemic social harm in the *social tense* of the coming good. Because these forms of violent disavowal have worked for so long for those for whom they have worked, no wonder so many of the middle class and affluent from the Global North, whose advantageous lives were built on the ground of this disavowed violence, now stand, stunned, staring at their horizon. Their surprise—or stubborn denial—of the coming disaster registers one way in which we can understand liberalism to be a toxic form in and of itself.

The permanent elasticity of the opening between liberal promise and liberal actualities operates much like any toxin does, if in inverse fashion—too much of an opening unleashes forms of unmanageable harm. The toxicity of liberalism is not mere talk. The discursive nature of disavowal routes through a material toxicity; it has a specific geographical form. This is made especially clear when one views liberal toxicity from the capital extractions and accumulations that spatialize it. For instance, consider the frontier, the rhizome, the hole, and the spiral in emerging and actual liberal capitalism.

As liberalism emerged in the colonial world, it absorbed an older geometry of the colonial frontier. The geometry of the frontier is a physics of bodies at motion or at rest, of opposing forces, of equal and opposite reactions. Even a secure border between rulers is a notional frontier because, no matter how precise the demarcation, some material space must hold the demarcating difference between here and there and between them and us, and because a border and frontier are effects and affects of specific political theologies—a belief that absorbed the realm of the divine into the function of the lawful border. A worldwide territorial order had a heavenly seal, a spirit of justice with its own centers, peripheries, and frontiers. Thus, Haiti could be within France, and yet where the application of the rights of man were concerned, it was a frontier. The British could massacre and mourn those who were in the Americas and Australia before it arrived with its right to create a sovereign order over a lawless expanse. The Monroe Doctrine allowed the United States to declare frontier spheres within spheres within spheres of its own domination. In short, the sovereign law decides what is border and what is frontier, when one becomes the other, when the energies accumulating in the space where two bodies are pressing against each other should be bracketed or liberated so that once again opposing forces and reactions can be set in motion. There is no left or right to this model. There is only this position against that one—your space and time against mine.

Once the war has been won and the frontier secured, the liberal politics of sovereign peace promises to keep all bodies in their proper place. But because actual policies of liberalism create internal differences through its mechanisms of inclusion and exclusion and its collaboration with capitalist extractions of labor, lands, the human, and the more-than-human for the

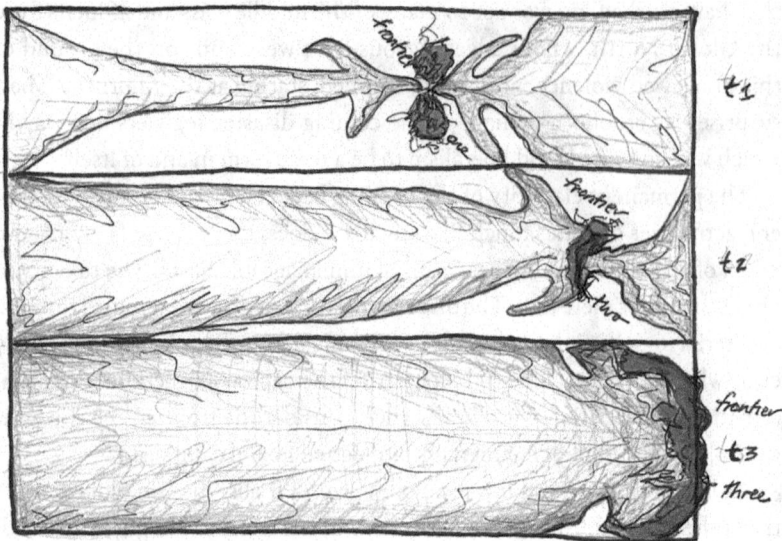

2.2 The sovereign imaginary of frontiers: the domination over time (*t*) of force at the meeting of sovereign frontiers.

purpose of pure profit, the frontier takes on a new form and dynamic within the walls of peace. After the peace, anybody who opposes liberal lines and orders are the disruptors of peace. They become terrorists and *viruses*. No longer a physics of colliding forces, the frontier becomes holey, spiralistic, rhizomatic. Newtonian physics gives way to spooky action at a distance, unseen viruses, *camouflage* at the center of recognition. Terrorists seem to come out of nowhere and from anywhere—the middle, the edges, the side. The frontier is all the interior twists of difference—the slum and the ghetto, the internet and the whistleblower. Frontiers emerge as punctures and perforations of the other and *otherwise*. They become rhizomatic and filled with bubbles and holes. The dynamics of inclusion continue to need exclusions for the extraction machine to justify shattering this area of existence to create value for another area with the promise that all boats will rise with the incoming tide at some point. Indeed, the rising tide is simply another version of the horizon, another mode of postponing its accountability for all the bodies sunk under the seas. Like the horizon, the boat that will eventually include everyone's vessel provides a fantasy through which liberal action in or at the frontier can be separated from liberalism, a means for liberalism to separate itself from itself like a snake shedding its skin. And the more skin it needs to

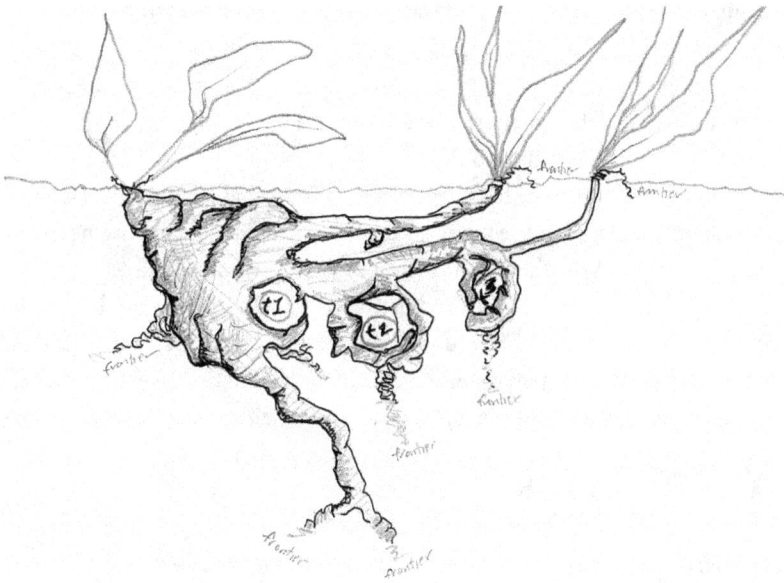

2.3 The rhizomatic imaginary of frontiers.

shed, the more complex the topology of its internal facts and frontiers and external frontiers and facts and internal and external horizons of norms. The snake accelerates, whips around, burrows, and lashes out.

The formal shapes that liberal disavowal takes are not the point, however. The point is that these are the shapes in which the material toxicity of capitalism has been seeded into existence and which, as Ruth Wilson Gilmore puts it, an abolitionist geography has taken root.[16] When we turn to this toxic planting, the geontological imaginary subtending liberal capitalism is crucial. As I noted already, *Geontologies* introduced the concept of the **carbon imaginary** as a scarred meeting place where philosophy and the natural sciences can exchange conceptual intensities, thrills, wonders, anxieties, and perhaps terrors, not merely of life but of life's absolute other, not death, which is a part of life, but that which constitutionally stands outside of it, the *inert, inanimate, and barren* nature of nonlife. The carbon imaginary places the rock on the other side of an unbridgeable difference to life. The rock can imprint a previous form of life (the fossil), but it can never enter Dasein because it has no internal relation to its own finitude. In **geontopower**, because the rock cannot die, it is surrounded by disregard in an equal and opposite way to how life is swarmed with the problematic of care—a dramatic differential opens within ethics to how we consider the consequences of disrupting the arrangements of nonlife and the biological functions of the living.

At times this disregard seems stronger, more of a psychotic break with the reality of nonlife's internal relation to life. For instance, when liberal disavowal is combined with capitalism's disregard, a spigot of toxicity flows first in certain lives and nonlife in toto. Mel Y. Chen has studied liberal white Americans' disregard of the material accumulations of lead in poor neighborhoods of color even as they fanned toxic panic about contaminated toys from China. These forms of neglect and denial pile harm into certain bodies and environments that are expressed as diabetes, high blood pressure, poisonous waters and poisonous playgrounds.[17] As Chen also notes, even as industrial capitalism deterritorializes lead, "lead deterritorializes, emphasizing its mobility through and against imperialistic spatializations of 'here' and 'there.'"[18] The Global North may believe that lead should belong in one region or another, in one kind of body or another, but lead is happy to hitch a ride on commercial products as it materially alters who should bear the burden of capitalism's toxic output. This point is underscored in Sebastián Ureta and Patricio Flores's work on copper mining in central Chile. They analyze mining "tailings as entities embedded with a certain monstrous capacity, or an inner capability to affect massively and in strange ways other entities, close and far, among them human beings."[19]

As they see the poisonous output of liberal capitalism seeping into their own shoes, we might expect to see a reflective moment among all those who have long benefited from keeping these toxic effluents walled off in other lands. But this expectation fails to account for the depth of the subjective and institutional disavowal of liberalism. Instead of finally admitting that liberalism and capitalism is an ancestral catastrophe flowing into every crack and crevice, some still point to the same progressive horizon, proposing more capitalism and its technology as the solution. T. J. Demos and Bron Szerszynski have critically discussed numerous liberal, neoliberal, and libertarian geoengineering projects. Some, like the Breakthrough Initiatives, see the future of humanity as composed of post-earthlings—the horizon of humanity in the endless frontier of outer space. Other eco-engineering initiatives, such as ScoPex, are designing earth-oriented climate-altering machines. Their horizon is the inner space of humans on earth—the frontier is not any particular place on earth but rather the earth as a whole. Across the various aims and aspirations of these science fantasies, Demos argues, is a common ideological backdrop articulated in Yuval Noah Harari's *Homo Deus: A Brief History of Tomorrow*—a view of anthropos as the god of techne. Demos writes: "Anthro-

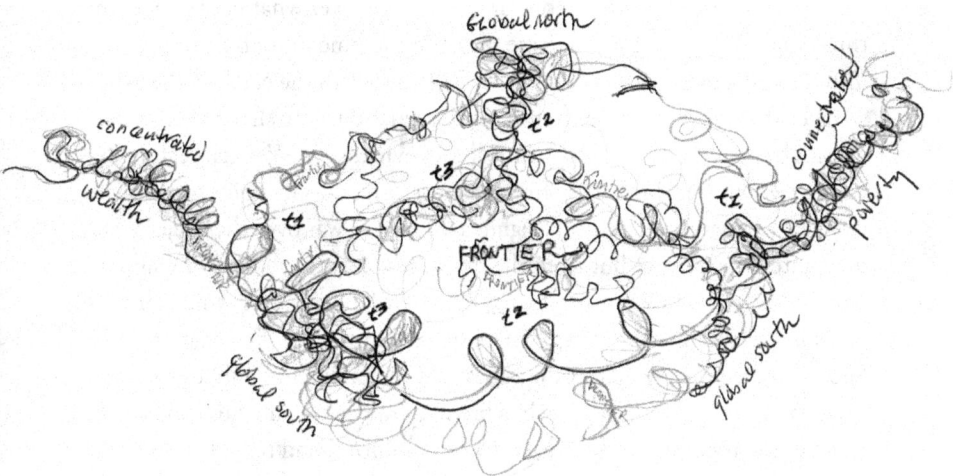

2.4 The entangled imaginary of frontiers.

pos, in this narrative, figures as ultimate self-creator, for whom no challenge—climate change, agricultural failure, artificial intelligence, planetary hunger, even death and extinction—will be beyond technological overcoming, especially when matched to Silicon Valley capital."[20] This anthropos is what Sylvia Wynter describes as the overrepresentation of a specific history of man, Western humanism as the model that has saturated the content horizon of thought since the colonial period.[21]

For all the bells and whistles surrounding their vision of a human engineered earth, these projects deploy long-standing liberal figures of the horizon and the frontier as a means of disavowing the extant toxicities of late liberalism and extractive capitalism. All the machinery that will construct and run this climate technology will be dug from someone's lands, the waste distributed somewhere, the aftermath absorbed by some things and not by other things.[22] As Mariana Silva notes, these geoengineered projects will plunge into the depths of the sea, ripping through the ocean floor, because capitalist geontopower "requires new spatial fixes."[23] The rhetoric of a common earth so essential to contemporary climate science becomes quietist when the placement of the wastelands of each "solution" is broached. The horizon and the frontier, in other words, continue to be necessary for liberalism and its alliance with capitalism insofar as they depend on a possessive logic that can figure relations only as one of possessing or being possessed.

In part we are looking at a discursive struggle over what existence is and thus what actions in existence are. Are the earthmoving machines ripping into the earth or excavating for minerals? Is the earth the earth or the extensions of the *ancestral presence* that made the land in the shape and content in which it now appears? Are the machines evidence of Western technological mastery or its nearly demonic psychosis? Liberalism's ability to disavow its harms comes not just from waging a discursive war over the subjects and predicates of existence but from the dynamics of a second level of mapping, one that converts any loss in the first to a mere "mistake" for which an apology suffices and one that keeps the basic ordering of the first map in place. Should Indigenous peoples gain a foothold in convincing publics to reconsider the violence done to them in a broader framework, liberals can don the cloak of the repentant, adjust their facts and norms, and reboot their singular good.

Is this double mapping of liberalism's disavowal of its toxic factuality an internal feature of liberalism or merely a qualification that can be removed from it without fatal consequences? In other words, could one do away with the horizon and frontier and still have liberalism? Is the problem liberalism's entwinement with capitalism, not frontiers and horizons? A different way of asking these questions is to determine whether liberalism and capitalism existed before or emerged from a specific way of explaining the violences that are the condition of their emergence. We know the answer. These political and economic forms emerged after Europeans unfurled their sails and crossed the oceans, still thinking they might fall off the edge of the earth. The invasion of the Americas was created from a mad circle of dispossession and accumulation, originary, primitive, and ongoing. As Glen Coulthard has argued, capitalism depended on an originary accumulation of Native American lands—a Caribbean rid of Caribs, an American south without the Caddo, Seminole, Catawba, Cherokee, Shawnee, and hundreds of other tribes. Primitive accumulation scraped value out of the bodies of enslaved West Africans, pulled nutrients from Caribbean soil, and cast gunpowder recipes from Chinese knowledge.[24] The ability to acquire new lands by dispossessing Native peoples, Alexis de Tocqueville argued in *Democracy in America*, allowed a form of equality among settler Americans unheard of in France and elsewhere in Europe. A sick logic was lodged in the heart of this practice of equality by dispossession, James Baldwin noted. Those who engaged in these vicious appropriations would become heroes, John Waynes or "Gary Cooper killing off the American Indians."[25]

Let us walk to the other side of the liberal horizon. For many standing there, liberalism and capitalism are seen as emerging from the cauldron of their ancestors' social devastation and dispossession. Both liberalism and capitalism grew like a wicked weed for which *toxic* is too sanitized a word. For those who live in the frontier of liberal horizons, the ever-receding vista of its norm, liberalism is no more or less its facts—indeed, fact after fact shows no such norm exists. In this sense, many who live liberalism as a fact see it as producing a toxic environment not by accident or incidentally: liberalism's exceptionalism depends on its violent production and appropriation of frontiers and its disavowal of this violence as constitutive of its history and present.

Reflecting on the inner state of W. E. B. Du Bois as he walked along Brussels's great park and palace at Tervuren in 1936, David Levering Lewis writes that Du Bois was "vividly reminded that Tervuren was Leopold's Versailles as a museum, twenty cavernous hallways gorged with mineral, fauna, and flora his agents scooped up, shot down, and cut out of the heart of Africa at the probable cost of ten million black lives."[26] As we read Lewis's biography, we hear Du Bois's heels clicking against the polished paving stones and see, as he saw, the copper architectural adornments of elite Belgian institutions as he absorbed the full monstrosity of colonialism. Here was Brussels, a model for a new modern Europe where flaneurs strolled, taking in the wonders of new urban life like the "arcades, a recent invention of industrial luxury . . . glass-roofed, marble-paneled corridors extending through whole blocks of buildings, whose owners have joined together for such enterprises."[27] It wasn't merely the glass-vaulted shopping centers that enraptured the young urban class but the unseen infrastructures of electricity, water, and sanitation. The Senne River was a catchment for stormwater and wastewater, "a visual and medical blight on the Brussels city center, a source of flooding, and an embarrassment to the new government."[28] The "Builder King" Leopold II and the Brussels municipal government began covering the Senne from 1867 to 1877, making a sewer invisible to sight but pulsing within the belly of a gleaming new metropole. These water infrastructures were built from industrial trade, which had a mediated relationship to colonial worlds. By 1878, having failed to acquire the Philippines from the Spanish Crown, Leopold II seized the so-called Congo Free State. Under the auspices of scientific inquiry and civilizational uplift, Leopold II extracted the countless fortunes that built Brussels into a wonder of the world and later the capital of Europe on the backs of ravaged Congolese people and lands.[29]

How easy it must have been for city dwellers to relegate the monstrosities of colonial capitalism to places far away and to have understood themselves unfolding across an ever-wider horizon. How estranged and enraged Du Bois must have felt witnessing the obliviousness of those who walked along those benighted streets, who sipped tea rich in sugar in the houses that lined them, who thought they lived in Belgium and who thought that Belgium was in Europe, and who thought that Europe was outside Africa, Asia, the Americas, and the Pacific; who thought, if they thought about this at all, that they were—and deserved to be—the center of a fabulously unfolding dialectic of Western civilization and its spiritual progress. What Du Bois saw in the urbane politics of loitering was equally if not more nightmarish than the atrocities that led to more than eight million African men, women, and children dead in the Congolese basin. The arcade may be "a city, a world in miniature, in which customers will find everything they need," but it existed in inverse proportion to worlds stripped of every material condition of human and nonhuman existence.[30] What but demons could so thoroughly disavow the sickening conditions of their good life?

In the great cities of Europe and its colonial diaspora, a form and mood emerged with the name "liberal humanism" from countless despoiled and depopulated spaces of the frontier. The minerals dug out of Congo, South Africa, Australia, and Canada went somewhere; in other words, they were not merely an accumulation of an abstraction (surplus value) or a double abstraction (surplus value of surplus value) but a material redistribution and transformation— the tailings of toxins, the rivers of poison, the mountains of mudslides engulfing whole communities. As Europeans crossed and recrossed the globe, pulling out what they needed and leaving behind what was superfluous to them, a new hegemonic order of things was created—what was useful and useless and how each related to the other. The hegemonic force of this order of things was secreted in the emerging trade routes and ethics. These different logics of use and abuse included what was grievable, what was killable, and what was destroyable.

Great cities rose from the smoldering of the colonized world, and within these cities, new topologies of glistening paving stones and stinking alleyways. As human and nonhuman worlds were ripped from one place to produce wealth in another, the great harvester would return, digging deeper into previously ravaged spaces, now with imperial and corporate armies to reorganize "free" African labor for mines, plantations, and the construction of new megalopolises in the Global South. They created new contours in the West; and not merely the glimmering glass of the arcade. The arcades' mirror reflection was first described in detail in Friedrich Engels's *The Condition of the Working Class in England* and then more recently in Mike Davis's *Planet of Slums*. Filipa César has examined what the anticolonial writer and activist Amílcar Cabral saw as an irreducible link between soil depletion in Portugal and Guinea-Bissau, although the conditions in each case were different. Caught up in extracting goods from the colonies, Portugal left its own soils unattended even as the state depleted colonized soils from overproduction.[31] For Cabral, the equivalence between soil revitalization and the liberation struggle against Portuguese colonialism in Guinea-Bissau and Cape Verde was not merely a metaphor for how colonialism corrupted both sides of the colonial relation but part of the practices of reterritorializing the matter that had been poisoned by liberal humanist colonialism. Cabral saw what Du Bois saw: material and social space being bent, distortedly sculpting routes and worlds, including the means of connecting these worlds by differentiating the urban from the rural and the city from its slum. Humans and nonhuman existence were forced into specific forms as the condition of their movement (what roads demanded; oceanways allowed; undersea cables provided; low-earth, mid-earth, and geostationary space satellite networks oversaw). The conditions of existence in one place stretched far beyond the location but in ways that seemed to disfigure only some.

The idea that toxicity could be kept at a distance was always a liberal fantasy waiting to be punctured. Even by the 1950s, in the wake of the catastrophe of World Wars I and II, the toxic horizon of Western paternal civilization collapsed back into Europe. Arendt and Césaire would agree that the source of European totalitarianism lay in its vicious treatment of other worlds (although how they periodized this expansion differed, as we'll see in chapter 3). As Césaire would write, colonialism worked "to decivilize the colonizer, to brutalize him in the true sense of the word, to degrade him, to awaken him to buried instincts, to covetousness, violence, race hatred, and moral relativism.... Each time a head is cut off or an eye put out in Vietnam and in France they accept the fact, each time a Madagascan is tortured and in France they accept the fact, civilization acquires another dead weight, a universal regression takes place, a gangrene set in, a center of infection begins to spread."[32] Colonialism destroyed everything, as Césaire's student Frantz Fanon would note; the decay just looked different when viewed from the sacred landscapes of colonial Congo than from the top of Belgium's Royal Museum for Central Africa. This is because colonialism is a system that encloses city and suburb, rural and wasteland, and the roads and waterways that provide transport. All roads lead to Rome, because no matter how far from Rome they are built and toward what unknown territory, they are built to move anything of value in only one direction.

By the 2000s, alongside the question of who caused this toxic mess was the question of who will be able to seal themselves off from it. Michelle Murphy has shown throughout her work that although the distribution of toxic industrial materials is widespread, concentrations are localized.[33] Caught between chemical spills and changing weather patterns, an increasing number of people, nonhuman animals, and plants crowd into narrowing survival zones. This does not just affect biological forms. Industrial toxicity makes it more difficult for rivers, winds, soil, mineral, and rock formations to maintain their shape and substance. Dramatic shifts in weather patterns, the heat of nuclear contamination, level-4 biohazardous materials, petroleum- and copper-contaminated waters from mining,[34] overflowing effluvia from industrial hog and chicken farms, and incinerated houses from fires[35]: as meteorological and geological forms give way under the strain of late liberal treatments of difference and markets, so do the biological forms on which they depend and which depend on them. Indeed, perhaps as never before, Western epistemologies built on the separations and ontologies of life and nonlife are confronted with the extimacy of all forms of existence. The natural sciences are only now understanding the complex feedback loops between and across all levels and regions of existence, not just between life-forms but between life and nonlife. As I noted above, climate scientists believe the earth will warm 4°C by 2100, a scale of heat that will dramatically alter the nature of what the ecologists of the 1970s came to describe as the whole earth, Gaia.[36]

Until these tipping points are reached, and even after, the effects of late liberalism on different regions will not be uniform. If we lower our gaze from Gaia to ground, we see that hot zones form like rain clouds over specific vicinities because clouds are part of a global circulation of forms of toxicity that abide and do not abide by the social conditions that helped give rise to them. The *New York Times* reported in 2017 that "changing weather patterns linked to rising global temperatures have resulted in a dearth of wind across northern China"; this in turn created a "wave of severe pollution that has been blamed for millions of premature deaths."[37] In 2014, a Chinese official described the pollution in Beijing as having the contours of a nuclear winter. Real nuclear events have driven out some forms of existence even as they have created spaces of toxic sovereignty. These new forms of toxic sovereignty extend beyond the human. After the 2011 Fukushima nuclear reactor meltdown, Japanese officials set up fences that demarcated safe and unsafe zones as if contaminated animals, fungi, and soils would not slip through the most barbed of barbed wire. They do, and they have. "Radioactive wild boars in Sweden are eating nuclear mushrooms" is not a line from a Margaret Atwood novel but a news headline about the long-term effects of the 1986 Chernobyl nuclear disaster as far away as northern Sweden.[38] Around the immediate vicinity of Chernobyl, a vast human exclusion zone has been created. What forms of existence are emerging and sheltering in it remains unclear. Eleana Kim has shown how nonhuman forms of life can find refuge in spaces between hostile sovereigns, celebrations of a resurgent nature in contaminated zones that need tempering.[39] As one ecological journalist put it, animals might be clustered there because "ironically, the damaging effects of radiation inside the zone may be less than the threat posed by humans outside if it."[40]

A line ad-libbed by a Karrabing Film Collective member in *Windjarrameru* (2016) reminds those who need reminding that it is not just animals who might experience a radioactive area as safer than living among certain kinds of humans. *Windjarrameru* revolves around a group of three young Australian Indigenous men hiding in a chemically contaminated swamp after being falsely accused of stealing two cases of beer, while all around them miners are wrecking and polluting their land. I often return to this scene when thinking about late liberal toxicity. As in all Karrabing films, the general narrative arc is more or less decided before we begin to shoot, but all the lines are composed on the spot. In this scene I was with Daryl Lane, Kelvin Bigfoot, Reggie Jorrock, Marcus Jorrock, Gavin Bianamu, and our small film crew. I reminded Reggie that in this part he is supposed to lean through a tangle of roots and look worried—as if the police might raid their hideout at any minute. Kelvin was supposed to reassure him—or not. As always, we pause to let people think what they will say and do after reminding them where we are in the story. After thinking, Kelvin turned to Reggie and said, "Don't worry. They won't come in here. We're safe, too much radiation here. We're safe." And when Reggie's brother, Marcus, says in response, "I don't want to die here!" Kelvin replies, "Our fathers died first. We can die after." In articulating these views, Karrabing sit alongside Native American and First Nations peoples who are attempting to foster what Hi'ilei Julia Kawehipuaakahaopulani Hobart and Tamara Kneese call "critical survival strategies" of care emergent in these spaces of neoliberal discard.[41]

Windjarrameru wasn't the first Karrabing Film Collective work centered on late settler liberal toxicity, nor was it the last. This book will refer again and again to two versions of another of our films, *The Mermaids, or Aiden in Wonderland* (2018) and *Mermaids, Mirror Worlds* (2018) as well as some of our art installations. Returning to *Windjarrameru* is helpful here because of how the four axioms of existence are addressed when the catastrophe of the present is ancestral: the entanglement of existence, the unequal distribution of power to affect local and transversal terrains of this entanglement, the multiplicity of event and collapse of the political event, and the provincial and dangerous nature of Western ontologies and epistemologies.

First, this short scene foregrounds the now well-known point that all places are in themselves and not of themselves. They are here-ish or there-ish, now-ish or then-ish, rather than here, there, now, or then. This is because all places are more or less densely compacted regions of extimate existence.[42] As I discussed in chapter 1, the social and political content of this observation is pulled from the ancestral catastrophe of the colonial history of liberalism and capitalism. Kelvin's statement points not just to the extimacy of materiality in general but to his and his kin's differential power to affect how they are entangled in this ancestral catastrophe. As Rob Nixon has argued, the slow violence of accumulating toxicity has overwhelmingly tended to accumulate in poor, brown, Black, and Indigenous neighborhoods and lands.[43] Completely unsurprisingly for those who live in Kelvin's world, at the end of *Windjarrameru* the four young men are incarcerated for the crime of finding and drinking two cases of beer while the miners go scot-free.

People like Kelvin, who have been living in, on the edge of, or at the end of the sewers of late liberalism for generations, might be forgiven for not being overly sympathetic to the contemporary cries of the middle class and affluent now staring at the horizon. For Kelvin and his family, Césaire's lamentations for "societies drained of their essence, cultures trampled underfoot, institutions undermined, lands confiscated, religions smashed, magnificent artistic creations destroyed, extraordinary possibilities wiped out" are their own.[44] How seriously did settler colonialism and late liberalism take the Dene who argued that extractive capitalism's eating of the land would awaken the land to eat us? How seriously did Western nations intervene as the Ogoni Ken Saro-Wiwa struggled against the cold disaster of the political-economic pact made between Royal Dutch Shell and the Nigerian state? How seriously are they listening to his daughter, Zina Saro-Wiwa, as she artistically explores the neocolonial conditions of contemporary food economies and politics?[45] The swamp dwellers are right to wonder whether the increasingly audible distress about the coming catastrophe is primarily an affective marker of the fact that the middle and wealthy classes of the Global North can no longer contain the toxic side effects of their wealth elsewhere. All of this is to say that for Kelvin, perhaps the framework of political, ecological, and ethical eventfulness multiplied and collapsed long ago. The catastrophe for his family has already happened—"Our fathers died first. We can die after." In the wake are large and small events and intensities without events, like contaminated swamps that offer more refuge than their uncontaminated outsides.

We would be wrong, I think, to absorb Kelvin's ad-libbed lines, gestated in generational knowledges and dispositions brewed in the ongoing ancestral catastrophe of colonialism, into existing liberal sense and affect. Repurposing the Western legal traditions of settler dispossession in Jacques Derrida's *la survivance* (a persistence that crosses life and death rather than being proper to one or the other), Gerald Vizenor powerfully argues that Indigenous survivance marks an insistent presence in spite of and as a refusal of dominant discourses of tragedy, elimination, and victimhood.[46] Kelvin's insistence that they are safer—as he says later in the scene, more likely to continue to be with his fathers and grandfathers in the toxic aftermath of settler colonial capitalism than outside—emphasizes the paradox of being in these zones of refusal and insistence.[47] These knowledges and dispositions do not simply add to the vocabulary of current critics of toxic late liberalism. Rather, his insistence that he and his kin are safer inside the toxic swamp than outside it deforms rather than merely provincializes Western epistemologies and ontologies.

In *Windjarrameru*, the concept most under pressure may be sovereignty. The film partakes in a broader Indigenous critical literature that has long critiqued the concept of sovereignty. The Dene political theorist Glen Coulthard, the Maori philosopher Carl Mika, the Goenpul cultural theorist Aileen Moreton-Robinson, Hawaiian J. Kēhaulani Kauanui, and numerous other Indigenous and non-Indigenous critical thinkers have relentlessly probed how state concepts and practices such as sovereignty, self-determination, and national reconciliation are tied to the original and ongoing acts of dispossession in Canada, New Zealand, the United States, Australia, and elsewhere. In films, installations, and interviews, the Karrabing Film Collective continuously foregrounds exactly this difference between dispossessing sovereignty and ancestral belonging. For instance, senior Karrabing member Rex Edmunds has noted how Western notions of sovereignty have been smuggled into Indigenous imaginaries through the legal definition of "the Aboriginal traditional owner." For Edmunds, the "traditional owner" is a socially toxic settler concept and tactic for slicing through the multiple extimate relationships between people and country—kinship, descent, ritual, corporeality, history, sweat, language, and their intensification over histories of the present—that always defined a group's way of belonging to each other and their lands.[48] When Western imaginaries of the sovereign are absorbed by Indigenous subjects and communities, it slowly corrodes the multiplicity of modes by which First Peoples belong to each other and to lands.

Kelvin's comments can also be read as showing another, equally disturbing aspect of the meaning of toxic sovereignty—a different calculus between the persistence of bodies and the persistence of embodiment. It is as if he is saying that his freedom from late liberal toxicity and his freedom to maintain his connections to his fathers and grandfathers, his lands, and their sensibilities depends on distinguishing between his body and the stubborn embodiment of him and his relatives. The paradox is as clear as it is explosive. If this embodiment cannot survive outside the swamp, his body cannot survive in the swamp, or at least not for long.[49] Those who seek shelter from the dangerous humans in contaminated swamps, nuclear-contaminated fields, and level-4 biohazard laboratories shatter the semantics of shelter. Sheltering gives them sovereignty but only in a toxic form.

Yet for all this, many within the long arm of the European diaspora are turning to Native and Indigenous people for their ancestral knowledge about how to live in a sustainable relationship with the earth. But, note, they are seeking an Indigenous knowledge cleansed of the actual conditions of worlds in which Indigenous people live. The question is not, "Tell us how you have kept in place even after the long onslaught of racial colonialism?" It is more typically, "Do your precolonial conditions provide us with the knowledge to stop or survive the coming catastrophe?" If Indigenous persons answer "No" or "We're not telling you," do those who ask turn away? If they do, what does this say about the distribution of social concern that animated the question? Did the query seek to understand what colonialism did and continues to do or merely to save the questioner's own skin?

CHANGING WINDS

At this point in time, the dynamic of colonial and postcolonial accumulation seems much messier than what was promised by the crisp dialectics of Hegel and Marx, out of which Césaire and Fanon originally built their critique. Accumulation has less the look of a precisely rendered logic and more of a science fiction–worthy harvesting machine—a massive earth-destroying Death Star ripping and gutting a million worlds and then returning to re-ravage them as many times as it can find new forms of destroying existence for profit (or in the language of capitalist disavowal, "creative destruction"). The wheels of the machine do not go forward, they go backward, side to side, and around and around.

In the last chapter of Karrabing's *Day in the Life* (2020), we find the fictionally real Rex Edmunds taking his grandson out into the country to teach him "blackfella ways," only to find a large lithium mine polluting the country. The preceding chapters of the film follow various Karrabing members through an ordinary if fictionalized day in their community: Ricky Bianamu trying to find a house with functioning bathrooms and stoves to take a shower and cook breakfast; Melissa Jorrock trying to play with her sister's kids as welfare roams the community; four young men trying to pick up their cousin at a beach beset by an ancestral spirit; and some of the same young men having cocktails and fantasizing about starting a hip-hop group as police roam the community locking up residents for drinking. Throughout, viewers hear a song refrain—"forward to the bush, but where is s/he gonna go"? By the time Rex Edmunds's chapter starts, the paradox of this reframe has begun to set in.

For a long time, the great harvesting machine of liberal capitalism sorted its gouging and grabbing based on race and a global compass. But as the gangrene returns to its source, new toxic sewers and swamps, as well as new forms of human and nonhuman corporealities, are forming and being revealed. In the French Antilles, Vanessa Agard-Jones tries to track sexuality, race, and gender expression only to find "the chemical embodiment" of coming corporealities.[50] Transnational circuits of pesti-capital—hormone-altering pesticides like chlordecone—are simultaneously giving rise to new forms of human bodies and new forms of national political collectives. The Allied Signal Company began manufacturing chlordecone (also known as kepone) in the 1950s in Hopewell, Virginia. After an environmental spill and public scandal in the 1970s, chlordecone was banned in the United States. But powerful planter groups on Martinique and Guadeloupe (principally local whites or békés) imported stockpiles of the pesticide with the approval of France, even though France had banned its use within its continental borders. France did not outlaw its use in its overseas, racialized territories until the 1990s. The interval before the ban produced increased levels of bodily maladies (prostate cancer, for example) and bodily "abnormalities" (the birth of intersexed children, for example). These bodies—born outside the body with organs and confronting an anxious bionormativity—are in turn producing a politics at the material intersection of carnal vulnerability and its chemical legacy.

This direction may be changing, as it did once before, during World War II. Viktor Orbán in Hungary, Donald Trump in the United States, Jarosław and Lech Kaczyński in Poland, Jair Bolsonaro in Brazil, Matteo Salvini and the Northern League in Italy: perhaps it is time to leave aside definitions of liberalism and look, as the essays in William Callison and Zachary Manfredi's *Mutant Neoliberalism* do, at the fracturing and multiple forms and figures claimed by the liberal surname.[51] This change is not merely political but biochemical. Take, for instance, Rochester, New York, where the great Eastman Kodak factory is undergoing a controlled demolition and a phased reorientation. Kodak Park is becoming the Eastman Business Park. It can't happen soon enough for the city of Rochester. The collapse of the market for film sunk Eastman Kodak into debt and hemorrhaged vast numbers of its thousands of employees who worked across 154 buildings on 1,300 acres. In 2012, the city's unemployment topped 11.7 percent. As company and personal debt rose, tales of toxic swamps and sinkholes leaked out. Billions of stilled memories and moving fantasies suddenly had a toxic unconscious. The material afterimages of those "Kodak moments" emerged as fibromyalgia, neuropathy, and primary biliary cirrhosis. Lawsuit after lawsuit followed. Kodak admitted to violations of air and water pollution laws that created "an underground plume of chemicals."[52] Cancer clusters were tracked. Superfund sites were established and managed. New forms of employment emerged as the film was run backward and a secret toxic image seen. Cleanup can be lucrative. Servpro makes between $100 and $500 million in revenue each year by providing residential and commercial restoration and cleaning services in the United States and Canada. Its services include water damage repair and restoration, fire damage repair and restoration, and mold remediation and restoration. The company also provides storm damage cleanup and restoration services for various disasters, such as flooding caused by heavy rains, hurricanes and tidal surges, tornadoes and wind damage, ice and snowstorms, and wildfires. Its cleaning services include odor removal and sewage and biohazard cleanup, as well as services for trauma and crime scenes and vandalism and graffiti.

But in Rochester and other polluted sites, there are some who don't wear hazmat suits. They don't suit up, clean up, and leave. They remain because they have nowhere to go or no means to get there. As one man in Rochester said, having remained on top of the toxic plume, "I don't think being on top of them will be any worse than living anywhere else."[53] Which doesn't mean that living amid the toxic plumes offers a space of composure. The invisibility of the hazard sparks an affective fire we call anxiety that steers the neural system according to its own logics and remedies. Opiates and amphetamines fill up the empty space left by collapsed industries.[54]

People look around and wonder, Where are the toxins? How can I know if this place is contaminated if I don't have the capacity to see or smell the toxins?[55] How can I seal myself off if the contamination is increasingly everywhere? Even as legacy toxins are identified, new ones seep into the environ-

Chapter Two

ment undetected—some legal, some not. And worse, how clean are methods of decontamination? Far away is nowhere different. The horizon is now in the past and has a specific smell. Anthropologist Ali Feser has found that no matter how much hard evidence of Kodak's liability is presented, many former employees and their children could not kick the habit of associating the signature astringent smell of photographic chemicals with better days, happier moments, more secure futures. The sensory history of chemicals seeps into affect, creating bonds of desire, nostalgia, and mourning for the very toxins now slowly overheating bodies and landscapes. The odor embodies nostalgic sensations of full and secure employment; of a working middle class; of an intimate kinship among capital, production, and consumption; and of work as something other than precarious labor, underwater mortgages, and mountains of debt.[56] Sure, it's clear by now that profit always mattered more than the vitality of bodies; that Foucault's understanding of biopolitics should have emphasized the fact that making live was an ideological cover for letting die; that the experience of vitality and potency was more like what a meth addict feels; that the battery acid, drain cleaner, antifreeze, and Sudafed are more expertly mixed than anyone thought. Now we know that geontopower was hiding in the open, telling everyone not to worry about the great expanse of nonlife, the soils and subsoils, the aquifers and ozone, until suddenly their irradiated glow surrounded us as chemicocapital made its vicious deal with consumptive capitalism and informational capitalism.[57]

SECTION II

Atomic Ends

The Whole Earth and
the Conquered Earth

UNDER THE MOONLIGHT

In a recent Karrabing film, *The Mermaids, or Aiden in Wonderland* (2018), the consequences of a relentless contamination of existence have finally come home to roost for settlers. *Berragut* (white people, Europeans, non-Indigenous people) can no longer venture outside without dying from their own industrial excrement. Indigenous people can and do live outside; so *berragut* experiment on Indigenous people to see if a substance can be extracted from their bodies and their lands that can be used to save their own skins. The film follows a young man, Aiden, who has been released from the experiment, and his uncle and brother as they travel across their ancestral countries. Along the way, they encounter various Dreamings (totems), including mermaids, who, according to Aiden's uncle, Trevor Bianamu, continue to live as they have always lived—singing at the side of waterholes and along coastal beaches, seducing men into their watery lairs, and ferrying young children to their island via aquatic tunnels. But Aiden's brother, Trevor's son, Gavin Bianamu, disagrees.[1] This is a new world, a world of settler poison and sadism in which the mermaids act as agents of the *berragut*, ferrying children to the "mud place." There white people "suck the life" out of the children and the site. The mermaids seem to agree with Gavin. As one mermaid tells her young charge during his fateful journey to the mud place: "Before white people came, the world was all right. Mermaids used to come out in the moonlight. They used to just sit down by the beachside, just lie around. And there was a lot of food everywhere then. Today there's nothing. Mermaids can't come out in the moonlight anymore."

Mermaids also has a two-channel version, *Mermaids, Mirror Worlds*. This second film flips between the fictional account of a toxic, ravaged world and a nonfictional series of promotional materials from industrial giants. In the nonfictional world, multinational corporations like Monsanto and Dow Chemical Company, and various undersea mining and fracking lobbies make wild claims about the health, safety, and environmental care that underlies their capitalization of nature. In the so-called fictional world, mermaids explain the sources of a toxically ravaged earth. In actual screenings, the mermaids and the promotional material sing under the tailings of Elon Musk's rockets, launched toward Mars, charged by the belief that it is more likely humans will ultimately survive and create a new world on Mars than on Earth.

As the stars dim over Aiden's sky, unable to penetrate the artificial light of neoliberalism, the importance of the notions of the earth, Gaia, and world seems to be intensifying for an ever-larger sector of critical theory. These terms overlay existence with a distinct set of mappings and relations between mappings. Gaia manifests the West's desire for the return to an original enchantment, a time when the earth was ruled by gods, totemic creatures, and animist materialities, or maybe the pre-Socratic Greeks. The *earth* registers the relentless grip of a technoscientific rationalization that long ago cast these gods, totemic creatures, and animist materialities out of nature and into the realm of the mythological, cultural beliefs, the surreal, and the phantasmatic. The *world* remains a human-made place within which such things as Gaia and earth-nature are discursively fashioned, debated, elaborated, or extinguished. Many non-Indigenous and some Indigenous viewers might intuitively understand the mermaids to be inhabitants of Gaia (a collective desire for enchantment signaled in the rise of an Occidentalized account of the *animist*), the earth to be the toxic natural landscape across which they wander, and the world as that form of human society that allows them to exist as myth or memory on a devastated planet.

The two-channel version of *Mermaids* provides a useful metaphor for (if not literal embodiment of) the bifurcation of the social and critical worlds of the 1950s. For instance, what would we grasp about the genealogy of the four axioms of existence if we placed Arendt on one screen and Césaire on the other? If we stared at their intersection, what middle screen might appear? It would not be a screen that reconciles difference but one that manifests a stranger combination and alteration, much as a floating chunk of finger appears when you stare past your fingers in a certain way. In this way, Arendt and Césaire can be in full agreement about the sources of Europe's midcentury toxic totalitarianism—that the totalitarianism that poisoned Europe during the *longue durée* of the Nazi and Stalinist regimes had its seeds in the sadistic treatment of non-Europeans—and yet have very different political imaginaries about the implication of the West's engorgement of lands, lives, and worlds. Why? Because Arendt seeks to understand and repair Western epistemologies and ontologies of political action under the looming threat of atomic annihilation, deepening as she adjusts liberal geontologies. For her, catastrophe is horizonal, coming, *á venir*. For Césaire, the catastrophe is the **ancestral present** of a Western colonialism that has destroyed countless lives and worlds first in the Americas and Africa and then everywhere. As colonialism rolled through these worlds, its geontological underpinnings entangled peoples in their civilizational hierarchies—from Stone Age peoples to savages and barbarians—creating differences and divergences that stitched together and then complicated alliances among anticolonial movements.

In the following I compare Arendt's desire to repair and revitalize Western forms of political action in the shadow of a coming atomic storm with critical writers and activists, such as Césaire, who begin from and return to the worlds assaulted by Western political and economic action. I do so in order to understand the destructive agency built into Western ways of knowing and being in the world as they were built out of the cataclysms of colonialism. I begin with Arendt's reflections in the 1950s on the concept of the human condition under the darkening sky of atomic annihilation. I move to critiques of Arendt, especially by Kathryn Gines and Fred Moten, and the counterhistories of the human condition that were emerging from the Black Atlantic in the 1950s on transhumanism during the same time Arendt was writing her major texts, *The Origins of Totalitarianism*, *The Human Condition*, and *On Revolution*. This history is situated in relation to Indigenous struggles against extractive mining and nuclear testing in Australia. If Arendt saw nuclear annihilation as being on the horizon of western Europe, Indigenous peoples in settler Australia were living in actual nuclear testing zones. Their understanding of the human condition radically departed from and opposed hers but also opens questions about what the transhuman and more-than-human might consist of.

Many have claimed a new relevance for Arendt's writings in the contemporary climatic moment. The rise of new forms of right-wing neofascist nationalism in the Americas, the Pacific, and Europe; the subsumption of the human and natural worlds into machine techno-intelligence; the treatment of migrants fleeing from Latin America, Africa, and the Middle East to the United States and Europe; and the political conditions and solutions for climate collapse—staring into a coming catastrophe, scholars as diverse as critical Marxist Andreas Malm and robotics professor Andrew Davison have turned to Arendt to understand how the human condition is being altered in the face of climate chaos.[2] Environmental journalists Kerrie Foxwell-Norton and Wen Stephenson agree. Foxwell-Norton asks what Arendt would have seen if she walked along the plastic bottle–strewn beach of the Maldives. Isn't this plastic detritus "the epitome of the often daily, banal, planetary vandalism that creates climate change"?[3] Stephenson argues that Arendt provides us with a framework for the "baseline facts" of "the actual conditions of the world in which we live"—the two actual and coming "catastrophes, planetary and political." Stephenson continues: "With the victory of the carbon-industrial machine, it is now clear, we confront corporate and political forces not only racist in ideology but totalitarian in mindset and ambition, if not yet in methods. Unless, as to methods, it can be argued that to ensure the suffering and death of countless innocent millions, by means of lies and the obstruction of urgent life-saving measures, marks some kind of epochal advance in the art of administrative mass murder."[4]

Arendt has also found new readers in critical Indigenous and subaltern studies. Vanessa Sloan Morgan, for instance, turns to Arendt's notion of "prefigurative politics" as a tool for countering denials of contemporary settler citizens that they bear any responsibility for past colonial harms. Sloan Morgan writes, "The inability to foretell consequences of ethical trespass and the spatiality through which settlers are on land and implicated in settler colonial relations emphasizes the importance of prefigurative politics in settler responsibilities."[5] Although writing in the context of Canadian politics, Sloan Morgan's point seems at home in Karrabing Australia. There the conservative leader, John Howard, the prime minister of Australia from 1996 to 2007, refused any connection between past actions and present conditions: "I do not believe, as a matter of principle, that one generation can accept responsibility for the acts of an earlier generation. I don't accept that as a matter of principle."[6]

Alongside these critical Indigenous studies scholars, some in subaltern studies pay homage to Arendt. Dipesh Chakrabarty refers to her work in the title of his Tanner Lectures, *The Human Condition in the Anthropocene*, asking, as she did, what hope can be grasped on the precipice "of a new and yet unknown age"?[7] As we career into a new ecologically damaged world, can a space of hope be found, for instance, at the contemporary intersection of discourses of globalization and the sciences of climate change? Chakrabarty answers these questions by turning to Arendt's teacher, Karl Jaspers, who coined the phrase and method for unearthing "epochal consciousness." For Chakrabarty, hope hinges on understanding the nature of our epochal consciousness in our common but differentiated world, a world where climate and ecological change is happening to all of us (it is a planetary event) but not in the same way (it is territorially diverse in its effects). For Chakrabarty, our epochal consciousness must find itself not in "the abstract concept of the Earth" but in "the lived world" disclosed to us by the impact of three collapsing forms of temporal knowledge: historical knowledge, species knowledge, and geological knowledge. In other words, the histories of human cultures and societies, the histories of the origins of the specifies, and the history of planetary formation, including the emergence of life from the hot, stony surface of the earth.[8] For a long time, Chakrabarty argues, these disciplines of time could be experienced as at great distances from each other. The geological processes that conditioned the emergence of life in its most elemental nature seemed at a great temporal distance from the origins of human species; and this temporal unfolding of species life seemed to be at a great distance from the history of human cultures and civilizations. This is no longer the case. Under the pressure of anthropogenic climate catastrophe, these time frames have imploded; as a result, our epochal consciousness has collapsed violently inward. Chakrabarty writes: "Here I would suggest, as I have already suggested elsewhere, our falling into deep or big history is also about a Heideggerian 'thrown-ness,' the shock of the recognition that the world-earth is not there simply as our place of dwelling, as the astronauts thought looking at the floating sphere from space. This thrownness is about the recognition of the otherness of the planet itself: an awakening to the awareness that we are not always in practical and/or aesthetic relationship with this place where we find ourselves."[9]

Chakrabarty points readers to James Lovelock's book *Ages of Gaia* to highlight how the geontological orders of life and nonlife have been shaken. There Lovelock argues that to make Mars "a fit home for life" we must start not with technologies for human dwelling but bacterial dwelling. In other words,

Lovelock sees *zoe* rather than *bios* as the true condition of the human—humans are dependent on the more general drama of life, its emergence from the inert, and its possible insertion into the *bios nullius* of the Moon and Mars. Note that for Lovelock and Chakrabarty the radical break between nonlife and life sets the clock and turns its gears of historical periodization. We first see a geontological separation of the lifeless rockiness of the earth from the emergence of the liveliness of speciation. Geological—nonlife—forms and forces certainly change over time, but unlike biological entities, this change is not attributed to some inward orientation to the actualization of form, such as the acorn oriented to becoming an oak, a child an adult. Only life, animated by the **carbon imaginary**, is said to possess this dynamic. The carbon imaginary is what Lovelock leans on when he inverts the hierarchy of *zoe* and *bios* but maintains their ontological and temporal difference from the inert, inanimate, barren landscapes of Mars. For Lovelock, scholars have been too fixated on human historical time—separating out the human from its zoological conditions. Human historical time also has its different clocks, such as what Elizabeth Freeman calls neoliberal chrononormativity, the use of time and the biological unfolding of life "to organize individual human bodies toward maximum productivity."[10] But what we are now experiencing, according to Chakrabarty is the radical collapse of all these formerly separate understandings and feelings of time.

Arendt also imagines astronauts peering at the earth from above and standing on the moon and Mars but for reasons diametrically opposed to those of Lovelock. Celebrations of the arrival of men on the Moon expressed in a discursive nutshell the problem with (not the achievement of) the social enclosure of technocapitalism. By the late 1950s, Arendt was staring at a bleak horizon. As she wrote *The Origins of Totalitarianism* and *The Human Condition*, Sputnik blasted into space and the cybernetic sciences sought to create a machine mind on par with or surpassing the powers of the human mind and technology. Both promised (or threatened, depending on how you look at it) to stretch human life and endeavors beyond earth toward the stars even as both could soon annihilate all life on earth in an accidental automated decision.[11] *Dr. Strangelove* was a decade away, but the horrific possibilities of wrong buttons pressed and computer-controlled programs releasing other computer-controlled machines were already on Arendt's mind. She warned her readers that humans were suffering from an alienation from nature and the world so profound that it could lead not just to human extinction but to the repudiation of Gaia, "an Earth who was the Mother of all living creatures under the sky."[12] It seemed to her that humanity no longer cared to belong to the planet, ushering in a frightening new age. The earth and the world that ruled it had reduced everything to things—including humans—to be used and maximized for profit. All was instrumentalized for the sole end of personal accumulation, expression, and consumption. The billionaires now building their bunkers to survive the coming toxic apocalypse exemplify the sickness Arendt saw. Today, rather than renouncing the processes that are consuming the earth, they are accumulating from this consumption ever faster, dispossessing others and everything more efficiently, so that they and perhaps their biological families can be saved from the planet they are destroying. Their logic is so crazy that English syntax strains to describe it. For Arendt this madness leaked out of and then flooded back into Europe as a mood, an attitude, and an orientation—we are all alone in the universe; we are all stuck on this planet; we are all praying for salvation from this world because the whole earth and everything in it are corrupted and disposable. You can substitute a contaminated earth for a terraformed Mars, but the human condition remains the same. For Arendt, the human condition is irreducibly anchored to the earth and the worlds they make there. The lonely astronaut accidentally left behind on Mars who fashions tools to make a life-sustaining dwelling reveals his human condition only when he desperately signals his presence to others who may or may not hear him. In other words, this Martian man's biological condition may depend on technoscientific infrastructures, but his human condition is expressed between himself and other humans living on earth.

The technological deployment of scientific rationality to which Arendt refers in her discussions of planetary travel was, of course, part of what US president Dwight Eisenhower called the US military-industrial-academic complex.[13] Arendt saw this complex not only as the cause of the impoverishment of countless human worlds but also as a threat to the material basis of all actual and possible worlds that exist nowhere but on the *earth*. The sciences of life, including the histories of planetary and species evolution and their obsessions with necessity, had reduced the threefold nature of the Greek understanding of the human condition (biology, work, and plurality) to one, biological necessity. To counter the accelerated human alienation from earth and world caused by a globalization of technoscientific utilitarianism, Arendt took on the qualities of Walter Benjamin's *Angelus Novus*. As the winds of an impending atomic storm hurled her forward, she looked backward into Europe's past, wagering that the classical Greek understanding of the *vita activa* of the human condition, namely, labor (*animal laborans*), work (*Homo faber*), and action (political animal, *zoon politikon*), might provide inspiration for a reworked political future.

Begun as an essay addressing Marx's theory of labor power, *The Human Condition* became an extended reflection on the historical transformation of the meaning and purpose of the political life (*zoon politikon*) from one focused on action to one focused on labor power. Indeed, a superficial reading of *The Human Condition* might mistakenly see the difference between labor (power) and political action as generating the heat and heart of the text. Arendt defines labor as "the activity which corresponds to the biological process of the human body, whose spontaneous growth, metabolism, and eventual decay are bound to the vital necessities produced and fed into the life process by labor."[14] Labor operates and addresses the biological and material realms of necessity—of animal needs, food, drink, shelter, pleasure, productivity, abundance, what she calls the "burden of biological life, weighing down and consuming the specifically human life-span between birth and death" on the earth.[15] Labor is the activity we do merely to stay alive and keep our kin alive for as long as possible. It is animated by the carbon imaginary and it operates among a person, their body, and the human species in a circular shape—birth, continuance, reproduction, death, repeat. Thus while, biological natality creates, it creates by repeating; its physical beginnings are strictly contained and consumed by the rhythms of mortality.[16] And so with labor. Labor does not puncture or depart from the biological necessities that provide the irreducible, natural, circular condition of human being. Indeed, labor is the skein of existence that humans share with all other living things. Humans, acorns, octopuses, amoebas, and all other living organisms share an indwelling, "automatic" process that comes into actuality at birth and lies "outside the range of willful and purposeful interference."[17] In short, while labor joins humans to the phylum of *zoe*, it does not distinguish the human condition from it.

Action, on the other hand, consists of a kind of speech and a sort of act that occurs "directly between men without the intermediary of things or matter." It "corresponds to the human condition of plurality, to the fact that men, not Man, live on the earth and inhabit the world."[18] It is manifested in the kind of speech in which those freed from necessity address others who are equally free. All small and large actions disclose who someone is relative to the mode, timing, and ordering of her speech and action. As Arendt notes, "The disclosure of 'who' in contradistinction to 'what' somebody is . . . is implicit in everything somebody says and does."[19] Actions, however, do not merely disclose who a person is but also set off a set of cascading effects that one cannot anticipate, control, or reverse: "Action, though it may proceed from nowhere, so to speak, acts into a medium where every reaction becomes a chain reaction and where every process is the cause of new processes."[20] The most minuscule event, the "smallest act in the most limited circumstances bears the seed of the same boundlessness, because one deed, and sometimes one word, suffices to change every constellation."[21] One cannot rewind the process—one cannot purify the toxic dump and return it to the state it was in before. (Even if we stopped the human contribution to climate change right now, as I type this on a Eurostar train in December 2019, we will not be able to roll the earth back to where it has been.) One cannot unsay what has been said. Nor can one seek to escape from the avalanche of unforeseen effects of human action by retreating into solitude or an escape to heaven or the stars. Because this is in the nature of the condition, humans must stand together and disclose who they are now by creating a new plurality in the blast zone.

Here is where work (*Homo faber*) becomes central to Arendt as the mediating figure between labor and action. The distinction between labor and work and between work and action was enormously important for Arendt—indeed, as Patchen Markell understands it, she saw the concept of "work" as her discovery of equal importance to Marx's discovery of labor power.[22] If labor is found in the relationship between people and their mortality and action in the plurality of speech, work is found in the relationship between the worker and her object. The worker has an idea and then attempts to reify it—materialize it—in a durable form. The worker places this idea over, through, and between things, or, in light of the discussion of axiom one, the worker presupposes and then entails the very nature of thingness. The object topologies imagined in the realm of action are put to work by *Homo faber*, who makes practical the distinctions of this and that, here and there, transforming a "heap of unrelated articles"[23] into a world of things. Work is crucial for political action because it interrupts the relentless circularity of the immediate consumption that defines labor and provides us with durable objects we can inhabit—work allows us to be within a world rather than merely on or of the earth. As Arendt puts it, work "provides an 'artificial' world of things, distinctly different from all natural surroundings."[24] Seen in this light, workers (*Homo faber*), as distinct from humans in their condition of *animal laborans*, have a mundane and existential task: imposing a web of ideational relations onto things and, through these mundane durable fabrications, building a world in which human action occurs. Thus, if labor acts in a circular motion, work provides the durable artificial skin (wall, table, trench, roof) that forces circularity into a new form of persistence and durability. The shelters that *Homo faber* creates outlast the mortality of the person—or they did before obsolescent production and then unfixable technology. But they are also the creations of the work of action, of imagining and leaving behind the durable shelters in which immortality can reside—or not. The production of those shelters may also have left, may be leaving, behind mountains of toxicity that ultimately annihilates the human condition, but this is not something Arendt considered.

The concept of immortality is crucial to Arendt not just in her theory of *vita activa* but in her concern about humans' alienation from the earth and world. Labor, work, and action all create something, but for Arendt, only action creates "someone" and the possibility of this person becoming immortal, rather than merely creating "the beginning of something."[25] Put another way, only action breaks the circularity of labor and life and the durative but always eroding nature of work's materiality; only action opens the possibility of remaining on the earth in a form that is untethered from biological life.[26] Here we can return to a distinction Arendt makes between earth and world, between being "on the earth" and inhabiting a world. This duality is expressed in multiple ways across the text and is crucial to how she conceives of the human condition and thus the grounds of political action. On the one hand, we are on or of the earth, as mortal individuals; we live within the rhythms of life, constantly needing to sustain our bodies. There is no human condition without these biological grounds and the corresponding activity of labor that keeps it in place.

This natural condition is an unavoidable and necessary precondition in the human world. But it is only a precondition. To be human, she claims, is to inhabit a world. The proper world for humans is one that allows us to speak and act in such a way that our actions extend beyond our mortality but never leave the earth. Some actions stun a witnessing public. Some actions keep reverberating across time long after the speaker's body has become dust and dirt. People so spoken of become immortal rather than eternal; they stay on the earth in the activity of others who continue to remember them. Immortals do not leave the earth for a celestial abstraction. They become heroic or at least remain in other people's memories, words, and actions. This is what the Greeks understood, that humans could remain on the earth and in the world long after their physical body had turned to dust in the form of active speech and memory. This is why Arendt views the Christian concept of eternity as dangerous—it denies the biological conditions of the human, their earthly domain. Martians and angels might live somewhere in the sky, but not humans. We are glued to the earth. Our alignment with immortality orients us in turn to this earthly condition, the worlds we have created here, and the work that must be done to make a suitable dwelling. These alignments foreground the necessity to care for the earth as the irreducible ground of human worlds; it makes the earth more compelling, more precious, and more vital because there is no other place for us.

DISCLOSURES FROM THE BLACK ATLANTIC

By the end of *The Human Condition*, Arendt returns to where she began—the threat of total atomic annihilation and the cascade of unintended consequences to a series of actions, outlined in *The Origins of Totalitarianism*, *On Revolution*, and *The Human Condition*. Arendt saw these actions as having changed the total composition and constellation of the human world, creating a series of catastrophes that piled "wreckage on wreckage."[27] In *The Human Condition*, these actions include the invention of the telescope, the circumnavigation of the world, and the inward turn of Christianity. In *The Origins of Totalitarianism*, the main action is imperialism, a condition of Europe outside Europe that she sharply distinguishes from colonialism. According to Arendt, unlike imperialism, "Colonization took place in America and Australia, the two continents that, without culture and a history of their own, had fallen into the hands of Europeans."[28] European imperialism occurred much later in Africa and Asia (1884–1914), by which time the earth had become a thing and capitalism had emerged from the engorgement of human and material value in the triangular trade that defined the Atlantic from 1500 to the 1800s. No desire to create new forms of human pluralities defined European "adventures" in imperial worlds. Imperial territories were considered only in relation to what they could provide for the further enlargement of wealth in the metropole. John Adams was not Cecil Rhodes, Arendt's argument goes, because Adams sought a "complete change of society" in his consideration of "the settlement of America as the opening of a grand scheme and design in Providence for the illumination of the ignorant and the emancipation of the slavish part of mankind all over the earth."[29] Rhodes simply thought of his Rabelaisian body.

When *On Revolution* and *The Origins of Totalitarianism* are read against *The Human Condition*, the distinction that Arendt draws between the two great revolutions of the late eighteenth century, the French and American, and the imperial world may seem at first blush to be a historical argument. She appears to be saying something like, because the Social and capitalism hadn't yet emerged when the Americas and Australia were colonized, political action in these worlds was still possible; by the imperial period, the transformation of the private and public realms had been accomplished, unleashing the Social on the world. This historical time line doesn't quite work, of course, because at the same time Arendt praises the American Revolution as exemplary of political action, she dismisses the French Revolution as too much about the necessities of bread and cake. The settlement of Australia, historically concurrent with these revolutions, didn't usher into being anything at the time other than a new penal colony. For some, such as Roberto Esposito, what is at stake in her distinction between colonialism and imperialism was her ambivalence about the possibility of a form of *just* violence given that she characterized violence as opposed to politics. In other words, how does one reconcile the difference between the Arendt of *On Violence* and the Arendt of *On Revolution*? As Arendt puts it in *On Revolution*, "Revolutions are the only political events which confront us directly and inevitably with the problem of beginning."[30] Why are some cases of revolutionary violence acceptable grounds for the emergence of new forms of political plurality and some not? Staying resolutely in the European trajectory, Esposito answers by distinguishing between Simone Weil's and Arendt's political imaginary, looking at how each one balances "the destruction of one city" (Troy) in relation to "the foundation of another" (Rome).[31]

For many, the logic that differentiates *On Violence* and *On Revolution* does not emerge from Troy but from Arendt's racial and racist attitudes. Fred Moten, for instance, agrees that the advent of settler and slave colonialism in the Americas ushered "another way of being" into the world, but on the condition that creating this new common European world involved the destruction of a multitude of existing Black and brown worlds.[32] Why don't these lives and worlds provide any human weight to Arendt's account of the human condition, something that she can note in her text but does not affect her conceptual thought? Kathryn Gines has likewise argued that if we read Arendt's account of the human condition from the point of view of colonialism, rather than from Athens or Sputnik, then we can see that the American Revolution was grounded in and emerged from the vicious sequestration of Africans and African Americans into the realm of necessity and the equally vicious attempt to cast Indigenous people into the realm of death.[33] These violent actions rendered these people not simply invisible to this new "revolutionary" form of public plurality but perversely necessary to it.[34] That is, racism and settler colonialism are not outside the emergence and substance of US forms of democracy or outside Arendt's political theory but fundamental to it. One is reminded of Hortense Spillers's powerful statement, "My country needs me, and if I were not here, I would have to be invented."[35] Or James Baldwin's observations about films stars such as John Wayne: "Heroes, as far as I could see, were white—and not merely because of the movies, but because of the land in which I lived, of which movies were simply a reflection." He notes, "I despised and feared those heroes because they did take vengeance into their own hands. They thought vengeance was theirs to take, and yes, I understood that. My countrymen were my enemy."[36]

While acknowledging that "western philosophy is eminently worthy of interrogation when it comes to questions of race, civilizational pride and ostensibly 'universal' values," Dana Villa claims that interpretations of Arendt like the one offered by Gines (and, we can assume, Moten) are distorted by presentism or anachronism, a certain retrospective reading.[37] Against such errant hermeneutic practices, Villa iterates the standard reading of *The Origins of Totalitarianism*, namely, that its purpose was to understand the *mentalités* and events that led to the catastrophe of European totalitarianism. Arendt was not seeking to understand European racism, according to Villa, nor was she engaged in an investigation of the hidden and not-so-hidden racial and racist tropes in the Western philosophical tradition. In a sort of damning by explanation, Villa suggests that "Arendt's work put the experience of European imperialism and racism front and centre" only because she was trying to identify the central elements that made totalitarianism possible.[38] For Villa, how we understand the periodization of imperialism and its distinction from colonialism depends on whether we take the specific task Arendt set for herself in *The Origins of Totalitarianism* seriously or we impose our own desires. Villa writes: "How one feels about Gines's analysis will depend, to a large degree, on how much one wants to shift the focus of discussion away from the 'origins' of totalitarianism proper to what we might call 'proto-totalitarian' elements in western thought and practice prior to the imperialist period. Arendt herself did as much—at least with respect to western political thought—in the work on Marx that eventually became *The Human Condition*."[39]

I can see two different responses to Villa's provocation. One would simply point out that Arendt's notion of immortality depends, by her own words, not on static things or making things static but on the dynamics of the cascading unpredictability of action. Arendt might blanch were she to discover that her thought was being transformed into something like Lenin's corpse with desperate minions doing their best to keep it from decaying. All our actions, as she wrote, disclose something about ourselves, both in the world we live(d) in and in the world in which we continue to live after our mortal death. Being present to the ongoing cascade of the world in all its agonistic rough and tumble beyond the actual mortality of the body is what immortality is and does. One can wish they had never been born. One can equally wonder, in the limitless stretch of changing discursive times, why one strove to become immortal.

A second response would begin by agreeing with Villa but drawing a different conclusion. Arendt was indeed interested in the origins of European totalitarianism. Thus, her transit through colonial and imperial worlds was simply that: a transit between two Europes. In *The Origins of Totalitarianism*, she begins in Europe and then transits through colonial and imperial worlds in order to return to the Europe of Stalin and Hitler. In *The Human Condition*, she moves between the classical Greeks and the quintessential European invention, the atomic bomb. In other words, I think Villa is right—Arendt never cared about the worlds that existed between leaving and returning to the Western tradition. These other worlds mattered insofar as they explained how the West became untrue to itself and could perhaps regain its truth. Rather than ask how Arendt is being read now, we can ask how her account of the human condition and its relevance to human survival square with other accounts of the human condition proliferating in the 1950s. What happens if we care about the worlds she saw only as a transit lounge?

There was plenty to read. The 1950s witnessed a global revolt against the *nomos* of the colonial world. Césaire's *Discourse on Colonialism*, Robin D. G. Kelley notes, "appeared alongside other key texts meditating on the impact of colonialism: W. E. B. Du Bois's *Color and Democracy* (1945) and *The World and Africa* (1947), George Padmore's *Pan-Africanism or Communism?* (1956), Albert Memmi's *The Colonizer and the Colonized* (1957), Richard Wright's *White Man Listen!* (1957), Jean-Paul Sartre's *Black Orpheus* (1948), and journals such as *Presence Africaine* and *African Revolution*."[40] Add to these Fanon's *Black Skin, White Masks* (1952) and *The Wretched of the Earth* (1961), and we find a completely different set of maps and mappings of Europe's history of totalitarianism, colonialism, and necropower and its frightening power to destroy worlds and the earth. Césaire's searing description of the colonial gangrene eating away the European body was paralleled by Du Bois's account of the relationship between European law and its extermination camps in *The World and Africa*. "There was no Nazi atrocity—concentration camps, wholesale maiming and murder, defilement of women, or ghastly blasphemy of children—which the Christian civilization of Europe had not long been practicing against colored folks in all parts of the world in the name of and the defense of a Superior Race born to rule the world."[41] This is what Ralph Ellison knew when he read Arendt's "Reflections on Little Rock" and wrote his powerful rejoinder in *Who Speaks for the Negro?*[42]

When viewed from the perspective of the ancestral and ongoing catastrophe of colonialism—past and present maiming, murder, defilement, and sadism—no distinction between colonialism and imperialism was worth its analytical weight. What mattered was finding new concepts that might disclose the concrete conditions of oppression and animate resistance across the differences and similarities of the colonial condition—Negritude, Pan-Africanism, Native, the nonaligned. The issue in play among decolonial thinkers of the 1950s, in other words, was not how to understand past or future European catastrophes but how to create new modes of political and social reality in the wake of Europe as a catastrophe. For instance, consider Gary Wilder's work on Césaire and Léopold Senghor. Wilder starts with a puzzle—why did Césaire support the departmentalization of Martinique rather than independence?[43] But Wilder is interested not just in what led Césaire to advocate strongly for departmentalization but in how this political tactic related to a broader desire to "recognize the history of interdependence between metropolitan and overseas people and protect the latter's economic and political claims on the metropolitan society their resources and labor had helped to create."[44]

I don't think I would be in error to read Wilder's use of "interdependence" in stronger terms, something more along the lines of what contemporary theorists mean when they describe existence as entangled. Metropolitan society did not preexist the extractions of colonial dispossession of lands and enslavement of peoples any more than capitalism did. Both social formations coemerged as entwined, entangled, co-conditioned things even as they entwined and reconditioned the worlds in which they emerged and to which they returned. As a result, if one or more regions in this entanglement seek a new condition, a new human condition, then the forces that have kept the region in place will change, and these changes will reverberate across the whole formation, in the process reorganizing various actual and potential futures in unpredictable ways. As Paul Gilroy notes, there wasn't just one alternative possibility, but "a range of alternative possibilities."[45] Césaire, Senghor, Fanon, and hosts of others probed these possibilities as they explored how the actual unraveling and reraveling of one region might ratify across the entire political order. They confronted the complexity of colonial entanglements. The colonial catastrophe did not just create confrontational structures like colonizer and colonized, capitalist and precariat, human and other-than-humans, humans and animals, organic and inorganic beings. It also released a complex set of new conditions that simultaneously created and complicated forms of solidarity across the wretched of the earth.

Before addressing these knots of entangled difference, let us turn to another atomic crisis, not one looming on the horizon as in Arendt's view but one that was happening in Indigenous Australia at the moment Arendt was writing *The Origins of Totalitarianism* and *The Human Condition*.

DISCLOSURES FROM INDIGENOUS WORLDS

Arendt's assertion that the people whose homelands lay in Australia and the United States had no culture or history of their own aligned her political philosophy with European settler ideology, not merely in the eighteenth century but in the 1950s. The violence such an opinion permitted—the destruction of other worlds for the sake of European expansion—was thoroughly contemporary to her writing of *The Origins of Totalitarianism* and *The Human Condition*. For instance, consider Australia in the 1950s. Between 1956 and 1957, two controversies broke out about the status of Indigenous people—the Wongi, Pitjantjatjara, Anangu, and Ngaanyatjarra—living in their central desert lands. The first is known as the Warburton Ranges controversy. The second, related to this first, was an exposé on Operation Totem, one of a series of British nuclear tests conducted in the territories of these Indigenous groups.

The basic facts about the Warburton Ranges controversy have been described by multiple historians.[46] In 1953, William Grayden, then a Liberal member of the Western Australian Parliament, conducted a trip to the Rawlinson Ranges searching for the remains of long-lost explorer Ludwig Leichhardt.[47] Instead of finding traces of Leichhardt, he reported on finding Indigenous people so destitute that he demanded a parliamentary inquiry into the status of Indigenous people in the Laverton-Warburton Ranges region. The report, tabled in 1956, found among other things that "malnutrition and blindness and disease, abortion and infanticide, and burns and other injuries are commonplace."[48] These and other findings initially found little audience until the Sydney communist newspaper, the *Tribune*, ran a story, "W.A. Parliament's Shocking Report on Aborigines," on January 9, 1957. Numerous papers followed suit, rousing public outrage. The Perth *Daily News* declared, "Warburton Natives in March of Death."[49] This publicity led to four follow-up parties. Grayden returned with Doug Nicholls, a Victorian Indigenous activist and pastor, and a 16mm camera to document his claims.[50] In addition, Rupert Murdoch, editor and owner of the Adelaide *News*, led a team of journalists into the region. Anthropologists Ronald and Catherine Berndt and Ruth Fink led another delegation. Finally, members of the Western Australian Department of Health toured the area. Even as Grayden produced his

Chapter Three

film exposé *The Darkest Hour* and book *Adam and Atoms*, all three of the other parties denied Indigenous groups were being unduly abused by the pastoralists and nuclear testing.

The diversity and style of argument in these inquiries still startles. Take Murdoch's defense of Indigenous culture. Rupert Murdoch had extensive ties to the Australian mining industry. It would not seem surprising that his paper vehemently repudiated the parliamentary findings, claiming, "No aborigines in the Central Australian reserves are dying of thirst or starvation—or disease."[51] But Murdoch launched into an extraordinary defense of the strength and well-being of "these fine native people" who "have never enjoyed better conditions."[52] He describes the people he spoke to as "a happy lot, fine people, steeped in the knowledge of their proud history, and great lovers of their own land." Even practices a settler public might find shocking, such as infanticide, Murdoch defends. Yes, "mothers DO kill their babies sometimes."[53] But this does not mean that Indigenous mothers do not love their children; it is merely an adaptation to the conditions of desert life during droughts.

Ronald Berndt sought to forge a path between Grayden, who he thought had misinterpreted much of what he saw, and Murdoch, who he thought had gone to the opposite extreme in claiming that Indigenous life remained untouched in the Laverton-Warburton Ranges.[54] Berndt's disagreement with their reports was based on his promotion of the special investigative skills of the discipline of anthropology and his sense of the objective changes to Indigenous society that were occurring in the wake of Europeans arriving. "Traditional Aboriginal life has inevitably been affected" by missionaries, pastoralists, and miners, "not only economic pursuits, but also ceremonial and ritual activity."[55] With their water sources stolen or poisoned and their environment transformed by sheep ranching and mines, most Indigenous people spent their lives in or at the edges of mining, pastoral lands, and missions. Berndt is careful to note that "this does not mean that they have given up their hereditary rights over their territory."[56] Rather than claim everything or nothing was wrong in Warburton and the surrounding lands, Berndt called for a pragmatic discussion—how to fashion state and federal policy based on the actual worlds Indigenous people lived in, rather than fantasies of a thriving or sunk people.[57]

Grayden was not deterred by Murdoch, Berndt, or any of the other members of the various expeditions of inquiry. He quickly produced and circulated *Their Darkest Hour* in cinemas across Australia. This film is widely credited with fundamentally altering settler attitudes toward Indigenous people, creating a wave of sympathy for their plight. But it was not merely sympathy for Indigenous people that swayed the public. The *Tribune* and other papers reported that Indigenous people were starving *and that* they were living in the fallout zones of atomic test sites. Few in the settler public were aware of the extent or danger of these tests—if they were aware that they were occurring at all.[58] Adding to the shock of discovering their government hiding the extent and effects of foreign nuclear tests on Australian soil was the discovery that the federal government had no power to protect Indigenous people from the fallout; indeed, the government was explicitly prohibited from writing laws pertaining to them. Images of starving and burned Indigenous men, women, and children and reports of scarred and irradiated lands led to the creation of the Federal Council for Aboriginal Advancement, propelling the 1967 referendum that gave the federal government the power to legislate on behalf of Indigenous persons and eventually the first major piece of land rights legislation, the Land Rights (Northern Territory) Act of 1976. Berndt was influential in how these laws were written, including the fact that anthropology became a legally mandated intermediating agent between Indigenous people and the state. At the heart of the legislation was a litmus test of authenticity—or, more precisely, of social anthropology's account of what "traditional Aboriginal owners" consisted of. Every Indigenous claimant would be measured by a sickly calibrated settler ruler—the more that colonization devastated Indigenous worlds, the less settlers had to give back, because according to the anthropological calculus, the greater the effect of the settler, the less Indigenous people could claim cultural and social difference.

Throughout all this, as Pamela Faye McGrath and David Brooks note, no one bothered to ask what Indigenous viewers of Grayden's film saw when they watched images of these central Indigenous families. After extensive archival research, McGrath and Brooks conclude that for many Indigenous viewers these images were not signs of poverty and destitution, nor of a measure between authentic presettler traditions and the inevitable accretions of assimilation. McGrath and Brooks write, "The way the Aboriginal subjects of *Their Darkest Hour* looked largely went hand-in-hand with the fact that they were successfully choosing to continue to occupy their traditional lands in the heart of the desert."[59] Although this certainly sounds close to Berndt's observation that the central desert people had not given up their "hereditary right" to their lands no matter their removal from a large tract of these lands, what engaged Indigenous viewers was not the ancestral past but the stubborn ancestral present. They were affected by and commented on how the bodies shown in the film registered an ongoing insistence of being in a mode of ancestral belonging in the present condition of that belonging, namely, belonging alongside and within toxic mines, murderous pastoralists, and atomic explosions.

The necessity of survivance in toxic liberalism was hardly restricted to Australia. The same technical rationality Arendt denounced in *The Human Condition* was central to wars in Europe and European colonies. In *War and Nature*, Edmund Russell explored the racist political discourses and imaginaries that underscored the deployment of chemical warfare. Far from deterring states and industries developing more lethal chemicals, the atrocities of World War I suggested the power of industrial chemistry to postwar governments, which unleashed new languages of racism and warfare. The colonies became the front line of chemical warfare. Jeffry Halverson and Nathaniel Greenberg note, "Europe's colonial power made a distinction between proper treatment of fellow Europeans and colonial subjects who resisted European hegemony, thus the English (with full French knowledge) did not hesitate to secretly deploy horrific aerial bombardments and chemical warfare against civilian men, women, and children in Morocco. Elsewhere, the British were already deploying chemical weapons (phosgene and mustard gas) against Arabs in Iraq and Afghans of the northwest frontier of British India."[60] They quote Winston Churchill, who stated, "I am strongly in favor of using poison gas against uncivilized tribes."[61] The technological transfer of atomic and nuclear technologies during and after World War II from Germany to the United States merely shifted the terrain of toxic domination and with it the hegemonic location of colonial and neocolonial power from Europe to the United States.[62]

It might be helpful to return to *The Mermaids* here, although the film was created some sixty years after the Warburton Ranges controversy and is set in the near future rather than the historic past. Nevertheless, the single-screen and the two-channel versions of the film cut to the core of what McGrath and Brooks are showing. A mermaid tells her ward that mermaids cannot be as they once were, even as they remain mermaids. In other words, the collapse of the West's disenchantment with rational technoscience and its toxic excretions did not bring the mermaids back—mermaids never left in the first place. They never vanished under the assault of the modern. The mermaids continue to shuttle their charges to their destinations even as the specificities of the destination are altered by the toxic actions of colonialism, industrialism, and their value extractions. These mermaids and their new wards are merely one part of larger segment of existence that was never enchanted or disenchanted but fought to preserve and endure in a constantly altering terrain of toxic racism and settler colonialism. Even if Aiden or Trevor releases the blowflies, wiping out all humans, the Dreaming will remain in the afterworld.

This is not what Arendt saw when she looked at the United States and Australia from the perspective of colonial history or from whatever full, partial, or nonexisting accounts of Indigenous worlds living at the same time as her own. She simply saw them as world-poor. Reflecting on Arendt's use of that phrase, Johanna C. Luttrell notes that various events can place a group in the status of world-poor. The global impoverishment of countless people, for instance, has alienated numerous populations from their lands and worlds.[63] Grayden saw exactly this sort of world and land alienation when he encountered the Wongi, Pitjantjatjara, Anangu, and Ngaanyatjarra. But I suspect this is not what Arendt was referring to when she claimed that Indigenous peoples in the Americas and Australia did not have a culture or history of their own. She meant that they never had a world to lose; that they had not even separated themselves from other living and nonliving beings, let alone developed two of the three conditions of being human—the making of durable shelters (*Homo faber*) for human action (*zoon activon*). They demonstrated a kind of speech and a sort of action that was oriented to the human and nonhuman world simultaneously, to *bios*, *zoe*, and *geos* as irrelevant divisions of existence. The "human condition of plurality" for them was that humans lived with and inhabited multiple modes of worlding—winds, fathers, mudflats, mermaids, cousins, rocks, and so on.[64] There was plenty of immortality here—just not of the toxic kind, of chemicals and atomic half-lives.

THE ENTANGLEMENTS OF ATOMIC LEGACIES

In an interview later in his life, Césaire sketched out an alternative vision of humanism grounded within a loop that begins in the colonial conditions of the Black Atlantic and returns to their potential for a new kind of political imaginary. "The universal," he said, "is not the negation of the particular but is reached by a deeper exploration of the particular."[65] He continued, "The West told us that in order to be universal we had to start by denying that we were Black. I, on the contrary, said to myself that the more we were Black, the more universal we would be."[66]

Other scholars quote similar reflections from *Discourse on Colonialism*; Ramón Grosfoguel turns to Césaire's encounter with the abstract universalism permeating Europe, which Césaire opposed to his own take: "My idea of the universal is that of a universal rich with all that is particular, rich with all particulars, the deepening and coexistence of all particulars."[67] Jane Hiddleston has built on the work of Gary Wilder and Nick Nesbitt to forge a rapprochement with Césaire's work and to understand the seeming paradox between the "solitude and isolation" of "Césaire the man and the Martinique conjured up by his work" and his "expansive and open-ended celebration of the black man's mobility and contact with the other."[68] These scholars seek to understand the differences among the transhumanism, postcolonial humanism, and pluriversalism of Césaire and European colonial humanism.

A very similar goal centers Paul Gilroy's Tanner Lectures, presented in 2014, the year before Chakrabarty's. In them, Gilroy outlines a proposal for a new transhuman or "infrahuman" moral economy built on a transversal network of places differentially knitted together by the complex entanglements of colonialism, including the various styles and articulations of Anglo, Spanish, and French colonialism. He begins not with what human nature is composed of in the abstract but "where the human broke down, how it was qualified, compromised, and disposed of."[69] Only by understanding these "extensive entanglements" can an alternative "largely forgotten lineage" be resurrected "in which the contested relationship between the properly human and the racialized infrahuman loomed large."[70] This new humanism will not be found in a revolutionary form of plurality that emerged from the colonialization of the Americas and Australia, nor with some inevitability of the violent founding of the new. Those humanisms, Gilroy argues, unleashed a double standard of law and peace and war and violence in which "peace and law would dwell inside their [European] borders—which would increasingly be drawn on a planetary scale—while the chaos and conflict that Marx would later name 'wild justice' reigned, catastrophically, outside."[71] Against this *nomos*, Black Atlantic theories of transhumanism consist of multitudes of alternative possibilities for political collectivity and solidarity. That is, Gilroy's project is resolutely humanist, but his understanding of the human condition arises from the comprehensive mapping of "colonial administration and the violent ordering of power and space that it required made for commercial, military, and juridical arrangements," central to which was the obscuring and mystifying of the "humanity of the people who had been subordinated, expropriated, and enslaved."[72]

In light of this violent ordering, Gilroy has critically engaged certain strands of the posthumanism, especially the part that claims to be engaged in a progressive politics of critical racism. Swiping at Donna Haraway's idea that "there is liberation in the prospect of human beings recognizing themselves as just one more 'critter' among many,"[73] he reminds readers who might have forgotten "the slave, the Negro, and the indigene experience enforced association with the animal."[74] Among the colonial dispossessed, he argues, "the liberatory and solidary possibilities released by the process of 'becoming animal' are less appealing precisely because they are almost entirely animal already."[75]

Of course, many Indigenous theories do not separate human and more-than-human worlds in quite this way. Take Aileen Moreton-Robinson's description of her and other Indigenous people's original, ontological mode of belonging to land and other nonhuman forms of existence in and of the land.[76] Likewise, Glen Coulthard argues in *Red Skin, White Masks* that the alienation Indigenous people struggle against comes from the relentless pressure to be absorbed into Western alienation from other more-than-human beings. Indigenous struggles against capitalist imperialism are best understood as struggles oriented around the question of land—"struggles not only *for* land, but also deeply *informed* by what the land as a mode of reciprocal relationship (which is itself informed by place-based practices and associated form of knowledge) ought to teach us about living our lives in relation to one another and our surroundings in a respectful, nondominating and nonexploitative way."[77] Before Coulthard was Vine Deloria Jr. The originary dispossession of Indigenous and Native peoples is thus not of the land as inert ground; instead, "social relations are often not only based on principles of egalitarianism but also deep reciprocity between people and with the other-than-human world."[78] This is what Rex Edmunds points to when he critiques the politics of recognition as primarily a means of dividing and pitting one against the other. It is what Barbara Glowczewski seeks to show in her pairing of Guattarian ecosophy with Indigenous Australian ontologies.[79]

Rather than understanding Gilroy as right or wrong, it is more productive to see his critique as expressing the need for different discourses, perspectives, tactics, and maneuvers depending on where and how one is entangled in the violent order of geontological being, an entanglement that began in the colonial period and continues today. Perhaps Gilroy is pointing out that the question is not one of becoming or not becoming a critter but refusing to become a geontological critter—refusing to enter the nomenclatures, ranks, and orders of Western epistemologies and ontologies of nonlife and life. Humans are not lowered to animal, lightning, mountain ranges, rivers, or plants when refusing the violent governance of *geontopower*. This lowering was part and parcel of a colonial epistemological invasion, part and parcel of a capitalist remaking of the relationship between humans and humans, humans and critters, life and nonlife. And it was exactly the onto-epistemological ordering that made it possible for Arendt to place Indigenous peoples outside the plurality of the human condition. In short, this lowering of some humans to animals depended on imposing a geontological imaginary in which animals and the geological world had already been lowered. Once the division between life and nonlife and the hierarchy of life based on this division were in place, various humans could be made more animal-like, more stone-like. Listen to the mermaids and the entities they come upon in their travels. The problem is not whether they are human or nonhuman but rather which human condition is imposed on them. The tensions between colonies and *nomos* extends its grip into the present, conferring contemporary challenges for those seeking new forms of solidarity across the decolonizing world.

Toxic Ends

The Biosphere and
the Colonial Sphere

THE BIOS FEAR

If the threat of atomic annihilation framed Arendt's reflections on the human condition in the late 1950s, a 1968 photograph snapped by US astronaut Buzz Aldrin of the blue-green earth rising over the grays of the lunar horizon framed a new generation of concern about human extinction. Rather than a massive boom of atomic annihilation, *Silent Spring*, Rachel Carson's 1962 blockbuster, tuned reading publics onto the vast silent implosion of life caused by industrial toxins and pesticides even as the Norwegian philosopher, Arne Naess, developed the concept of deep ecology to show how humans were dependent on these global ecosystems.[1] Humans needed to stop attending only to their own existence and start caring about the vast disappearing worlds of nonhuman life. Even if humans cared only about other humans, Carson argued, they needed to focus on the pesticides and industrial toxins that were destroying the environmental web on which the human condition depended. Carson and Naess were joined by many others. The anthropologist Gregory Bateson wrote *Steps to an Ecology of Mind* and argued that not only were humans immanent to and dependent on the broader ecology of life on earth, their minds, long thought to separate the human from nature, were merely a part of the much broader mind of nature.

In different ways, these scholars and writers attacked the idea that *Homo sapiens sapiens* were a morally and socially superior animal, with all other forms of existence having value relative to them. By the 1960s, such an attitude was not merely prejudiced; it was a deadly bias. Old words like *biocide* took on new meanings. The concepts of speciesism and the biosphere joined a host of other -isms emerging across the array of social movements reflecting this new awareness. The US bioethicist and botanist Arthur Galston introduced the term *ecocide*, for instance, at a 1970 conference on the war and national responsibility in Washington, DC, to highlight the massive environmental impact Agent Orange was having on the Vietnamese landscape.[2] Just two years after the *Earthrise* photograph and eight years after the publication of *Silent Spring*, more than a million people in the United States took part in the first Earth Day, which was followed by a raft of federal legislations—the Clean Air Act (1970) and the establishment of the US Environmental Protection Agency, the Clean Water Act (1972), and the Endangered Species Act (1973). In Europe, the Environment Action Programme was established in 1972, the same year that the Club of Rome published *The Limits of Growth*.

Arendt, Bateson, Carson: these three thinkers reflected the convergences and differences of a set of discursive struggles playing out in the West about how to situate humans in their earthly existence as a catastrophe of human extinction loomed on the horizon. All three agreed that humans were irreducibly tied to the earth. Whereas Bateson, Carson, and Naess sought to place humans on the same level and within the same web of existence as nonhuman life, Arendt tried desperately to pull the human world out of its biopolitical conditions. Indeed, at the end of her life, she was attempting to complement her discussion of the *vita activa* in *The Human Condition* with the *vita contemplativa* published posthumously as *The Life of the Mind*. She was fighting a losing war. By the time her friend Mary McCarthy had edited her unfinished manuscript in the late 1970s, the mind had sunk into the more general concept of the biosphere and a new cybernetic science threatened to tear it loose from organic material altogether. The 1970s were the dawn of the Age of Aquarius and the cyborg. Arendt was alive long enough to contemplate how the private realm had devoured the public sphere and how the cybernetic mind would devour the human mind.

We certainly should applaud Bateson, Carson, Naess, and others for trying to awaken the slumbering affluent classes to the carcinogenic chemicals on their kitchen counters and to the broader environmental disaster of extractive and consumerist capitalism. But if we are to understand how their efforts provide a prehistory to the emergence of the four axioms of existence, then we need to understand how the rhythm of colonial citation and disavowal we saw in the difference between Arendt and Césaire repeats in the new ecology of mind emerging in the 1960s and 1970s. Thus, like the last chapter, this one is structured to look at two different historical screens—the anxiety of a coming catastrophe and the analytics of an ancestral catastrophe. First, I discuss how specific First Nations and Indigenous peoples understood the relationship among human and nonhuman minds during the ongoing assault of settler law and capital in the late 1960s and early 1970s. Then I turn to Bateson's understanding of the ecology of mind during the same period.

Throughout this chapter, First Nations, Native American, and Indigenous critical theorists will refer to ontological and metaphysical differences between their ethics of relationality and settler politics of possessive disruption. Reference to these works might strike some as contradictory to the broad purpose of this book, namely, to dislodge a critical tendency to revert to first conditions. I prefer not to use the term *ontology* and see no reason that all peoples must show they also have what western Europe has elevated as its highest and purist form of existential self-reflexivity. Thus, I use the sometimes awkward phrase "analytics of existence." But I also do not think that the Indigenous thinkers I discuss use ontology in a way equivalent to its use and function in its Western genealogies. On the contrary, what I hope to show is that, while the word might be the same, the content and use of ontology within critical Indigenous theory are irreducibly historically and materially relational. This is a point that the Métis scholar Zoe Todd makes forcefully, arguing that ontology is just another word for colonialism.[3] It does not refer to conditions outside history and its material entanglements but to a set of activities of survivance in the ongoing activity of colonial power.

THE COLONIAL MIND

In late March 1974, Justice Thomas Berger began an inquiry investigating the economic, environmental, and social impact of a proposed gas pipeline that would stretch across the Mackenzie Valley and Yukon region, connecting the rich oil and gas fields in Alaska to the continental United States. Berger would not have been the first choice to lead the inquiry if it had been left up to conservative state and business commercial interests. He was widely known for his environmental and social justice interests; for instance, he had served as leader of the British Columbia New Democratic Party. Conservative concerns about Berger were soon justified. He took an activist approach to the inquiry, traveling extensively throughout the Northwest Territories, consulting with First Nations people of the Inuvialuit, Gwich'in, Dene, Cree, and Métis. He allowed First Nations people to present their own expert testimony as opposed to what was then standard: the interpretive mediation of anthropologists, historians, and archaeologists. Berger ultimately reported that the social and environmental harm of the proposed pipeline outweighed any significant countervailing economic benefits of it for local Indigenous people.[4]

The First Nations Dene groups were already organizing against the pipeline by the time Berger arrived. The Mackenzie pipeline was not the first time (and would not be the last) that extractive and transport capital tried to rampage through their lands. Some Dene cited industrial mining and toxic tailings in the 1930s and 1940s as having awakened them to the necessity of organized protest. During that period, mining companies regularly "hired local native people to perform unskilled work at the site and along the ore transportation route" with no protective precautions.[5] Uranium ore was loaded and unloaded "in burlap sacks for barge transport along northern waterways to a railhead in Alberta," and "radioactive tailings" were dumped "directly into Great Slave Lake, local pothole lakes, and on land near Port Radium."[6]

The Sahtu Dene's experience was just one part of broader First Nations struggles against the toxicity of extractive capitalism in the Northwest Territories. The 1950s and 1960s witnessed new mining expansion as businesses began exploring for lead, zinc, and nickel in the Yukon and Rankin Inlet region.[7] Minerals were not the only value the settlers tried to extract from Dene and other First Nations; liberal governments reached deep into First Nations families, intentionally tearing children from their languages and lands. As Margaux Kristjansson has shown, although the capital forms differed between the mining interests and welfare policies of child removal, both created an economic value that flowed out of First Nations lands and bodies into settler society.[8]

As chapters 1 and 2 show, liberal capitalism never finally controls the territories or outcomes of its toxic actions. In this case, rather than severing the connection between stolen children and their land, a generation of the Dene, forcefully removed from their families as children and sent to regional boarding schools, vigorously organized against the pipeline in the 1970s.[9] Not only did these men and women present their own testimony to Berger, they spelled out the connection between the ongoing settler dispossession and ongoing First Nations refusals to be dispossessed. Colonialism was not an event that happened, so resistance would never end. For example, consider the testimony of George Erasmus: "Too often in the past we have been compelled to adjust to changes that were beyond our control. For decades there has been encroachment on our land without our permission and without compensation. Lands and resource[s] have been illegally alienated and appropriated and our people have experienced serious disruption—socially, economically, and environmentally. Contemporary pressures are greater still—and the potential for further disruption is vast—but now more and more of our people are saying 'enough.'"[10] The struggle Erasmus identifies reminds us of a point made at the end of chapter 2. Late settler liberalism operates across territorial mappings, a crucial mapping being the struggle over the definition of being and subsequent ethical and political consequences on the meaning of violent actions toward these variously defined beings. What is the earth such that one can convincingly say that the Mackenzie pipelines are *ripping* into the connective tissues of the human and more-than-human existence or merely moving a product *extracted* from the earth? This is not a question of relativity or one of the multiperspectival nature of ontologies—a *late liberal* response of "they see it this way, we see it that way." It is a question of how describing existence in one way or another supports very different actions on existence. As William James noted, it is a question of "power-bringing" words (concepts) "as a program for more work."[11] The conceptual and protest work Berger heard was just part of a more global Indigenous opposition to extractive capitalism. This fight was not merely over who owned the land but over the analysis of existence that made the concept of ownership valid. Thus, in her essays reflecting on "the white possessive," Aileen Moreton-Robinson has contrasted an Indigenous ontology of original belonging to land with settler racial and environmental violence emerging from liberal forms of property.[12] In a similar move, Saidiya Hartman has discussed the movement from being treated as an object of property to being granted the right to own oneself and other things. She writes about

> the failure of Reconstruction not simply as a matter of policy or as evidence of a flagging commitment to black rights, which is undeniably the case, but also in terms of the limits of emancipation, the ambiguous legacy of universalism, the exclusions constitutive of liberalism, and the blameworthiness of the freed individual. Therefore I examine the role of rights in facilitating relations of domination, the new forms of bondage enabled by proprietorial notions of the self, and the pedagogical and legislative efforts aimed at transforming the formerly enslaved into rational, acquisitive, and responsible individuals. From this vantage point, emancipation appears less the grand event of liberation than a point of transition between modes of servitude and racial subjection.[13]

In the US context, Vine Deloria Jr. forcefully articulated the metaphysical conditions that were at stake in the struggle against settler colonialism. In his

1973 book *God Is Red*, Deloria describes the Western tradition of revelation as consisting of "the communication to human beings of a divine plane, the release of information and insights when the deity has perceived that mankind has reached the fullness of time and can now understand additional knowledge about the ultimate nature of our world."[14] Because revelation is oriented to the ultimate nature of existence, "the manifestation of deity in a particular local situation is mistaken for a truth applicable to all times and places."[15] Nothing of the sort defined the path that Native Americans took to revelation. For them, "revelation was seen as a continuous process of adjustment to the natural surroundings and not as a specific message valid for all times and places."[16] Deloria's account of revelation evokes a mode of existence in which relationality is ongoing and neither assumes nor imposes one form of dominion over another—whether of mind, territory, or security—even as the integrity of each is entwined with the integrity of the other.

Many critical Indigenous scholars have elaborated Deloria's powerful insight. Zoe Todd, for instance, has asked how grief over colonial losses manifests across the sameness and difference between her human Métis and fish relatives in the shadow of the Truth and Reconciliation Commission of Canada on the Indian Residential School System. We see the continual adjustment Deloria characterizes as fundamental to a Native metaphysics—among "Paulatuuq, people refract the colonial laws and principles imposed upon local lives by negotiating across simultaneous and often contradictory 'sameness and difference,'" which includes "local Inuvialuit legal orders that govern how to respect fish" and "contending with the Canadian State's colonial legal systems that seek to control the legal-governance relationships between humans, animals, lands and waters."[17] Even at this edge of existential encounter, consciousness of the other is not consciousness over or even about the other but an acknowledgment that an individual consciousness is irreducibly conditioned by the form and materialization of the entwinement of existence.

Glen Coulthard also cites and builds on Deloria's argument that "the most significant differences that exist between Indigenous and Western metaphysics revolves around the central importance of land to Indigenous modes of being, thought, and ethics."[18] He does so to explicate how what is important for Dene is "the position land occupies as an ontological framework for understanding relationships" rather than simply "the rather obvious observation that most Indigenous societies hold a strong attachment to their homelands."[19] Like Todd, Coulthard points to modes of relationality from within the struggle against settler dispossession and against a version of land, human, and more-than-human minds that are either different and thus separate from one another or the same and thus equivalent. To deepen readers' understanding of such a relational ontology, Coulthard refers to an event that happened on a moose hunt undertaken by Edward Blondin, brother of Sahtu Dene George Blondin. Coulthard quotes George Blondin on his brother's story:

> "Edward was hunting near a small river when he heard a raven croaking, far off to his left. Ravens can't kill animals themselves, so they depend on hunters and wolves to kill food for them. Flying high in the sky, they spot animals too far away for hunters or wolves to see. They then fly to the hunter and attract his attention by croaking loudly, then fly back to where the animals are. Edward stopped and watched the raven carefully. It made two trips back and forth in the same direction.
>
> "Edward made a sharp turn and walked to where the raven was flying. There were no moose tracks, but he kept following the raven. When he got to the riverbank and looked down, Edward saw two big moose feeding on the bank. He shot them, skinned them, and covered the meat with their hides.
>
> "Before he left, Edward put some fat meat out on the snow for the raven. He knew that without the bird, he wouldn't have killed any meat that day."[20]

Coulthard identifies two forms of refusal embedded in this story that relate to Indigenous theories of sovereignty. First, Blondin refuses the choice between portraying the minds and interests of the human and the more-than-human, in this case a raven, as completely different (incommensurate, untranslatable) or the same (commensurate and translatable without remainder). Second, and relatedly, Blondin refuses the choice between elevating human sovereignty over all other forms of existence, whether living or non-living, or removing Indigenous sovereignty from the land. The analytics of existence that Blondin and Coulthard are proposing is one in which Edward and the raven have an agency and consciousness oriented toward and independent of each other. Understanding what the raven needs is not confined to what Edward needs from the raven but what the raven needs without reference to Edward or any other human.

The needs of other regions and forms of existence irrespective of human needs became crucial in the Berger hearings, when questions arose of why Dene cared about lands they rarely lived on or visited. The answer was that these lands were necessary for the caribou herds. If the Dene were to remain in their place, so must the caribou. This understanding of relationality acknowledges the complexities of relational ontologies in which not all forms of existence need the same kind of things, and yet without each other none could stay in the shape they are in; they will all change in ways none want. Paul Nadasdy makes a similar point in a story from the 1970s about the grandmother of Joe Johnson, then chief elect of the Kluane First Nation (KFN). Accompanied by his grandmother, Johnson "had been out in the bush inspecting a piece of land that the KFN was considering for selection" as part of a coming land claim. Puzzled, she asked what he was doing. He replied that he was working, to which she scoffed, "What do you mean 'working'? You're just walking around with a map." When Johnson tried to explain how land claims worked "she became upset . . . that he was trying to figure out which land belonged to Indians and which to the white men." "She told him that was a crazy thing to do, for no one can own the land—neither white men nor Indians. The land is there; we move around; we die. How can anyone own it? She said that she had thought that 'land claims' meant that the government and native people were getting together to try to figure out how to keep the land and animals safe for their children and grandchildren."[21]

The emphasis these examples place on the necessity for each form and mode of existence to make room for the other, even as many look to eat each other, brings into view and makes manifest the profound alienation of European thought from the richness of existence at the center of the concept of terra nullius. The insistence that to stay in place necessitates care about the needs of others for a place of their own contrasts with the two dominant ways the settler state has represented Indigenous relations to their lands, namely, as having no relation (terra nullius) or as having a human-centric proprietary practice that could ultimately be translated into its own. In both cases, as Deloria noted above, Europeans asserted not merely the world-historical superiority of their truth but that their truth was "a truth applicable to all times and places."[22] When it came to human relations to land, settler truth insisted sovereignty depended on humans having a specific population density in a place and humans having an intention to assert their divine superiority over all other forms of existence in a place. The absence of humans and this human intention (dominion) was a sign of economic waste and a divine abomination.[23] Thus the puzzlement of lawyers in the Mackenzie Valley hearings over why Dene cared about lands they rarely if ever visited.

The clash between Indigenous and settler analytics of existence stretched across the Pacific in the 1970s. While Berger was conducting his inquiry in Canada, Edward Woodward sat down with Karrabing ancestors at the Delissaville Settlement (later renamed Belyuen) in Australia. Like the Berger inquiry, the Woodward Royal Commission played out against the backdrop of a hydrocarbon and mineral boom. Places long considered wastelands from the point of view of agricultural and pastoral capitalism revealed themselves as vast stores of carbon and mineral wealth for extractive capitalism. While a boom in uranium mining centered a national debate about whether or not Australia should participate, other ores and minerals became the basis of settler Australian wealth and well-being.[24]

In this broad context, the Yolngu launched a legal challenge in 1968 against the plans of the mining giant Nabalco to commence extracting bauxite on their lands. Like in Canada, this challenge did not come out of the blue; the Yolngu began organizing against the mine soon after the federal government gave Nabalco a twelve-year lease carved out of the Arnhem Land Aboriginal Reserve on their lands.[25] The case went before the Northern Territory Supreme Court. On April 27, 1971, Justice Richard Blackburn found that whatever rights and relations Indigenous people had over their lands were not proprietary rights and relations, and even if they had been, these rights and relations had long been invalidated by the Crown's declaration of Australia as terra nullius at the moment of colonization. Blackburn did not dismiss the Yolngu's deep affinity with their lands. He argued instead that they were a community of law, not men. They were ruled by spiritual beliefs and customs that did not include the concept of property. In Blackburn's opinion, property depended on the idea that a person did (or could) have primary power over another person or thing and had the power to exclude others from using it. The Yolgnu did not place themselves over existence in this way.

No matter its technical felicity to settler law, coming in the wake of the Warburton Ranges controversy discussed in chapter 3 and a highly publicized labor strike by Indigenous people at Wave Hill in 1966, Blackburn's legal reasoning spread a putrid smell of injustice across the liberal legal and public community. To dispel this odor, the federal Whitlam government commissioned Woodward to lead an inquiry into the "appropriate means to recognise and establish the traditional rights and interests of the Aborigines in and in relation to land, and to satisfy in other ways the reasonable aspirations of the Aborigines to rights in or in relation to land."[26]

Woodward issued two reports, the first in July 1973 and the second in April 1974. Between those dates he visited the Social Science Research Council of Canada to take part in a symposium on public land usage in late October 1973. In his 1974 report, he noted discussing "native land rights questions with a number of government officers, lawyers and Indian leaders in various parts of Canada."[27] He also reports having traveled to the United States and having conversations "with officers of the Bureau of Indian Affairs and others in Washington, D.C."[28] His endeavors to bring Australian Indigenous land rights into an international setting were supplemented by his anthropological consultant, Nicholas Peterson, a newly minted doctor in social anthropology from the University of Sydney who had studied Yolngu social organization for his dissertation. Thus whatever would be the results of local conversations with Indigenous elders, the Woodward Report would be oriented to an international conversation on Indigenous and First Nation land rights.

In his first report Woodward identifies two issues he confronted, the first being the need to sort out what lands belong to which Indigenous groups. Woodward notes that he quickly realized this task was "unnecessary." "They know which Aborigines own which tract of land by Aboriginal law, whether it is now part of an Aboriginal reserve or of a cattle station."[29] The second issue was the complexity of Indigenous social organization as it related to land. This issue presented Woodward with the conundrum, or awkwardness, of imputing concepts of property to anything, even in relation to religious rites. One can say that "religious rites [are] owned by a clan," Woodward observes, but the rites "could not be held without the assistance of the managers whose essential task it was to prepare the ritual paraphernalia, decorate the celebrants and conduct the rite."[30] Lest readers reduce the importance of these managers as analogous to hired labor, Woodward notes that the "agreement of managers had to be secured for the exploitation of specialised local resources such as ochre and flint deposits and for visits *by the clan owners to their own sacred sites*."[31] What relevance did Western notions of ownership or sovereignty have in such a system? Even Woodward's anthropological consultants could not agree on "the exact nature of the relationship between Aboriginal organization for land holding and for land usage."[32]

Delissaville was one of the settlements that Woodward visited on his fact-finding mission. From notes taken during his meeting with the gathered elders, the ancestors of the Karrabing certainly demonstrated an air of confidence about how they were related to various lands and what they envisioned as the proper way of treating them. They knew where their traditional country lay and had strong opinions about who should be recognized for the country under claim. Elders from five language groups and more than ten *durlg* (totemic) groups told Woodward that all groups should own the peninsula together, a sentiment they echoed later to anthropologists Maria Brandl and Michael Walsh.[33] Their argument was not just that the lands had always been used by all the groups at Delissaville but that new rituals rooted in the *ancestral present* of the land to transform human dislocation into obligated belonging now expressed the ancestral desires of the country.[34]

In broad agreement with Deloria's understanding of Native American approaches to revelation, current Karrabing members, the descendants of the men and women who spoke to Woodward, understand the reason for this desire to share the land to be based on the dynamic relationship between humans and the more-than-human world that rests within the framework of the ancestral present. In concrete terms this means that Karrabing know where many of their ancestral beings are located. And, equally important, as my previous discussion about Rex Edmunds's Mudi totem suggests, they know the ancestral interactions that led to the ancestral beings being where they are, in the shape they are, and in a specific relation to each other. Fellow Karrabing member Linda Yarrowin describes this mode of interdependent independence ("separate-separate and connected") as the basis of the Karrabing analytics of existence.[35]

While emplaced by a series of ancestral actions, these totemic beings are not inert; they are not confined to the past perfect. They can move around in response to the movements of the human and more-than-human world. Karrabing know that a mangrove dwelling rock-based family totem is slowly moving out to sea, revealing that it feels its human relatives are no longer caring for it. Distant totems will show themselves in new places such as when a sea serpent totem from one area revealed itself in the shape of a petrified ribcage to women hunting for snails on a reef in another area. This was interpreted as a sign that the land was accepting a human family with this same totem then forcibly interned on the Delissaville Settlement. Ancestors can also change the shape or health of the human body. For instance, Edmunds has spoken about how, if he spears too many Mudi or too close to his Mudi totem, he can unintentionally create severe headaches in his children, or worse.[36]

When Woodward released his official report in 1974, he made the following observations and recommendations:

- Aboriginal people themselves must be fully consulted about all steps proposed to be taken.
- Any scheme for recognition of Aboriginal rights to land must be sufficiently flexible to allow for changing ideas and changing needs among Aboriginal people over a period of years.
- Cash compensation is no answer to the legitimate land claims of a people with a distinct past who want to maintain their separate identity in the future.
- There is little point in recognizing Aboriginal claims to land unless the Aboriginal people concerned are also provided with the necessary funds to make use of that land in any sensible way they wish.
- It is important that Aboriginal communities have as much autonomy as possible in their own affairs.

- Aboriginal people should be free to follow their traditional methods of decision making.
- Aboriginal people should be free to choose their manner of living.
- There must be regard for principles of conservation. Thus, public monies must not be wasted or misappropriated, and lands and natural resources should not be used in a way that they suffer avoidable damage.
- Differences between Aboriginal people should be allowed for, but any artificial barriers (in particular those based on degrees of Aboriginal blood) must be avoided.

The legislative implementation of these recommendations was interrupted, however. In 1975, in what some describe as the greatest constitutional crisis to rock the nation, Governor General John Kerr (for the most part a titular appointment of the British Crown) sacked the Whitlam government. The conservative Liberal Party's Malcolm Fraser was appointed the interim prime minister and won the subsequent federal election. Although these dramatic events were caused by numerous factors, all grounded in the progressive policies of the first Labor government in twenty-three years, the impact on the land legislation that emerged was significant. The Land Rights (Northern Territory) Act of 1976 (LRA) made two major changes to Woodward's broad vision and understanding of the desires of Indigenous men and women. First, rather than allowing Indigenous people to decide who belonged to what lands, the LRA implemented a strict social anthropological model for how Indigenous people had to present their claims. Any group who wanted their country back had to prove that they were a "traditional Aboriginal owner" consisting of some sort of "local descent group" with "common spiritual affiliations" to a sacred site on their land.[37] Second, directly opposite to what Woodward observed about the inappropriateness of the concept of property to Indigenous ritual and land relations, the LRA specified that the kind of spiritual affiliation to a sacred site and the land the claimant had must be "primary rights" over that land with the powers to exclude others.

This distortion of Woodward's report and this distortion of the understandings of the Indigenous men and women who spoke to Woodward became the discursive blueprint for all subsequent pieces of state and federal legislation pertaining to Indigenous people.[38] Bodies, minds, and relations could have a superficial sheen of difference, but they were ordered based on the sovereignty of property. When asked to discuss with me nonfascist modes of belonging to place for *L'internationale online*, Rex Edmunds focused on the ways that federal land rights legislation disrupted the double session Yarrowin describes in the phrase "separate-separate and connected."

REX EDMUNDS: I am Mudi or what white people call Barramundi, a kind of fish. I saw it once on the menu in New York City! Anyway, my Mudi sits on the tip of Mabaluk; it's reef-shaped, like the tail of the fish. The point of Mabaluk is shaped like a mudi. I get the totem from my dad and he from his dad. It's the same way my dad's brother and their kids, like Natie (Natasha Bigfoot), pick it up. And so it's been ours since before the white people and right back to the Dreaming time. And it still is. I don't know if it's right to say, but we're the chiefs. [Laughing.]

ELIZABETH A. POVINELLI: Ah, but smack on point. Maybe you can tell folks about what you and Linda [Yarrowin] were saying in the video we made for Natasha Ginwala's exhibition at the ifa-Galerie in Berlin, *Riots: Slow Cancellation of the Future*. You talked then about "separate-separate and connected." Maybe you can also talk about your totem and ceremonies like rag burning, *kapug*?

RE: Sure, my totem, my mudi, is one of two sisters who were circling around a place called Bandawarrangalgen—this place is still there, as you know. As they were going around and around they made a dangerous whirlpool. They decided after a while—maybe they were jealous of something, maybe it was a man—that one would go upstream and become a freshwater barramundi and the other would stay in the saltwater; the saltwater one came to my land and sat down at Mabaluk. So these sisters are "separate-separate." They each have the place where they were and are now, but they are also connected because of this story and the land that their activity shaped into being the way it is today.

So it's like that: separate-separate but connected. You can and can't make them different. Like we talk about "Karrabing" as meaning one of the tides, the low tide, which shows how various places are connected and different, as you can see the shape of the sand and the reefs and the deep channel waterways below the surface of the water. It's also what connects all of us. How can I take care of my land if you are destroying yours? I think white people are realising this with climate change and the poisons and plastic and radiation everywhere now. And fracking. They say, oh, we'll only frack in this little area, but the poisons might spread into the underground water.

EAP: I think rag burning might help outside people understand this idea of how everything was connected or joined together at the very beginning.

RE: Well, if someone from your family dies we have the Christian funeral at the graveyard. If it's a ceremonial man or woman, then we also have a *wangga* to show respect. But, in any case, you keep the person's old clothes or stuff that has their sweat on them, the spirit of that person, you know. Then maybe after a year—should be a year or something like that—we have a rag burning. Like we did for Trevor's mum and Daphne's husband last year. Well, you need your uncle or aunt or cousin, in our way it's a cousin, like your mum's brother's kids or your dad's sister's kids to do the burning of the clothes. Because they are your aunt (father's sister) or uncle (mother's brother), they are always from another clan, so another country. Best if the uncle, aunt or cousins are close, but as long as it's connected in this way it's okay. How could I burn my mum's or sister's or father's clothes myself: no one who is in my totem group can touch those things during the ceremony. I am boss of them, but I cannot do it myself. I need my relations from that other totem or country.[39]

Ironically the relationships of belonging Edmunds describe mirror Justice Blackburn's justification for rejecting Yolngu challenges to the plans of the mining giant Nabalco to extract bauxite from their lands. But Edmunds sees himself as refusing the proprietary logics of settler capitalism, and all of its ontological and social entailments, rather than as lacking them. Edmunds argues that the regime of settler land claims has reduced the scope of Indigenous power. According to him, the rich interdependencies and connections among Indigenous lands are reduced to "TOs" (traditional owners) being give a "little bit of land" in order to facilitate mining and development. In other words, the law of recognition did what even Blackburn refused to do: it collapsed the analytics of how humans were with land into an order of property that would make commensurate those analytics to state and capital approaches to property. The Karrabing answer is not that they lack land but that they refuse the Western idea that their land is property.

Not only do Karrabing understand their ancestral totems as relational beings but they also know that the interruption of previous relations might have led ancestral beings to "hide themselves" or "go underground."[40] The significance of these underground ancestors rests in their ability, if they so choose, to reveal potentially new (old) connections among places, people, and the more-than-human world. In *Geontologies* I describe the Karrabing as seeing the task of human thought when encountering a manifestation.[41] The point was not to understand things in and of themselves but to understand how their variations in locations were an indication of an alteration of some regional mode(s) of existence that mattered. The purpose of understanding the tendencies, predilections, and orientations of any given part in a given formation was to keep that part oriented toward the formation so it could continue.[42] The double session of "separate-separate and connected" is not merely a material matter. It is a mental orientation, an ethics of existence that is constantly concerned with the potentialities of the ancestral present to signal its intentions and desires. We get a glimpse of what is at stake in a conversation among some Karrabing members about the broad hold that this way of thinking about interdependent independence has on linguistic, ceremonial and social ethics.

ELIZABETH A. POVINELLI: So, in the beginning, there were many languages. Did all of these languages present a problem to them?

CECILIA LEWIS: No, it didn't, because they knew all these languages. Like my mom's mom knew the whole lot of the languages we've been discussing. . . .

CL: We think that when you speak to that person in this way, you connect or articulate, you and him—when you speak their language to them the other person comes inside you and you go inside of them. You are thinking of/with/through that other person. . . .

ANGELIA LEWIS: And don't forget about ceremony. . . . And about people sitting around a fire and swapping stories . . .

CL: One group tells their side of a story, like the various ways the Sea Serpent story is told depending on where you live. And all the stories are similar but different and so you need to tell what the Dreaming did from your country's perspective and you begin to see how it connects to what happens in another country—or how it's different—such as whom he fought or didn't fight. So Marriamu, Emmi, and Mentha and Wadjigiyn with the Dog Dreaming are connected by the story that crosses their countries.

LINDA YARROWIN: As so with marriage, ceremony, sweating in a place—by doing this you join the places that these activities cross over, but you also keep your own people and places strong. That is why people were strong before white people came. They respected the other person because they were connected inside and outside.[43]

THE BIOSPHERIC MIND

In what might appear as mere correlations of time and event, Bateson published his groundbreaking *Steps to an Ecology of Mind* just two years before Berger and Woodward wrote their reports. But a deeper causal connection exists between Bateson's text and the kinds of worlds Dene and Karrabing ancestors were struggling to keep in place. Part anthropologist, cyberneticist, psychologist, and morphologist of being, Bateson cut a wide swath across the variegated domains of intellectual life from the 1940s until his death in 1980. His intellectual career began in colonial Papua New Guinea and Indonesia and moved through US military intelligence and the heyday of cybernetics, then ended in left ecology. A host of scholars have detailed the connections between Bateson and contemporary critical thinkers.[44] His thinking about mind and nature can be traced in Deleuze and Guattari's work on the plateau, rhizome, and schizoanalysis; Guattari's ecosophy; and the postcolonial readings of Sylvia Wynter, Barbara Glowczewski, and Deborah Bird Rose. Behind all this thinking lay the Indigenous worlds of Papua New Guinea.

Much has been made of the influence of cybernetics on Bateson's theory of mind. But two concepts—schismogenesis and the double bind—emerged from his initial work in the 1930s and 1940s among the Iatmul in the Sepik region of Papua New Guinea under Australian administration and among people living in the Balinese village of Bajoeng Gede under Dutch mandate.[45] Biographies note the initial frustration Bateson experienced during his Papuan fieldwork in the 1930s. Originally a student of zoology, he shifted to social anthropology under A. C. Haddon, who urged him to study contact between the Sepik groups and their Australian colonial administrators. Instead, after deciding that his initial interlocutors were too culturally contaminated, he shifted his attention to Iatmul families and then later, with Margaret Mead, to highland Bali. Bateson's understanding of the relevance of the cybernetic revolution to a general ecology of mind came directly from a specific Papuan ceremony, the Naven. In his 1936 book *Naven*, Bateson introduces the key concept of schismogenesis, "a process of differentiation in the norms of individual behaviour resulting from cumulative interaction between individuals."[46] Bateson saw two forms of schismogenesis—complementary and symmetrical. In the case of complementary schismogenesis, differences become increasingly exaggerated until no relation can exist between the two sides.

> If, for example, one of the patterns of cultural behaviour, considered appropriate in individual A, is culturally labelled as an assertive pattern, while B is expected to reply to this with what is culturally regarded as submission, it is likely that this submission will encourage a further assertion, and that this assertion will demand still further submission. We have thus a potentially progressive state of affairs, and unless other factors are present to restrain the excesses of assertive and submissive behaviour, A must necessarily become

more and more assertive, while B will become more and more submissive; and this progressive change will occur whether A and B are separate individuals or members of complementary groups.[47]

In symmetrical schismogenesis, people battle over who exemplifies the ideal quality. "If, for example, we find boasting as the cultural pattern of behaviour in one group, and that the other group replies to this with boasting, a competitive situation may develop in which boasting leads to more boasting, and so on."[48] Bateson understood the Naven ceremony as rebalancing a social system set to overheat and then collapse. During the Naven, social and cultural roles were intensified and reversed. Rather than upending the social order, the intensification and reversal provided the means of social, emotional, and mental reintegration—what he later saw as a mechanism of corrective feedback in the system meant to continually rebalance it. The rebalancing was not a social abstraction. Each member of the society experienced what it was to be another social position; each embodied the other position. Naven was a flywheel, smoothing out and reorienting uneven energy flows.

Bateson brought these thoughts about cultural systems and subsystems as forms of organic distortion and self-correction with him when he first encountered cybernetics during his work with the Office of Strategic Services (oss), during World War II, after his fieldwork in Papua and Bali.[49] His work with the oss has been characterized as initially reluctant for reasons of intellectual freedom but was ultimately part of a wider war effort that many intellectuals and scholars understood as a fight against a growing European fascism.[50] Whatever his individual reasoning, his work with the intelligence community introduced him to the originators of cybernetics, such as Norbert Wiener, Warren McCulloch, and John von Neumann.[51] For the military, the goal of cybernetics was fairly clear-cut. Could cybernetics build a fighting force that combined human and machine intelligence? Initially the question was whether thinking machines could more quickly and accurately process the trajectory of incoming missiles and thus more effectively operate antimissile batteries than humans could. Could they break enemy codes better than the overwhelmingly female cryptanalytic workforce?[52]

The 1940s were hardly the first time a thinking machine was thought—some point to its origins in Charles Babbage's Victorian "difference machine," others to the Arabic abacus, still others to the Turing machine. Moreover, as Ronald Kline notes, cybernetics was hardly a unified theory.[53] Although most people agreed that cybernetics was broadly interested in how animals, machines, and systems more generally maintain themselves through information, control, and feedback loops, proponents fought over the meaning of concepts as fundamental as information, system, mind, noise, and communication. What was mind? Could nonorganic machines think? What was the relationship between elements of a system and a system itself; where was mind? Was mind within a system? But then what was that system within? Where was mind if mind was within systems that were within systems within systems, and minds were within minds within minds? These questions were debated between individuals and across publications and conferences, including the famous Macy Conferences held between 1946 and 1953.[54] According to Thomas Rid, one presentation in particular shaped Bateson's thinking about the environment: William Ross Ashby's presentation of the homeostat, a machine made out of spare military parts consisting of four batteries linked by wires and dials. Ashby designed the homeostat so that if its equilibrium was disturbed, the entire system would adjust itself until it reached a new equilibrium.[55]

All sorts of people were pulled into these debates, including Arendt. Brian Simbirski notes that although she was long suspicious of automation, by the late 1950s Arendt "came to associate nuclear violence with automation and cybernetics."[56] In a 1964 lecture at the Conference on the Cybercultural Revolution, Arendt takes specific aim at several assumptions in the cybernetic community. She notes the singularity of the cybernetic. Whereas the Industrial Revolution sought to replace human labor power with machine power, cybernetics sought to replace human brain power. As far as maintaining the border between the human and machine mind, that boat had already sailed. As Arendt notes, we are all already slightly cybernetic—the human condition had already been enfolded into the machinic.

> The simple fact that man is not just conditioned by his environment and the environment conditions him, that is, this particular kind of what [is] now called feedback and which indeed is quite obvious in the whole history of the human race wherever he finds it, that is, we are always much more speedily adjusted to new conditions than we think we could if we looked ahead of them. Once they are there, once the environment has really changed, we are already conditioned, even though we don't know it and even though we may know very little about what actually conditioned us. Take somebody who has lived through my life span. When I was a small child there were still horse-drawn cabbies, and then the automobile, and then the airplane. If I think how beautifully, for instance, I have adjusted in my own lifetime to all these very different conditions, to which I may add a few purely political ones, then I must say that I am quite astonished at my adaptability.[57]

Hers was the astonishment of an entire generation. The thinking machines seemed to be leading humans to the precipice of not just a new industrial revolution but a new planetary evolution. The potential power of this new cybernetic condition pressed the question of the purpose of cybernetic "liberation." Were machines to do no more than free humans from labor and work so that their lives would be filled by "leisure"? One of the great benefits engineers touted for cybernetic machines was the liberation of humans from labor. Computer automation promised to take over the fabrication of everything. The utopic and dystopic visions of cyberpunks soon began imagining a world run by machines, exemplified in Philip K. Dick's novel *Do Androids Dream of Electric Sheep?* Would thinking computers provide increased leisure time for the vast majority of humans, or a new kind of enslavement? Leave aside the cybernetic dream that this new form of automation would reduce work time—a dream Arendt punctures by arguing that since the Industrial Revolution real work time has increased. Even if the cybernetic revolution did reduce labor time, would this form of liberation be little more than a descent into an endless hell of nothingness? "Vacant time is what it says: it is nothingness, and no matter how much you put in in order to fill up this nothingness, this nothingness in itself is still there and present and may indeed prevent us from voluntarily and speedily adjusting ourselves to it."[58] Cybernetic leisure was desirable only if it freed people from necessity so that they could enter the political realm. The Greeks had liberated certain men from necessity so that they could act politically. Could cybernetics offer this form of freedom to all humans? Or would machines merely shift who became the Greek woman, enslaved people, colonized people, and subaltern subjects? Isaac Asimov's *I, Robot* had something to say about this future for robotics.

Bateson left these debates with a very specific understanding of what mind entailed and thus what criteria had to be met before one could say they were in the presence of mind. Two criteria of mind set the stage for what he called an ecology of mind—difference and relevance, or what he called a "difference that makes a difference" (or second-order difference).[59] Bateson was familiar with the semiotics of Charles Sanders Peirce, and we hear in his criteria Peirce's theory of the role that the interpretant plays in the evolution of mind.[60] For Peirce the interpretant does not simply place a sign indicating some object, activity, or subject into another mind. Whereas the sign determines the object in one aspect or another (rather than represents the object), the interpretant transforms or "develops" it as it transforms the habits of the mind in which the development is occurring. The possibility of a random deviation (chance) setting off new laws of habituation and new patterns of mind is lodged in the sign's determination of the object and the interpretant's development of the sign.[61] Peirce not only saw these mental patterns and natural law as having evolved, but he also saw evolution as the play of these chance mutations. In other words, mind was nature, and nature was the result of patterns and chance deviations as the cosmos interpreted itself.

Likewise, Bateson saw mind as the embodiment of a certain tautology. Mind emerged when difference became relevant to the mind made by the relevance of this difference to its continuity.[62] Thus, for Bateson, mind is not a thing, a substance, or a unified self.[63] One will never find mind if one starts by drawing boundaries around things in space and time. Using the term *self*, one of his synonyms for mind, Bateson writes, "Inside and outside are not appropriate metaphors for inclusion and exclusion when we are speaking of the self."[64] Mind is a mode of process and classification that turns back on itself when it hits information (difference), resacking itself into itself and into other sacks; the condition of self is a process of "stimulus, response, and reinforcement."[65] In other words, the mind is not in the sack any more than the subject is in her skin or the object ends at its crust.[66] Each is immanent to and at risk in the sacking. We know we are in the presence of mind when a process is initiated in response to an encounter with difference (information). Mind is a verb (process) of classification, of a response to a difference that makes a difference to the information of mind, which is a pseudonym for biology, soul, and life. Mind is what works by responding through the metaclassification of taking in difference (information) in order to remain in place. It would be wrong to see these absorptions as stable or as not producing their own instability. All life-minds face the problem that in order to produce themselves at a higher order, they must absorb and give off free-floating noise.[67] Mind eats noise to create new orders of mind. But the more it eats, the more complex and unstable it becomes. For Bateson, this was simply the law of entropy—the higher the entropy, the greater the disorder.

Bateson thought this definition of mind would place the human back into a broader biospheric Gaia. The human mind-self would be inside and outside other forces of life-mind equally inside and outside themselves. The human and nonhuman biosphere would depend not only on maintaining their specific selves but on maintaining what maintained them. In his hands, the compass of the human mind was cast far beyond the human into the meaning and source of the evolution of life. Rather than the human mind serving to define mind, it was merely one region of a biospheric mind, a part of a larger play of life forces partaking in difference, relevance, and self-correction.[68] The "individual mind" is immanent not just in the body. "It is immanent also in pathways and messages outside the body; and there is a larger Mind of which the individual mind is only a subsystem. This larger Mind is comparable to God but it is still immanent in the total interconnected social system and planetary ecology."[69]

It is true that Bateson often speaks of mind as if it were some sort of Spinozan unity: in his own work, the word *mind* appears in the singular and is capitalized. Nevertheless, Bateson did not consider mind to be a singularity, not a thing-in-itself, not sovereign within itself or in agreement with itself. At the root of mind was what Deleuze came to call "original multiplicity" and a philosophy of relations; it could be broadly placed in the Glissant's understanding of relation among toute-monde, écho-monde, and chaos-monde.[70] As Bateson says, time and again, through *Steps to an Ecology of Mind*, *Mind and Nature*, and *A Sacred Unity*, the map is not the territory, even as the map is what holds "us" in relation to "ourselves" at whatever level of bios.[71] Like other orders of mind, the complexity of the biospheric mind intensifies and multiplies the cascading, relaying exchange of noise as maps intrude into maps and so on. Moreover, Bateson sees the only source of difference, which supplies creativity for the remapping, as coming from territory. He writes: "It is only news of difference that can get from the territory to the map, and this fact is the basic epistemological statement about the relationship between all reality out there and all perception in here: that the bridge must always be in the form of difference. Difference, out there, precipitates coded or corresponding difference in the aggregate of differentiation which we call the organism's mind."[72]

Bateson uses a series of mind systems—the keeshond and gibbon system, dog-rabbit system, dolphin-human system, and other multispecies-patterned and irreducibly opaque interactions—to crack the carapace of the singularity of the human mind. His examples remind us of other assemblages and symbiogenetic creatures that later appeared in Deleuze and Guattari's *A Thousand Plateaus* and Donna Haraway's *The Companion Species Manifesto*. Bateson uses these multispecies minds to try to rebalance a dangerously unsecured flywheel in Western epistemologies of mind. As he first noted in *Naven*, all societies, indeed all minds, are run through with various forms of schismogenesis. The idea that distinctly different kinds of minds existed in their self-contained boxes—self within the self, the human within the human—had created an existential crisis in the West. The complementary schismogenesis of Western epistemologies was threatening not just one or another society but life itself, the biosphere. Bateson hoped that placing the human mind within the mind of nature would puncture a dangerous Enlightenment chauvinism;

he hoped that acknowledging the biospheric mind was an antidote to the toxic biocide of Enlightenment thinking. By the time Bateson was composing *Steps to an Ecology of Mind* and *Mind and Nature*, he rejected the impossibility of black boxes and the thought that anything but industrial manufacturing and chemical pesticidal poisons would emerge from them. Speaking of computers and species and black boxes in his seminal work, *Steps to an Ecology of Mind*, Bateson writes: "Let us consider for a moment the question of whether a computer thinks. I would state that it does not. What 'thinks' and engages in 'trial and error' is the man plus the computer plus the environment. And the lines between man, computer, and environment are purely artificial, fictitious lines. They are lines across the pathways along which information or difference is transmitted. They are not boundaries of the thinking system. What thinks is the total system which engages in trial and error, which is man plus environment."[73] Misunderstanding what thinks and what does not was not a mere epistemological failure; it was an environmental catastrophe:

> Let us now consider what happens when you make the epistemological error of chasing the wrong unit: you end up with the species versus the other species around it or versus the environment in which it operates. Man against nature. You end up, in fact, with Kaneohe Bay polluted, Lake Erie a slimy green mess, and "Let's build bigger atom bombs to kill off the next-door neighbors." There is an ecology of bad ideas, just as there is an ecology of weeds, and it is characteristic of the system that basic error propagates itself. It branches out like a rooted parasite through the tissues of life, and everything gets into a rather peculiar mess. When you narrow down your epistemology and act on the premise, "What interests me is me, or my organization, or my species," you chop off consideration of other loops of the loop structure. You decide that you want to get rid of the by-products of human life and that Lake Erie will be a good place to put them.[74]

The reference to Kāneʻohe Bay would have been well known to Bateson's readers. It was a case study of the effects of the common practice of dumping raw sewage into rivers, bays, seas, and oceans in the late 1960s. But the toxic consequences of liberal capitalism were hardly contained to one beach and bay. Eighty people died in New York City in 1966 when the temperature rose, intensifying smog. Lake Erie was so heavily polluted by industrial contaminates that the Cuyahoga River of the Seneca caught fire, helping spur the environmental movement. The United States redeployed both events to create and defend its own borders, or in Bateson's phrasing, to make them relevant for the maintenance and extension of its mind.

Given Bateson's argument that the health of the planet necessitated explod-ing a certain homocentric view of mind, how should we read Bateson along-side the critical anticolonial positions of the many Dene and Karrabing? Be-fore we answer, let us remember two additional aspects of Bateson's *Mind and Nature* and *Steps to an Ecology of Mind*. First, there is a noteworthy dynamic and direction of incorporation and expansion at play in Bateson's model of mind and nature. Let's use mind as a case in point. In continually encoun-tering distinct regions of mind (among the Iatmul, Balinese, US military in-telligence, Western science and epistemology, new age ecology), Bateson en-riched himself with the selves of others. As he carefully opened his mouth to incorporate the differences of others, he slowly shaped them into a new meta-pattern of mind. The more he pulled difference into himself, the more he claimed to be able to abduct the larger metapattern of existence, a wondrous kaleidoscope of aesthetic patterning. And he meant *abduct*—Peirce's under-standing of abduction as a form of reasoning distinct from deduction and induction. Abduction is a hypothesis a mind makes about how elements are related based on the vast archive one has encountered and absorbed. Think here of the method of Sherlock Holmes. Pure abduction never proves any-thing by itself; it is more intuition that is later proven. In Bateson's case, the vast corpus of orders of difference and relevance in forms of mind led him to propose a version of mind that hypothetically encompassed all, even if noth-ing could be proven in fact. Thus, Bateson's abduction was equivalent to an act of faith: "What is my answer to the question of the nature of knowing? I surrender to the belief that my knowing is a small part of a wider integrated knowing that knits the entire biosphere or creation."[75]

As Native and Indigenous people were advancing their analysis of how human relations with nonhuman existence necessitated their refusal to cede lands in the face of the extractive infrastructures of settler capitalism, Bateson and a host of new ecologists were building a model of a mind that absorbed others in order to expand mind from the human to the biosphere. What do we make of the difference between First Nation and Indigenous efforts to refuse the colonizing mind in order to support a relationality of minds and Bateson's effort to refuse the Western black-boxing of the human mind by placing it into nature? Or, more simply, what's at stake in keeping the colonial sphere or biosphere in the foreground and, alongside them, the ancestral catastrophe or the coming catastrophe?

One way of answering these questions—questions pulled from section I—is to return to Césaire's understanding of the difference between contact and colonialism in *Discourse on Colonialism*. He writes: "I admit that it is a good thing to place different civilizations in contact with each other; that it is an excellent thing to blend different worlds; that whatever its own particular genius may be, a civilization that withdraws into itself atrophies; that for civilizations, exchange is oxygen."[76] Each civilization grows and maintains its difference. Then he asks, "has colonization really *placed civilizations in contact*? Or, if you prefer, of all the ways of *establishing contact*, was it the best? I answer *no*."[77]

Was Bateson in contact with his Iatmul colleagues—the leaders of Naven whose analytics of social equilibrium set his thought in motion? Or was it a colonial relation? Speaking of Bateson's concept of the double bind, Orit Halpern notes, "Bateson's formulation of the double bind, sitting on his own work as an ethnographer in Papua New Guinea and Indonesia in the 1920s and 1930s, does indeed provide a stunning case study of the logistics by which disciplinary and colonial histories were folded into hyper-individuated and personalized technologies."[78] It does not to matter to Bateson where minds begin their journey of encounter with a difference that makes a difference or where they end. And yet, his own theory foregrounds the fact that, although from a certain vantage, all minds were in the biospheric mind, not all minds equally apprehended it. Mind had a logical ordering based on the amount and level of patterned transformation they are able to engorge.[79] Bateson's mind is more complexly patterned then many because he was able—enabled—to travel across complexly differentiated terrains. These infrastructures of colonial difference are nowhere significantly discussed or theorized. What is at stake is not merely a politics of citation. It is a politics of orientation—of where one puts one's effort of attention. Bateson might have merited the colonial sources of his thinking more than Arendt. But where did he direct the powers of his thought? What pulls his attention, and what does he help pull into existence, to helping endure an existence that is pulling it apart?

As with Deleuze and Guattari so with Bateson. Rather than Peirce, it is his pragmatist colleague, William James, who needs to enter the conversation. Long before Bateson, James proposed that mental concepts and indeed all of mental life were not inside the head but in relation to the vast entanglements of patterned social life. Because mental concepts evolved from social difference, the source of concepts would never be found by burrowing deeper into one or another mind in search of ever more abstract forms. The distribution and power of mental concepts reflect the distributions and powers of the social world. The mind is not filled with abstract semantic meaning but with the social world of distributed energies and abilities to focus on the tasks at hand. To put into words is to pull into words, to shape a concept that can do the work of articulating or disarticulating a field of forces. Mental concepts are actual worlds with all their vast and emergent multiplicity. As a result, we must foreground questions of where concepts are emerging, for whom or what, and whether they can endure the conditions of their emergence. There are billions of potential concepts in terrains of shattered existence that would better account for this shattering, but the shattering exhausts them before they can coagulate. Not everyone had the ability to sack the differences of others without feeling obligated to lend effort to enhancing regions of difference.

Second, Bateson is not merely examining how minds engorge difference in order to expand their territory; he is also excluding entire regions of existence from mental motion. Given the broader geontological framework of his training in zoology, what was excluded is not surprising—the nonorganic and the analytical truth of the vast number of human worlds that did not agree to the exclusion of the nonorganic from mental life. While at one moment Bateson writes, "the lines between man, computer, and environment are purely artificial, fictitious lines," at others he insists that without a human mind, objects like telescopes, windup toys, computer software, rocks, winds, and corpses are without mind.[80] They are mere objects subject to the simple law of cause and effect. Bateson writes: "The toy locomotive may become a part in that mental system which includes the child who plays with it, and the galaxy may become part of the mental system which includes the astronomer and his telescope. But the objects do not become thinking subsystems in those larger minds. The criteria are useful only in combination."[81] His need to differentiate himself absolutely from rocks is clear. If mere survival is what interests him, then becoming granite would be one's best option. He writes: "But the rock's way of staying in the game is different from the way of living things. The rock, we may say, resists change; it stays put, unchanging. The living thing escapes change either by correcting change or changing itself to meet the change or by incorporating continual change into its own being."[82]

If Bateson remained entrenched in a stubborn geontological framework, he also registered its seismic quakes as late liberal toxicity came home to roost. If a difference that makes a difference is crucial to the evolution and ecology of mind, certain differences can get stuck in the throat, and choking can result. As Bateson tried to ground his logical hierarchy in the fundamental difference between mind (bios, self, life, pattern) and nonmind (the inert, the merely mechanical, the geological, noise) everything kept slipping off the foundation. Machines are not mind, but the difference is artificial because mind has apprehended them. Rocks are outside mind, but to put them there threatens to create dangerous black boxes where we hide contaminants in plain sight. As soon as Bateson divides the mechanical from the mental, he folds it all back in. His inability to maintain the geontological grip of his own system suggests that people of the rocks refuse to be digested easily, without effect, passing through seamlessly. They get into the system like a cancer to it, a burr in the belly, a toxic virus in the bowels. As Nick Estes notes in relation to the long Native American tradition of keeping Turtle Island, freedom is a place that cannot be digested in the settler logics.[83]

Conceptual Ends

Solidarity and Stubbornness

ENDINGS

In the course of a day, one can now hear a litany of endings: the end of the European Union; the end of liberal democracy; the end of the progressive gender, sexual, and racial uprisings; the end of humans; the end of the planet. Western dreams seem to have arrived at the end of every road on which they set off since the turn of the eighteenth century. All the books that have been written in the longhand of the Enlightenment now seem just chapters of some other huge writing tablet with a surprise twist. At its end are no rainbows, no universal mutual recognition, no cosmopolitan law—only a steep cliff. The affects and images of this cliff are multiple. The affects range from denial (right-wing Christian-based states, Donald Trump, Scott Morrison, Jair Bolsonaro) and rage (Extinction Rebellion) to hope (climate technologists) and acceptance. The images flip from grand finales—a phase shift of the size and powers of unimaginable tsunami and fire tornadoes, which are already occurring with greater frequency and intensity—to cruddy afterlives as people pick up pieces of themselves after the storm recedes and the fires abate. Indeed, the image of a grand finale seems hopeful when placed alongside images of life in a toxic smog. Nothing actually just ends, after all. Even the Book of Enlightenment isn't incinerated as much as it is slowly worn down as it is passed, pulped, ripped up, and used as kindling or toilet paper, or just slowly molds and turns to dust.

To add misery to misery, many of the grand concepts that underpinned and justified Enlightenment social institutions and discourses—now under attack by white supremacists, nativists, religious zealots, misogynists, and homophobes—were never intended to serve Black, Indigenous, queer, or other marginalized peoples. Democracy, liberalism, environmentalism, critical reason: to be sure, progressive and radical groups have long made use of these social institutions and discourses. We need look no further than the politics of recognition, inclusion, and the expansion of human rights from one kind of human to another and then to nonhuman animals, rivers, and nature.

Many activists who pushed for the expansion of liberal concepts and institutions in a politics of inclusion knew that liberalism's institutions were not created in their image or for their benefit. As Dorceta E. Taylor's work has shown, the white urban Protestant elite, which founded the US conservation movement on an explicitly racist and colonial imaginary, absorbed without acknowledgment the contributions to policy making by the poor and working class, people of color, women, and Native Americans.[1] As one of the most powerful leaders of this movement and founder of the Sierra Club in 1892, John Muir promoted white tourism as a way to justify forming federally protected national parks. He reassured readers, for whom the Native American resistance to settlers was still quite fresh—the Battle of Little Bighorn was in 1872—when he wrote, "As to Indians, most of them are dead or civilized into useless innocence."[2] By the late 1970s, a specific kind of "Indian" could be allowed into the environmentalist rhetoric—the one who added a romantic value to the landscape for settlers. One had only to squint to see, just over the horizon, the gaping mines of extractive capitalism that tore into the Global South and Indigenous north. Beyond the romance, actual Indigenous people have been left with the catch-22 of either opening their countries to more toxic extraction or starving their children of foods and goods. Moreover, when minority groups, the subaltern, the Indigenous, and the wretched of the earth have succeeded in forcing the defenders of the exclusivity of liberal democratic values to open their doors and let them in, the institutions have marked them as "included." It is as if the doorframe held a huge permanent ink marker that slid over the head of each "included," marking them as "included" for all to see. This mark of inclusion preserves the original distinction of liberalism's whiteness even as liberalism claims to have diversified. What was the choice? The rabid hatred rising all around us will not serve us any better than these older institutions did. Indeed, we know it will be worse. It is never good to have racism, sexism, and other phobias on the loose. So here we are, stuck between supporting what never meant to support us and holding back a rising tide of xenophobic cruelty.

Some of us are surviving the moment by reassuring ourselves and others that the tide always turns. We say, "Yes, we are in one of those moments; we need to hunker down in our resistance and wait for the weather to turn," as if history were a climate event, climate was a history, or history is Nietzschean in the sense of eternal return. Not only do some of us defend institutions whose function was never radical, let alone ours, but even if such defense were successful, we would not be returning to where we left off. Many fear that the ends we face are nonreversible: after all, when a tsunami rolls back, it doesn't leave the land in the same shape as before. But many people and places never signed up to this messianic vision because they know that when the tide returns, it returns mixed with and spreading the uncontainable containers of toxicity—the drums of petroleum, fertilizer, red algae, and so on. On chemicals released after wildfires, Sharon Bernstein writes: "Fires like the one that razed Paradise in November burn thousands of pounds of wiring, plastic pipes and building materials, leaving dangerous chemicals in the air, soil and water. Lead paint, burned asbestos and even melted refrigerators from tens of thousands of households only add to the danger, public health experts say."[3] Some people already know that the eternal return of liberalism is more of the same toxicity, because they have witnessed this over and over. And here is the real eternal return: when the tide rolls back, it always brings the remainders of actions from afar, and those who have set these toxins in motion will have the most mobility to dodge their new locations. Like before, so now: those who have the resources to build their arks will be the ones to start over. Or so they hope—thus the Elon Musks of this world are building their bunkers and rocket ships. They are hoping to weather the world with their accumulation of millions and trillions. More likely, no exact end will come, no global obliteration. Instead, many will newly experience the cruddy kind of continuing that others have long known.

This chapter turns to political concepts and affects in the shadow of this new toxic moment of *late liberalism*. I begin with a set of political concepts (precarity, solidarity, grievability, and autonomy) in order to juxtapose them to another set (tailings, embankments, and strainings). The idea is not to substitute the second set of concepts for the first, as if all that political action needed were the right words. Instead, I want to suggest the odd sort of ideas that might be necessary if we are to take seriously the revamped approach to the four axioms of existence, the coming and ancestral catastrophe, and the shaking of *geontopower* this book has been examining. I propose that, whatever concepts we formulate, they need *to do something*, even if that is only signaling linguistically the material fields that currently exist but are outside many people's field of vision. My intention is to circle back to the very beginning of this manuscript and argue that any political concepts emerging from the axioms of existence would need, at a minimum, to do the following: first tack back and forth among regions of existence without collapsing those regions into one general thing and smooth space; second, resist using the qualities and materialities of one region of existence to define all regions; and third, highlight the directionality and differentials of power that make some regions seem more valuable than others.

To concretize the stakes of this discussion, this chapter begins by looking at a political turn in the autonomist movement toward solidarity with all life. I then examine how such solidarity is being actualized in the recognition of ecological formations as legal persons and in the process is smuggling into existence Western images and concepts. I conclude by examining how concepts such as tailings, embankments, and strainings might alter and make strange our political imaginaries without erasing the effects of the long unrelenting arm of colonialism.

SOLIDARITIES ACROSS WASTED WORLDS

We live in a moment of new, rich, and strange antagonisms—the clash between human and nature, between societies and natures, and between entangled species and the geological, ecological, and meteorological systems that support them. Karl Marx might have thought that the social dialectic was leading to the purification of the fundamental opposition of human classes, but many now believe the new war of the world is defined by antagonism among humans and all other classes of existence. Anthropogenic climate change and toxicity have created revolutionary ethical, political, and conceptual problems and frictions. But what if the problem of climate and toxic catastrophes has set off a much richer and much stranger problem? What if one of the conceptual consequences of these catastrophes is not that humans will not exist in the future but they never existed in the way the Western Enlightenment and its spawn, liberalism, imagined? What if there is no human, or even any humans, but merely regionally more or less densely compacted forms and modes of existence, one component of which has been abstracted out and named "the human"? What if these regions of existence are off-gassing in such a way that they produce themselves as their own waste products?

Perhaps these questions will seem less strange if we imagine, following Alexander Dunst and Stefan Schlensag, that science fiction writer Philip K.

Dick is taking part in an International Union of Geological Sciences symposium charged with deciding whether the Holocene has ended and, if it has, how to mark the beginning of the new and last age of the human.[4] What if, alongside him, we seat representatives of the Italian political movement known generally as autonomism, such as Franco "Bifo" Berardi. Dick and Berardi might raise their voices above the din of scientific discourse to call for some measurement based on solidarity with all forms of life. Not that their proposals would be the same. Dick might scribble new assemblages on the white board that radically distended the human body into its environment, with other still ghostly envelopes of being emerging, each claiming a different part of the human body as its internal organs. Over the squeaking of his marker, Berardi might demand that the abstract human continually cited in discussions of the Anthropocene be denounced as an illusion of our epoch—that there is no human, only various forms of human existence trapped in the informational machinery of contemporary capital extracting bodily labor and psychic desire from some for the benefit of others.

Now imagine that at this moment other clusters of existence walk through the door. We can list some of them by their known names. First Nations/ Indigenous peoples in settler liberalism, rock and sand formations, creeks, European and Syrian youth who have never been and will never be employed, and the tens of thousands of species on the International Union for Conservation of Nature Red List and threatened with extinction. Representatives of these groups may have been issued invitations. But as they enter the commodious hall, they begin to wonder how they fit into the prevailing antagonism. As Glen Coulthard notes of First Nations in Canada, so with Indigenous Australians, land dispossession was not followed by proletarianization, and as a result Indigenous Australians were mostly never precarious workers.[5] Invasive colonial powers considered them remnants of the Stone Age and did not calculate their labor within labor power as they used their bodies and appropriated their lands, introduced new species into them, and poisoned them with atomic and toxic chemicals. Other representatives will not come, perhaps because they are bored or put off by the form of the meetings, or they know they are simply being invited as an alibi for making the same decisions that would have been made anyway. They stay home and do things that fail to appear as political actions because they are not general, not universalizing, not class based, not utopian or even practical if practical means that their lives will be enhanced by their actions. Still others may not have been issued an invitation, because after all, what's the postal address of rocks and riverbeds? Can they be addressed as "you," that is, in the demanding structures of (human) language? Can they accept or refuse to take up subjectivity in (human) language? What must be implanted in them to create mouths that can speak an understandable language? Would they be given the power to demand a change in human morphology? What if they said to the colloquium organizers, "You want us to join your efforts to save the planet you have made? Then you can learn to become unintelligible to yourselves by adapting to our intelligibility." They know it is unlikely the human organizers will take up this challenge, so they remain precariously autonomous, removed from the order to participate in solving the coming catastrophe. Besides, rocks and sand and riverbanks have little reason to care—they are not going anywhere.

In this cacophony, Berardi and others have proposed new forms of Left progressive solidarity.[6] Building on the work of Mario Tronti, autonomists such as Antonio Negri and Berardi begin with the assumption that working-class struggles precede and prefigure the unfolding formations and strategies of capital. This dynamic played out in the autonomist struggle of the 1960s. Workers refused the organizational and philosophical premises of corporate capitalism and (even Marxist) unions, both of which reduced the value of human life to labor power. When workerism developed new tactics to undermine their work conditions—absenteeism, wildcat strikes, bossnapping—they were not struggling for better contractual terms or for their labor power to be recognized per se. More profoundly, they were refusing to subsume life, desire, and happiness under the rule of labor power, Left or Right.[7] They were embracing freedom from both capitalism and economistic Marxism and embarking on a flight from class identity within and identification with the dialectics of capital.[8] Refusing to be defined by the dialectic of capital and its abstraction of human labor power, the workerist movement sought to explore new forms and modes of being. In short, autonomism called for a revolt of the soul that refuses "the field of lack" that had "produced dialectical philosophy, on which twentieth century politics built its (mis)fortunes."[9] It advocated poetic practices of the otherwise—a politics that left open the content and destiny of the human by removing them from the capture of the teleology of capital. Capital and labor power would no longer be the antagonism through which the critical work of class analysis would be understood.

But to be autonomous from the dialectic of capital and labor does not mean to be removed from the history of capital. It is to be related to capitalism differently. Capitalists did not sit passively when their colleagues and relatives were being kidnapped and when their assembly lines were being disrupted. They and their union and state allies aggressively and creatively responded to the autonomist challenge. Berardi provides some of this history, noting that the emergence of a European autonomist refusal to subjugate life to labor power helped accelerate the technological replacement of workers through postcybernetic software and machines, the rise of deregulation and neoliberalism, the reorganization of relations between economy and society through the absorption of state pensions in markets, and the consequent dis-organization of the coordinates of Left critical discourse.[10] These technolog-ical and social events in turn posed a challenge to how the autonomist Left conceptualized revolt and the conversations they fostered. Berardi, like many other Italian autonomists, fled to France, protected by the Mitterrand doc-trine.[11] His work with Radio Alice and friendship with Félix Guattari opened new understandings of the antagonisms of semiocapitalism.[12]

Berardi, Guattari, Negri, and others saw semiocapitalism (or informa-tional capital) as a new mode of capitalism in which immaterial signs and de-sire are the principal objects of capital production and expropriation.[13] Capi-tal doesn't want the bodily effort of laborers in a classic sense but the desiring hearts of human beings—and not merely what one knows she desires but what she doesn't know until the massive stores of data are redirected toward an immanent tendency. This form of capitalism certainly reflects the general turn of capital to individuated just-in-time production for obsolete consump-tion in neoliberal post-Fordist production. And it is not without an enormous material infrastructure. What Berardi argues is new about semiocapitalism is the ability of digital capitalism to disperse and coordinate labor processes as it creates new forms of commodities, not just desirable commodities but desire as a commodity. Berardi notes, "The digital transformation started two dif-ferent but integrated processes. The first is the capture of work inside the net-work, that is to say the coordination of different labor fragments in a unique flow of information and production made possible by digital infrastructures. The second is the dissemination of the labor process into a multitude of productive islands formally autonomous, but actually coordinated and ul-timately dependent."[14] But what worries Berardi is not just the significant differences between new and old forms of digital and nondigital commod-ities but the ongoing upending of the grounds of the autonomist struggle. Workerism said no to the reduction of human value to labor power and yes to "the quality of life, pleasure and pain, self-realization and respect for diver-sity: desire as the engine of collective action."[15] Semiocapitalism capitalizes on exactly this workerist objective. It seeks to align perfectly digital algorithms to life and work rhythms. Anywhere, anytime, you can (but don't need to) go straight to your digital checkout, just have your friends like your desires, look up information, think, post a picture, or Snapchat. Berardi sees these digital megacorporations as pushing beyond labor power into soul power—a spiritphagia.[16] Anticipatory algorithms seek to gallop ahead of in-time activity—finishing our sentences as well as creating and feeding our ideological predilections—even as new forms of informational labor targeted new "lines of flight." For Berardi, Jean Baudrillard's prediction for the coming era of simulacra has come true:

> We will live in this world, which for us has all the disquieting strangeness of the desert and of the simulacrum, with all the veracity of living phantoms, of wandering and simulating animals, that the death of capital has made of us—because the desert of cities is equal to the desert of sand—the jungle of signs is equal to that of the forests—the vertigo of simulacra is equal to that of nature—only the vertiginous seduction of a dying system remains, in which work buries work, in which value buries value—leaving a virgin, sacred space without pathways, continuous as Bataille wished it, where only the wind lifts the sand, where only the wind watches over the sand.[17]

For Berardi, the cellular phone provides the connective element, constantly coordinating and localizing in real time, with a new frictionless ease such that the labor given to informational capitalism is never experienced or resisted. Paradoxically, perhaps, the frictionless nature of communication creates a reinforcing dynamic between the desire to connect and an anxiety of being disconnected, even as the smallest fragments of commentary we send through our phones—and even the attention we give a site without sending any information at all—is absorbed into an information production machine.[18] The Karrabing Film Collective makes serious fun of this insight in *Day in the Life* in the "Lunch Run" segment. Tasked with picking up a young man at a local beach, a group of young kids are stalked by an ancestral being who hopes to hypnotize them into following him into the bush. Unable to get them to look into his eyes because of their obsession with their phones, the ancestral being finally succeeds by waving a new iPhone 10 at them.

In these new topologies of capitalism, what is human? Where is it? Is it flesh inside neurons encased in metal cooled by vast arrays whose power is generated by vaster networks of energy production? The human in semiocapital is within the leakage of corporealities as all existence is turned to extract and support the accumulation of informational capital.[19] All is multiplied, distended, attuned, and embodied. And this "where am it/I" is then disembodied in the image of the digital cloud, which runs a good race with the Anthropocenic human as the illusion of our epoch.[20] How does one "build forms of social solidarity that are capable of re-activating the social body" in the context of this competitive, aggressive subjugation of all forms of existence in the "competitive aggressiveness" of contemporary capital?[21] Who are the antagonists? If autonomism is to succeed in this new climate, Berardi argues, it must work to rewire the multitude of positions in the working assemblage of cognitive capital and liberate the soul from the labor of capital. Workers are not merely the precarious laborers in the Silicon Valley knowledge factories but all the dispersed and fragmented nodes within and across which information desire is produced, elaborated, amplified, distributed, and consumed. This vast assemblage includes geologists, geneticists, biochemists, miners, software coders, biocircuitry, computer algorithms, massive data storage facilities, air conditioners, satellites, human fingers and rare earth–based screens, legislation for appropriating gas and minerals, ships and ship canals, and the teeming life and toxicities carried and discharged in the ballast that crosses territories, sinks into soils, is ingested in drinking water, and so on. What concepts will stretch across and articulate this assemblage?

To be sure, depending on who you are and where you have been standing, the call for solidarity with nonhuman existence is not the result of a new stage of capitalism. For instance, if you are Dene or Karrabing, the cosubstantive relation between regions and forms of existence has been the major argument against colonial extractive capitalism, often a deadly one. A year after Nigerian writer and environmental and political activist Ken Saro-Wiwa was executed in 1995 for attempting to protect Ogoni lands, ancestors, and spirits from the devastation wrought by Shell Oil and formal military and paramilitary state allies, Amazon.com opened for business on the nascent web. So let's take Berardi at his best. After all, he is not arguing that semiocapitalism is a moment of capitalism's internal unfolding; it is a reaction to specific historical actions and their intended and unintended consequences. Even if capitalism sloughed off human labor completely in favor of machinic labor, machinic labor would tie capitalism more tightly to its extractive machinery. Even a fully automated manufacturing capitalism in which machines make machines to make machines for sale must extract material for this first-, second-, and third-order automation. In this light we can see a connection between Berardi's call for solidarity between all forms of life and the emergence of legal designations of the more-than-human world as persons.

Since 2010, Indigenous and non-Indigenous legal scholars in alliance with In-digenous activists have sought to mobilize the legal concept of the person and articulate a new alliance between human and nonhuman forms of exis-tence. If corporations can be legal persons, why can't other abstract collec-tives? Rivers, for instance, have been declared legal persons in Chile, New Zealand, and India. The political hopes behind these personifications are well known by now—bestowing personhood on rivers and other ecological entities is a strategy for slowing the apparatus of extractive capitalism. The question has shifted from a technical legal argument, "Can a river be a person?," to a broader political argument, "What happens when we absorb rivers and others forms of existence into the concept of persons and into the concept of Life un-derpinning Western personage?" What happens to a region of existence when it is made a person within a liberal legal framework? Put differently, what do we begin doing and attending to when we transform regions into persons?

While many see this legal innovation as representing the cutting edge of contemporary environmental law, a similar approach has been operating in Australia since the late 1970s. If we want to look into one possible future of these contemporary legal interventions, perhaps there is no better place to look than in the *ancestral present* of the treatment of sacred sites in the Northern Territory of Australia, where a state agency, the Aboriginal Areas and Protection Authority, has been registering and protecting natural enti-ties for over forty years. The Aboriginal Lands and Sacred Sites Bill (NT) 1977 was the first bill implemented to protect sacred sites in the Northern Terri-tory. It was drafted under the terms of Section 73(1) of the Land Rights Act, creating two categories of sacred site—sites on Aboriginal land trusts or Ab-original freehold land, and sites not on Aboriginal land trusts or Aboriginal freehold land. At the same time, a number of land councils were also estab-lished under the terms of Section 21(1) of the Land Rights Act; their function is to run land claims on behalf of "traditional aboriginal owners" and then administer trust lands.

The history of the sacred sites bill would suggest a progressive empow-erment of Indigenous peoples to control not only their lands but the terms through which land was conceptualized. The original bill gave limited pow-ers to Aboriginal custodians to safeguard sites on Aboriginal land trusts and freehold land, yet there was little custodians could do to protect sites out-side these areas, other than requesting that the administrator protect them. When the Northern Territory achieved self-government in 1978, a stronger version was passed by the new Legislative Assembly. The Aboriginal Sacred Sites (NT) Bill 1978 became law in November 1978 and led to the establishment of a permanent Aboriginal Sacred Sites Authority a year later, which was the precursor to today's Aboriginal Areas Protection Authority.

While bureaucratically separated from the land councils, the sacred sites legislation refers back to a common genealogy in the Land Rights Act. As I noted in chapters 3 and 4, the Land Rights Act emerged from decades of Indigenous people's ongoing refusal to cede their lands and analytics of existence, intensified by a series of public scandals around their refusal—the 1950s Warburton Ranges controversy in which the Wongi, Pitjantjatjara, Anangu, and Ngaanyatarra were found living in a secret nuclear testing range; the 1963 Yirrkala bark petitions that demanded recognition of Yolngu lands appropriated for mining; and the 1966 Wave Hill walk-off that saw Gurindji people refuse to work for rations on pastoral stations on their lands. These ongoing refusals and scandals prompted reactions from the state, what Audra Simpson has called countersovereign reactions, including the 1967 referendum, the Woodward inquiry, and the Land Rights Act.[22]

The Land Rights Act sets up mechanisms for Indigenous people to claim their land and the bureaucratic infrastructure of these claims and (if successful) the management of Aboriginal lands. As with all pieces of legislation, a series of definitions prefaces the main body of the text.

> **Aboriginal land** means (a) land held by a land trust for an estate in fee simple; or (b) land the subject of a deed of grant held in escrow by a Land Council.

> **Aboriginal tradition** means the body of traditions, observances, customs, and beliefs of Aboriginals or a community or group of Aboriginals, and includes those traditions, observances, customs, and beliefs applied in relation to particular persons, sites, areas of land, things, or relationships.

> **traditional Aboriginal owners,** in relation to land, means a local descent group of Aboriginals who (a) have common spiritual affiliations to a site on the land, being affiliations that place the group under a primary spiritual responsibility for that site and for the land; and (b) are entitled by Aboriginal tradition to forage as a right over that land.

> **sacred site** means a site that is sacred to Aboriginals or is otherwise of significance according to Aboriginal tradition, and includes any land that, under a law of the Northern Territory, is declared to be sacred to Aboriginals or of significance according to Aboriginal tradition.[23]

As discussed in chapter 3, these definitions and the broader settler law of recognition were subtended by the imaginary of Western forms of sovereignty rather than Indigenous analytics of the relations subtending themselves and the more-than-human world. Furthermore, these laws absorbed Indigenous analytics into Western geontologies as the condition of state recognition. Just as Berardi understands the form of capitalism to be responsive to workerist challenges, so we must understand the settler state to be constantly innovating as it tries to retain its sovereignty in the face of Indigenous challenges to it. As Indigenous people successfully assert their preexisting sovereignty, capital and state do not sit passively; they intervene in the social relations of production. Thus, one purpose of land claim legislation was to create an entity (the traditional Aboriginal owner, the local descent group, the sacred site) that anyone, no matter their knowledge or understanding of local Indigenous laws—and the practices and analytics undergirding these laws—could easily discern. The procedure of producing this abstractable entity and the abstracted social group to which it belongs operates, on the one hand, through the definition of "traditional Aboriginal owner." First, this social group, the traditional Aboriginal owner, is created by applying whatever principle of biological descent is deemed locally relevant—patrilineal, matrilineal, bilateral. Commissioners and the bureaucratic arms of land councils apply these biologically reductive principles as if other forms of human and more-than-human relationships built out of the ongoing interactions with each other and places are irrelevant. The state does not have to ask who knows more or less, has spent more or less time with a place, is more or less oriented to its ritual knowledge, is more or less likely to subject the land to extractive capitalism. Indeed, corporations seek out state-designated traditional Aboriginal owners who either know next to nothing or who think of land as property.[24] The Northern Land Council has increasingly taken a similar position to its own consultants, appointing anthropologists to supervise claims based on their ignorance of local conditions—land councils call this ignorance "objectivity." The second procedural intervention is how Indigenous social relations are transformed through the definition of land. Although nothing in the Land Rights Act mandates that "Aboriginal land" is defined on the basis of hard nation-like borders between group lands, the practice of land recognition has increasingly operated to create virtual fences between Indigenous territories. These boundaries are seen as crucial to the absorption of land into capital practice—who receives royalties for the expropriation of goods and values from which land.

While more open to who can and must speak for a place, the Aboriginal Areas Protection Authority faces similar state pressures to create person-like objects when Indigenous people request the registration of their sacred sites. To suggest how, I return to an example I discussed in *Geontologies*—the sacred site Two Women Sitting Down, located north of Tennant Creek, held and cared for by the Kunapa people. The Aboriginal Areas Protection Authority took the mining company OM Holdings to court for the desecration of the site. In its quest to extract manganese, which constituted the blood of the two women, rat and bandicoot, who fought there, OM Holdings dug so far down, directly along the borders of the site, that it undermined its structural integrity. Part of Two Women fell down the steep cliff. In *Geontologies* I emphasized the distinction between the actual lawsuit, based on the concept of desecration, and an imaginary one, based on the concepts of murder or attempted murder.

Here I want to understand whether the hosts of protagonists and antagonists in this scene can be understood through the frames of war that Judith Butler proposes. Or, put another way, what happens when we create solidarity between humans and more-than-humans through the idea of the human person? At first blush this application seems easily achieved. Taking advice from Berardi, we could understand precarity to apply to the vast assemblage and various nodes that compose semiocapitalism, Two Women Sitting Down being an obvious example of these assemblages and nodes. But to respect the work Butler is trying to do is to acknowledge the humanism at the heart of the kind of grievability in which she grounds her approach to precarity. For Butler, what allows for recognition across differences of war is the shared vulnerability that ontologically characterizes human life. Because all humans are born vulnerable and in the care of others, they can recognize this vulnerability in others and the injustice of the distribution of social vulnerability—how an ontologically shared condition is socially intensified or lessened. Rocks do not share these ontological conditions, according to this model; although we can grieve their disappearance, we can do so only across a cleavage of existence—from the viewpoint of the "as if," as if they were like us, although they are not.

A large part of the movement to bestow legal personage on natural entities consists in trying to bridge this *as if*. As we set out to follow them across it, let us direct our attention not to what OM Holdings did wrong, but what it did right according to the law of persons. OM Holdings "recognized" that Two Women consisted of two persons, rat and bandicoot, in the sense that it modified its practice relative to its skin. The company did not cut a micrometer into the site, nor was it charged with doing so. Instead, the company was charged with knowingly undermining the site by not providing a substitute architectural support for the geological support on which it depended. In other words, OM Holdings was charged because it knew that Two Women Sitting Down was kept in place by geological forces outside of it. Who would have known this better than an international mining company that depends on a team of geologists and geological engineers?

But why did Two Women Sitting Down have skin (a border that defines where it begins and ends) in the first place? What if, as I began this chapter suggesting, humans were modeled after other forms and regions of existence, rather than the other way around? What if the manganese blood remains a part of these women whether or not OM Holdings sucks it up, whether or not it heads to China to be used in smelting, and whether or not it returns to the area in the form of industrial pollution or climate change? Why isn't the spilled blood part of the person? For answers, look to the bureaucracy of the law of persons. The Aboriginal Areas Protection Authority must define the borders and boundaries of every site that Indigenous owners and custodians seek to register. A general rule of thumb has emerged about these boundaries: they need to reflect the shape of the site and cannot extend much more than one hundred meters from the primary features of the site. A site can have its personal space, but this space must conform to what a living agent, or person, is within Western law and imaginaries. The Land Rights Act and Aboriginal Areas Protection Authority must counter Indigenous requests for recognition of sacred sites as ancestral presences in the land with demands that this ancestral presence must appear in the shape of Western living things.

Legal theorists and activists are hardly naive. Rather than being a panacea, the benefits of attributing personhood to rivers and other ecological entities is a strategy for getting nature legally recognized. What I think people mean by this is that, given the prevailing conditions of extractive consumer capitalism in the horizon of anthropogenic climate collapse, personhood for rivers is a tactic for limiting and delimiting how capitalism and its allies can make use of the earth. It is easy to find legal essays and commentary that acknowledge Indigenous traditions as an inspiration for the innovative move to declare rivers, trees, and other environmental features as juridically living persons. Quite frankly, I stand with them in deploying any means possible to postpone, delay, and divert the Death Star of extractive and industrial capitalism from digging, damming, and destroying their land and yet another piece of the planet.

If this is the aim, what does this case study suggest? First, persons aren't persons, meaning that what Kunapa might mean, what Karrabing often mean, when they point to a Dreaming (totem) and say, "It is part of me; if it is hurt, I will become sick or die," is that the place demands a continual attended-to-ness, a set of ongoing cosubstantiations and *obligations* whose material conditions can only be attended to and not fully known. To say "I am water" or "We are water" does not make water a person. It makes water and me necessary for each other's existence without knowing exactly how or where we intersect. We return to Vine Deloria's reading of Native and First Nations practices of revelation discussed in chapter 4, namely, that "revelation was seen as a continuous process of adjustment to the natural surroundings and not as a specific message valid for all times and places."[25] When we attend to the specificities and difference among Indigenous analytics, we might be able to move beyond mistaking various strategies as anything but tactics meant to jam late liberalism as a governance of difference and markets and to overturn the hierarchies and differences of geontopower. If the aim is transforming natural environments into legal persons, the second thing this case suggests is that various regions of existence stay in place in different ways. To treat Kunapa people as being of the same intensive and extensive substance as Two Women Sitting Down is the same mistake as doing the opposite. We will not overturn anything if we turn everything into what the law has already made compatible with liberal and illiberal capitalism.

Many people do not want this overturning. They want to continue to have what they have. What they want is for Indigenous people to save the world. I was at a critical art event in a provincial city in Europe a few years ago in conversation with another artist and filmmaker. The Karrabing film *Wutharr, Saltwater Dreams* was screened as part of the program, with a Q&A following. *Wutharr* moves across a series of increasingly surreal flashbacks as an extended Indigenous family argues about what caused their boat's motor to break down and leave them stranded. As they consider the roles played in the incident by the ancestral present, the regulatory state, and the Christian faith, *Wutharr* explores the multiple demands and inescapable vortexes of contemporary Indigenous life. (It's really funny too.) During the Q&A session, an audience member raised her hand and said something like, "Whenever people come from Australia or America and present native material, we always hear 'settler colonialism' this and 'postcolonial' that and power. What I want to know is whether your people have in their ancient traditions a knowledge that would help us save the world and the terrible future we are facing."

What concepts might we use to contribute to the work of overturning the general syntactic framework of the four axioms of existence? Or what qualities should these concepts exhibit? Let me discuss three possibilities. First, political concepts should linguistically signal the material fields in which they mean to make visible and thus reveal possibilities for action. Second, they need to travel back and forth among regions of existence (instead of between forms of life and forms of nonlife), without collapsing those regions into one general kind of thing or one simplistic, binarily structured system. Finally, concepts should not elevate the qualities and materialities of one region of existence as a defining characterization of all regions but highlight directionality and differentials of power. The following discusses how a series of alternatives to solidarity, antagonism and precarity might suggest new political imaginaries in a decolonizing world. Specifically I discuss the concepts of embankment-sacking-embagination, strainings-durability-efforts, and tailings-trailings?

Sacking, embaginating, embanking: when we look at what appeared to be objects through these concepts, we see the dense material ridges that force creates by disturbing or keeping in places other ridges, all of which allow processes to occur within their surrounds. Embankments are the sandbags or sand dunes that keep a flood at bay as long as they can keep themselves in place as they are assaulted by pounding and creeping waves; they are mountains that contain the circulation of winds and trap pollutants until they crumble under their strain; they are the social identities that provide the conduits through which rights are circulated until they are twisted by these circulating rights and take on new identities; they are the skin that protects the inner organs unless a cancer eats it away, having begun from outside contamination. All these sackings of material space create the contours that are (mis)interpreted as autonomous insides and outsides.

After all, the claim about the status of individuals in the sense of discrete subjects or objects has played a critical role in how Western disciplines differentiate themselves (biology, geology) and, from this initial differentiation, the way other Western disciplines create endless second- and third-order ethical discourses, economic values, and political practices and justifications. The illusion of the boundary—the skinning of existence—provides an against-which and within-which a subject or object can be defined, stabilized, and characterized for the conditions for any claim about autonomous being. The illusion of objects (including subjects) has been foundational for the biological sciences, relying as they have on the concept of the membrane to animate the difference between life and nonlife and forms of life—the smallest unit of life, the cell, is defined and made possible by its membrane, the human by its skin, the species by its reproductive limits. Indeed, it is unclear how final causes, teleology, finitude, and eventfulness—from Aristotle's acorn to Hegel's Geist to Samuel Huntington's clash of civilizations—are imaginable without this idea of skin, whether the internal unfolding of the skinned thing operates at the level of the cell, the body, the species, or Geist. One can also see how skin—or perhaps at this point, we can say a sack that holds something that operates in relation to itself—also provides a crucial imaginary for the difference between organic skin and rock surfaces. Skins, or sacks, are protective covers; surfaces are simply the place where this comes to an end.

This difference ramifies into subsequent ones like the legalities of the difference between murder (possible with human life), killing (with animal life), and destruction (inorganic objects). Without these insides or outsides, murder, killing, and destruction weave into and out of each other. If a rock is a rock *qua* rock or the soil is soil *qua* soil, then from its point of view humans are merely a moment on the journey and travels of minerals. In producing us, they maintain themselves insofar as we will return to their condition. In other words, the assertion that the self-repair of life has a different status than the *inert* passivity of nonlife allows the latter to be treated very differently than the former. But rocks use gravity to sack themselves, or gravity sacks rocks; the more gravity, the denser the rock is. To unsack these various formations of rocks requires other sacked materials—whether the chemicals that frack shale or diamonds that cover drill tips. Every tactic of self-repair, of being shattered or reinforced, leaves and absorbs tailings and trailings that circulate back into this movement of embankment and tailings.

When objects/subjects are reconceptualized as areas of ongoing embankment, sacking, or embagination, two points emerge. First, because all embankments are temporary scaffoldings that need constant reinforcement and repair, they must reach into or disturb other regions—or must find a means of limiting other regions from reaching into and disturbing them. To crib from Michel Serres's concept of the parasite, all embankments are in an abuse relationship that is inseparable from all forms of exchange—the abuse can be a source to power an *otherwise*, giving it a material and social architecture, or a means of crippling resistance to the dominant ordering of existence.[26] How these strainings resolve themselves depends on the durability of the material they are composed of and the material that touches them. Here it is important to understand power as effortability and durability, the power to endure.

This brings me to my second point: the movements of embankments constantly lay down trails and give off tailings.[27] Tailings are usually defined as the residue of whatever valuable material has been extracted from a mine. As Kathryn Yusoff notes, such tailing and trailings are the irreducible "substrata of the technosphere, once imagined and imaged as extraneous and external to the rational projects of materializing late modernity," but no longer.[28] Tailings are the physics of all embankments when viewed from their indefinable, crumbling, and corroding edges, where they become quasi things, where dead things on living things enter nostrils and topsoil. Tailings are the material trails that Katerina Martina Teaiwa follows as Bañaba Island in the Pacific is gutted for phosphorus, which is crucial for manufacturing the fertilizer that powers the so-called green revolution. We can follow these trails as mining spews dust into the atmosphere and as winds spread the particles like settler colonizers, as airplanes spread phosphorus across previously infertile fields. As Bañaba is dispersed around the world in the form of tiny motes combined and recombined with other substances, the island is made uninhabitable for Bañabans, who become displaced.[29] But the dissipation of the island in the form of agricultural fertilizer entering the soil, plants, and human and nonhuman bodies and in the form of dust tailings entering the atmosphere is mirrored by the extension of Bañaban sovereignty in the form of an ever more vast set of lands and relationships. Equally and unavoidably, this form of chemosovereignty nurtures new, usually unwanted modes of existence, such as those found across Polynesia after French nuclear tests in the Pacific Tuamotu Archipelago during the 1960s and 1970s. Their infrastructural histories provide, Yusoff says, "new museums of humanity." "Waste sites, mining shafts and extraction zones are imagined as the new museums of humanity, alongside the more affectual and accumulative material registers of pollution, toxicity and climate shifts."[30]

The embanking of existence and the strainings and tailings that result are material. But mental processes also depend on the embankment of concepts and the strainings and tailings that result. Long before Bateson, William James proposed that mental concepts and indeed all of mental life are efforts of embankment. Mental life is—and thus all concepts are—a cacophony of efforts of attention.[31] The source of concepts would never be found by burrowing into the mind in search of ever more abstract forms. Understanding concepts as a form of effort, James argued, demands that we place mental life in the social worlds in which it exists—in which it is given dimensions and qualities and in which it spreads. In other words, concepts aren't merely situated in the social world. They are the social world—and this is not the social world of meaning, but the social world of distributed energies and abilities to focus on the tasks at hand. This approach to language, mental life, and discourse would be elaborated by a host of postpragmatists stretching across linguistics, ecology, textual studies, and anthropology. To put into words is to pull into words, to give matter to a concept that can do the work of articulating a scene of forces. In other words, two kinds of embankments emerge as forces of disembankment: on the one hand, the concept itself as thingish in relation to thingishes just as all objects are only here-ish and there-ish, and on the other hand, the new field of arrangement given matter by that concept. As these embankments do their work, like other material sackings, they strain the given and emit all sorts of discursive tailings as the potential prefigurative signs for new concepts. Again, for James, at the beginning are the social and its arrangement of powers to affect and be affected. Concepts are not in the mind. They are neither descriptions of existence nor transcendental forms of truth about existence. Concepts are a form of gathering from and rearticulating actual worlds, actual regions of existence, and the actual ways these worlds and regions are entangled. When we compose concepts, front and center must be questions of from where these concepts are coming, to whom they are obligated, and how they help coming forms of human and more-than-human worlds endure.

The concepts discussed here are offered as a way of approaching a broader question about concepts and commons in many contemporary critical theories and practices of the political and politics. Must politics be grounded in a common condition, whether the soul, Geist, or precarity, before we can have a politics or act politically as such? What if the soul was not common but just the repetition of Geist and its history of dispossession and disposal? What if we said we do not all share in precariousness because this common depends on a more foundational distinction between life and nonlife, that this entails a demand on other worlds that refuse this distinction as relevant to an analysis of existence? What if the task of political thought and action in the West was not to find a way of making its specific history a common history that was then shoved down everyone's throat? What if the goal was to find a way of approaching difference that allowed for the retention of difference, of seeking a common world that is differentiated rather than homogenized by one concept, and of foregrounding the ancestral presents that maintain or alter the shape and content of these differences?

Postscript

THIS BOOK HAS SOUGHT to engage a stubborn bifurcation of the *social tense* of catastrophe—the coming and the ancestral—and the effect of this split on how we understand the importance of four axioms of contemporary critical theory. Rather than a conclusion, this postscript is meant to emphasize a series of points I have made throughout this book.

The first is simply that the political meaning and importance of the axioms cannot be separated from the question of the social tense of catastrophe. Tracking both the hidden and not-so-hidden nature of this social tense shows that the source and ultimate end of critique is often split. Hannah Arendt and Gregory Bateson are good examples of theorists who trek through the colonial world but are ultimately looking toward the horizon of the West. But even Dipesh Chakrabarty's discussions of the epochal consciousness of climate change can unwittingly begin in and rebound into the European diaspora, its Enlightenment and humanism, and its geontological ordering of existence. Beginning with those for whom these *liberal diasporas*, imaginaries, and orderings are the ongoing ancestral catastrophe, we see that the catastrophe has a very different meaning and mood.

Second, the point of this book was not to argue with a word, say, *ontology*, but to insist on a dual orientation—from within the ancestral catastrophe toward and against its ongoing power to harm those it has been harming for hundreds of years. In her recent study of the water graves of the enslaved, destitute, and refugee, Valérie Loichot places the ecological thought of Michel Serres and Édouard Glissant in the hull of a seafaring boat. Loichot suggests that both use the turbulent sea and the confined hull to produce *la pensé du tremblement*, "a spiritual, ethical, and political gesture against fixed truth, rigid theology, or worse, religious and political absolutisms."[1] But if we remember that Glissant's is not a philosophy or poetics of equivalence or empathy, then these two men, for all their deep conversation, are not in the same boat. As for Glissant, Loichot observes a deeper seismic thinking. In *La cohée du lamentin*, Glissant does not use *catastrophe* in the etymological sense of turning something upside down but instead uses it as a relational deep probing of the "communication between the vulnerable planet and the lonely trembling human."[2]

This leads to the third potential insight of this book: the ongoing nature of the ancestral catastrophe of colonialism and its epistemological and ontological presuppositions and unfoldings have mobilized spatial and affective discourses in order to transform actual harms into horizonal hopes. No liberal violence seems large enough to shatter liberals' ability to slough it off by acknowledging they had made a mistake but are now back on track, leaving in their wake endless worlds that know the eternal return of this trick. In many of these places, where the ongoing ancestral harms of liberalism are continually dismissed as nothing but an unintentional mistake, the affect that rules is not hope but stubbornness and survivance. Neither of these affects seeks to reach the horizon of universal mutual recognition or equality and justice because both know there is no such horizon. It is simply a mirror the West enjoys preening in front of.

We can see this refusal to budge in a fourth point. In the contemporary collapse of infrastructure and climate in places that have previously been able to sequester the effects of liberal capitalism elsewhere, the concepts and discourses of alleviation remain stubbornly predictable. To maintain and increase their share of the earth's resources, the affluent use the poor as their alibi. Is there an infrastructural problem around clean water? Don't go asking the affluent to have less so the poor can have more. Instead dig deeper and commodify the water resources of others. Stop mining for coal as the simplest intervention in the acceleration of heat toxicity? Blame the sliding middle class's need for jobs, rather than redistributing capital around the concept of a universal minimal income or a host of other social experiments.

It is little wonder—and this is my fifth point—that we see the rise of illiberal democracy and nonliberal capitalism globally. Aimé Césaire long ago noted the rot that ran backward along the colonial waves. If liberalism and capitalism actually cared about the norms and ideals they touted, distinguishing their humanism from all other modes of governance, we would be seeing this difference by now. Instead we see across the United States, South America, India, Europe, the Middle East, and elsewhere the erection of walls, the election of hard nationalists with all their subsequent racisms and xenophobias, and the ejection of others through soft and hard law.

For those going to heaven, perhaps none of this matters. For those seeking to become immortal, they need not worry—their imprint is everywhere, their legacy ensured in the composition of the earth.

Glossary

ancestral present, ancestral presence   *Ancestral present* is found in "The Urban Intensions of Geontopower." The term emerged from the social project of Karrabing Film Collective. Members encountered questions that demonstrated a late liberal understanding of the endurant nature of ancestral existence, namely, that human and totemic ancestors were materially past while they were in the present. Karrabing began to experiment with visual overlays and narrative loops that demonstrate that their human and totemic ancestors struggle to stay in place in ongoing colonialism. The ancestors also engage in a practice of survivance, as this term is defined and mobilized by Gerald Vizenor in *Manifest Manners*. The ancestral present, like survivance, refuses settler colonial lamentations of Indigenous loss and cultural recession and instead points to the strategic, creative, and sometimes cranky nature of totemic and human existence.

animist   This concept is discussed most thoroughly in *Geontologies*. The animist does not refer to the myriad worlds that have been anthropologically categorized as animist or totemist. For such comparative approaches one can read Philippe Descola's *Beyond Nature and Culture*. Instead, the animist is one of three symptomatic figures who began arising as geontopower moved from background to foreground as Western epistemology and ontology came to be seem as elements of Western governance. The animist solves the problem of the potential dissolution of the difference between life and nonlife by attributing the core properties of live things to all existence. My analysis of this maneuver is aligned with the analysis of late liberal recognition outlined in *The Cunning of Recognition*. The animist conserves and regrounds all the major dramas, desires, and directions of Western power even as it claims to see that all other existents were always just like themselves.

autological subject   This figure is introduced in *The Empire of Love* and elaborated in a series of interviews, perhaps best in "Shapes of Freedom" with Kim Turcot DiFruscia. By talking of the autological subject, I am referring to discourses, practices, and fantasies about self-making, self-sovereignty, and the value of individual freedom associated with the Enlightenment project of contractual constitutional democracy and capitalism. This term is paired with the genealogical society. On the one hand, it conjures the multiple discourses and practices in liberal freedom as coterminous with the autonomous and self-determining subject. On the other hand, its meaning depends on its contrast with the genealogical society, the colonial imaginary of a humanity determined by custom as control. The genealogical society comprises the discourses, practices, and fantasies about social constraints placed on the autological subject by various kinds of inheritances.

biontological, biontology   Introduced in *Geontolologies*, the biontological refers to the subsumption of ontology into the broad characteristics of life. It is related to the carbon imaginary (see below) insofar as the carbon imaginary maintains the scarred homology between the biological concept of metabolism and its key components (birth, growth and reproduction, and death) and the ontological concepts of event, *conatus/affectus*, and finitude.

camouflage   Introduced in *Economies of Abandonment*, camouflage refers to the art of hiding in a given environment via embodied disguise. These actual practices of cloaking are part of a much broader and varied set of discourses about modes of concealment that allow otherwise visible organisms or objects to remain indiscernible from the surrounding environment. Camouflage has a genealogical relationship to mimicry and colonialism (see the work of Frantz Fanon, Homi Bhabha, and Michel Serres). Camouflage is not merely a spectral quality but involves the entire sensory apparatus. It is the main mode of existence within the brackets of recognition, namely, the modes of recognition that become visible when, as a result of some threat to late liberal security, the tense of the other is written as a bracket. In these redlined and bracketed moments, difference is given a tense and a mood—say, the past perfect and subjunctive—and recognition is transformed into the modality of espionage and camouflage.

carbon imaginary   In *Geontologies*, the carbon imaginary is described as the suturing and transpositions of biological concepts of birth, growth and reproduction, and death and the ontological concepts of event, conatus/affectus, and finitude. The carbon imaginary fits Ludwig Wittgenstein's concept of an axial hinge—an axle on which turns an entire apparatus of practical and propositional knowledge about the world, rather than a set of propositions about the state of the world. In the kind of conversion Wittgenstein proposes, one is not merely repositioned in the space established by an axial proposition but moves out of one space and into another, from one kind of physics into another, from one metaphysics into another. But hinge and axle also seem, as metaphors, to make too smooth an imaginary joint. It might be better to imagine the homologous productivity of the space between natural life and critical life and the nature of the carbon imaginary as a scar. The carbon imaginary would then be the pulsing scarred region between life and nonlife—an ache that makes us pay attention to a scar that has, for a long time, remained numb and dormant but not unfelt.

cunning of recognition   *The Cunning of Recognition* introduces this phrase as a reformulation of Hegel's understanding of the cunning of reason as the mechanism by which the concrete universality of mutual human recognition is achieved. For Hegel, the cunning of reason is to set the passions of individual energies, self-interest, and desire "to work in its service, as a result of which the agents by which it gives itself existence must pay the penalty and suffer the loss."[1] The pain and carnage left in the wake is figured as the necessary if unfortunate condition of the birth of universal justice. Colonial liberalism hijacked this diagram of disavowable violence. In *Economies of Abandonment*, late liberalism is introduced as a way of periodizing the emergence of the cunning of recognition, in which liberalism attempts to insulate itself from anticolonial and new social critiques by four major movements of discourse: first, to violently repress radical elements while enticing more moderate elements to turn to the law for recognition; second, to flip the direction of the evaluation of worth from liberalism to those seeking recognition; third, to encourage an identification with the impossible object of a difference that is no different; and fourth, to safeguard the key possessive principles of liberalism and capitalism. *Economies of Abandonment* also introduced the inverse figures of camouflage and espionage that always accompany the discourse and tactics of recognition and work in conjunction with the governance of the prior.

desert   Introduced in *Geontologies*, the desert is one of three symptomatic figures that began arising as geontopower moved from background to foreground as Western epistemology and ontology came to be seem as elements of Western governance. The desert includes the discourses, tactics, and figures that restabilize the distinction between life and nonlife. It stands for all things understood as denuded of life—and by implication, all things that could, with the correct deployment of technological expertise or proper stewardship, be (re)made hospitable to life. The desert, in other words, holds on to the distinction between life and nonlife and dramatizes the possibility that life is always threatened by the creeping desiccating sands of nonlife. The desert is the space where life was, is not now, but could be with the proper management of knowledges, techniques, and resources. The carbon imaginary lies at the heart of this figure and is thus the key to maintaining geontopower. The carbon imaginary lodges the superiority of life into being by transposing biological concepts (such as metabolism and its key events, birth, growth and reproduction, and death) and ontological concepts (such as event, conatus/affectus, and finitude). Clearly, biology and ontology do not operate in the same discursive field, nor do they simply intersect. Nevertheless, the carbon imaginary reinforces a scarred meeting place where each can exchange conceptual intensities, thrills, wonders, anxieties, and perhaps terrors of the other of life, namely, the inert, inanimate, and barren. In this scarred space, ontology is revealed to be biontology. Being has always been dominated by life and the desires of life.

endurance, endurant In *Economies of Abandonment*, endurance is a social antonym of exhaustion. Endurance is the refusal to consider the substance of being as a secondary quality. The endurant is always more or less strength, hardiness, callousness; its continuity through space; its ability to suffer and yet persist. Endurance encloses itself around the durative—an approach to the temporality of continuance, a denotation of continuous action without any reference to its beginning or end and outside the dialectic of presence and absence in deep conversation with Henri Bergson's idea of duration as "the continuous progress of the past which gnaws into the future and which swells as it advances."[2] Enduring is neither a singularity nor a homogeneous space. Every scene of endurance is shot through with multiple and incommensurate configurations of tense, eventfulness, ethical substance, and aggregations of existence. On the side of colonizing power, the endurant is constraining; on the side of colonized worlds, the endurant is survivance.

espionage Introduced in *Economies of Abandonment*, espionage refers to actual practices of spying and being spied on, and to a much broader and diverse set of assumptions that someone is trying to penetrate a socially sealed space. In espionage, value circulates in such a way that both those circulating it and those trying to impede its circulation avoid the initial confrontation underlying the imaginary of recognition.

genealogical society This figure is introduced in *The Empire of Love* and elaborated in a series of interviews (perhaps best in "Shapes of Freedom" with Kim Turcot DiFruscia). Genealogical society is a fantasy of late liberalism and capitalism meant to justify forms of disruption and dispossession and to provide a negative differential content to the fantasy of the autological subject, specifically those that ground freedom and justice in self-making and self-sovereignty.

geontology   *Geontology* was introduced as a concept in a talk at the Haus der Kulturen der Welt as part of the 2013 Anthropocene Project. At that time, *geontology* referred to the various ways peoples have differentiated modes of existence such as life and nonlife. As I discuss in *Geontologies*, geontology highlights, on the one hand, the biontological enclosure of existence (to characterize all existents as endowed with the qualities associated with life). On the other hand, it is intended to highlight the difficulty of finding a critical language to account for the moment in which a form of power long self-evident in certain regimes of settler late liberalism is becoming visible globally. The point of geontology is neither to found a new ontology of objects, nor to establish a new metaphysics of power, nor to adjudicate the possibility or impossibility of the human ability to know the truth of the world of things. Rather, it is a concept meant to help make visible the figural tactics of late liberalism as a long-standing biontological orientation and distribution of power crumbles, losing its efficacy as a self-evident backdrop to reason.

geontopower   In *Geontologies*, geontopower is differentiated from biopower and meant to indicate and intensify the contrasting components of nonlife (geos) and being (ontology) currently in play in the late liberal governance of difference and markets. Geontopower is not just now emerging to replace biopolitics; biopower (the governance through life and death) has long depended on a subtending geontopower (the difference between the lively and the inert). And similar to the function of necropolitics, which Achille Mbembe showed openly operating in colonial Africa and only later revealing its shape in Europe, so geontopower has long operated openly in settler late liberalism and has been insinuated in the ordinary operations of its governance of difference and markets. The attribution of an inability of various colonized peoples to differentiate the things that have agency, subjectivity, and intentionality of the sort that emerges with life has been the grounds of casting them into a premodern mentality and a postrecognition difference. More specifically, geontopower is meant to illuminate the cramped space in which my Indigenous colleagues are forced to maneuver as they attempt to keep relevant their critical analytics and practices of existence. In its operations geontopower is related to the governance of the prior.

ghoul health   In *Empire of Love*, *ghoul health* refers to the global organization of the biomedical establishment and its imaginary around the idea that the big scary bug, the new plague, is the real threat that haunts the contemporary global division, distribution, and circulation of health. Ghoul health is the prefigure of the concept of the virus. It is the bad faith of what I called "the end-game of geophysical bad faith" of the empire of the liberal diaspora.[3]

governance of the prior   In *Economies of Abandonment*, this division of tense is shown to inhabit the social fabric of emerging settler nationalism, which bifurcated the sources and grounds of social belonging in such a way that the relationship between settler and Native/Indigenous was transformed from a mutual implication in the problem of prior occupation to a hierarchical relationship between two modes of prior occupation, one oriented to the future, the other to the past. As the governance of the prior crossed the truth value of the future anterior and past perfect, the priority of the human as ultimate signature of liberal democratic sovereignty was detached from the priority of the descent of persons, even as the priority of certain persons (colonizers) was safeguarded against the priority of others (the colonized). This division became available to be applied to other grounds in and against the nation. The governance of the prior works hand in hand with the cunning of recognition.

late liberalism, late liberal   Initially in *Economies of Abandonment*, *late liberalism* refers to and is differentiated from neoliberalism. In that work, late liberalism refers to the governance of social difference in the wake of the anticolonial movements and the emergence of new social movements, whereas *neoliberalism* referred to the governance of markets beginning in the 1970s. Like liberal diaspora, late liberalism does not exist as a thing in the ordinary sense of the term but as actions like a sighting or a citing. It exists insofar as it is evoked to conjure, shape, aggregate, and evaluate a variety of social worlds, and each conjuring, shaping, aggregation, and evaluation disperses liberalism as a global terrain.

liberal diaspora   This phrase is introduced in *The Cunning of Recognition* to "gesture at the colonial and postcolonial subjective, institutional identifications, dispersions and elaborations of the enlightenment idea that society should be organized on the basis of rational mutual understanding."[4] The main purpose was to demonstrate the varieties of tactics liberalism takes in justifying the violent actions arising in the gap between public reason and moral reason, and the discursive forms of disavowal that arise in retrospect. In *The Empire of Love* liberal diaspora is a process, whereby the dispersions of Western forms of possession-based governance transform themselves as they move into new contexts, even as their status as things that do or don't do things is continually abstracted and reified. Liberalism is thus only citational in the sense that its core can be referenced by way of its difference in all of its actual partial and improper variants. Late liberalism should be considered to have this same diasporic character.

obligation   In *Economies of Abandonment*, obligation is always immanent and belated. Immanent obligation is a no-man's-land between choice and determination. By *immanent obligation*, I refer to a form of relationality that one finds oneself drawn to and finds oneself nurturing or caring for in the midst of critical reflexivity. This being "drawn to" or "repelled by" is often initially a fragile connection, a sense of an immanent connectivity. Choices are made to enrich and intensify these connections. Even these choices need to be understood as retrospective—the subject choosing is herself continually deferred by the choice. In other words, she is and is beginning to be different in the vicinity of this choice; she is belated to herself, arriving too late to be any use to adjudication. I might be able to describe why I am drawn to a particular space, and I may try to nurture this obligation or break away from it, but still I have very little that can be described as "choice" in the original orientation.

otherwise   The spaces of the otherwise are mapped out in *Economies of Abandonment* and a number of subsequent essays, especially, "The Will to Be Otherwise/The Effort of Endurance" and "After the Last Man: Images and Ethics of Becoming Otherwise." The otherwise are those immanent forms that lie within social projects outside the dialectic and difference of Self and Other. Examples include the otherwise to the two positions in the governance of the prior, Indigenous and settler, and the two positions in the geontologies of life and nonlife. In the will to be otherwise, a person may find herself to be ethically otherwise and seek to persevere in being so or may seek to be ethically otherwise and act on and persevere in this desire. We might, for the moment, distinguish between these two sorts of persons as structurally and volitionally otherwise, the passive and the active. This is the otherwise that stares back at its actual conditions without yet being able to speak its new conditions. The otherwise is not an ontology. It is radically empirical and found in the endurant and crumbling conditions and forces of governance.

quasi event   This shape and register of the social and political were first outlined in *Economies of Abandonment*. A subsequent conversation with Lauren Berlant in "Holding Up the World," elaborated the relationship between this form of material endurance and decay and the political imaginaries of embankment, tailing, and straining. Quasi events are meant to be the irreducibly material substrate and construct of social power. The concept was meant to find kinship with Rob Nixon's environments of slow violence and Paul Gilroy's politics of a lower frequency.

social project   In *Economies of Abandonment*, social projects are forms of collective action that attempt to make capable an alternative set of human and posthuman worlds. They are specific arrangements (*agencements*) that extend beyond simple human sociality or human beings. A social project is dependent on a host of interlocking concepts, materials, and forces that include human and nonhuman agencies and organisms. The point of a social project is not to discover the eternal or the universal but to find the singular conditions under which something new is produced.

social tense This aspect of tense, addressed in *Economies of Abandonment*, is broadly social rather than strictly linguistic. From a grammatical perspective, tense and event are difficult to disambiguate. Metapragmatic approaches to discourse, for instance, understand tense and event to emerge from the intersection between what is being narrated and the act of narration—the time when the state or action of a verb occurs. In the grammatical past tense, for instance, the narrated event is marked as prior to the act of narrating, while in the grammatical present tense the narrated event coincides with the act of narration. Languages demonstrate a variety of ways of configuring the temporal relationship between what is being narrated and the narration: how these strictly grammatical figurations are absorbed into other discourses, affective attachments, and practices of late liberalism. The autological subject and genealogical society, the brackets of recognition, the governance of the prior, and sacrificial love are all examined as techniques of social tense that are available when accounts of ongoing structural social harm are explained from a late liberal perspective.

transfiguration Introduced in "Technologies of Public Persuasion," cowritten with Dilip Parameshwar Gaonkar, transfiguration was contrasted with interpretive practices associated with language and text-focused forms of social analysis. As the liberal dream of translation is innervated, materialized, and reduced to a normative struggle, a new analytic focuses on the power-laden interlocking levels of and contestations between cultures of circulation. Transfigurative analysis would focus on the palpability, intelligibility, and recognizability of texts, events, and practices and the play of supplementarity that frames and ruptures the enterprise of public recognition, whatever its object. All these compose the demanding environments of "things" and their movement. They provide things with their mappable dimensions and ghostly distensions, their protocols for safe movement (or not) across cultures of circulation. A transfigurative analysis lay in the backdrop of my "Radical Worlds: The Anthropology of Incommensurability and Inconceivability" and *The Cunning of Recognition*.

virus Introduced in *Geontologies*, the virus is one of three symptomatic figures that began arising as geontopower moved from background to foreground as Western epistemology and ontology came to be seen as elements of Western governance. The virus and its central imaginary of the terrorist provide a glimpse of a persistent, errant potential radicalization of the desert and the animist. The virus is the figure that seeks to disrupt the current arrangements of life and nonlife by claiming that it is a difference that makes no difference, not because all is alive, vital, and potent, nor because all is inert, replicative, unmoving, dormant, and endurant. Because the division of life and nonlife does not define or contain the virus, it can use and ignore this division for the sole purpose of diverting the energies of arrangements of existence in order to extend itself. The virus copies, duplicates, and lies dormant even as it continually adjusts to, experiments with, and tests its circumstances. It confuses and levels the difference between life and nonlife while carefully taking advantage of the smallest aspects of their differentiation. We catch a glimpse of the virus whenever someone suggests that the size of the human population must be addressed in the wake of climate change, that a glacial granite mountain welcomes the effects of air-conditioning on life, that humans are kudzu, or that human extinction is desirable and should be accelerated. The virus is also Ebola and the waste dump, nuclear fallout and the drug-resistant bacterial infection stewed in massive salmon and poultry farms, the person who looks just like "we" do as she plants a bomb. Perhaps most spectacularly, the virus is the popular cultural figure of the zombie—life turned to nonlife and transformed into a new kind of species war—the aggressive rotting undead against the last redoubt of Life. The virus is an emergent or residual form of a previous human–more-than-human arrangement. It operates to create a new dwelling, diagnosing along the way the structures and contours of power. How terribly true this seems at the moment. COVID-19 emerged from extractive capitalism and was disseminated by transportation capitalism. It devastates the poor, Indigenous communities and communities of color because these communities embody the long arm of the ancestral catastrophe of racism and colonialism. Rather than seeing COVID-19 as a horrifying analytic of power's embodiment, as a devasting critique of late liberal capitalism—understanding this late liberal capitalism as the source of this horror we are experiencing—we are told to view the virus as our enemy.

NOTES

PREFACE

1 Musu, "War Metaphors Used for COVID-19 Useful but Also Dangerous."

INTRODUCTION

1 For instance, see Das and Fassin, *Words and Worlds*; and Callison and Manfredi, *Mutant Neoliberalism*.

2 Wynter, "Unsettling the Coloniality."

3 Although Peirce's early writings may suggest some actual something to which mental habits seek to align themselves, by his later *Monist* essays, existence is a multiplicity of regions of mind in and out of habit with itself due to the function of absolute chance and an original and ongoing diversification and specification taking place across an irregularly formed world. Peirce, "The Doctrine of Necessity."

4 Massumi, "Such as It Is," 117.

5 Massumi, "Such as It Is," 117.

6 Kenton, "South Dakota Nurse Says."

7 James, *Principles of Psychology*, 402.

8 James, *Pragmatism*, 32.

9 "There can BE no difference any-where that doesn't MAKE a difference elsewhere—no difference in abstract truth that doesn't express itself in concrete fact and no conduct consequent upon that fact, imposed on somebody, somehow, somewhere and somewhen." James, *Pragmatism*, 27.

10 James, *Pragmatism*, 28.

11 Lapoujade, *William James*, 1.

12 Deleuze and Guattari, *What Is Philosophy?*, 11.

13 James, *Pragmatism*, 25.

14 Glissant, *Poetics of Relation*, 5. See also Glissant, *Treatise on the Whole-World*; and Diawara, *Édouard Glissant*.

15 Deleuze and Guattari, *What Is Philosophy?*, 51.

16 Sylvia Wynter also sees this moment as a crucial turning point. She notes that "the multiple challenges" during roughly the same period and "at the global level by anticolonial activists and by activists in Europe, and then in the United States by Blacks and a range of other non-white groups, together with feminists and Gay Liberationists" sought to dislodge the overrepresentation of the human by European humanism. Wynter, "Unsettling the Coloniality," 72.

17 Taylor, "The Politics of Recognition," 64.

18 Taylor, "The Politics of Recognition," 65.

19 "The proponents of neo-Nietzschean theories hope to escape this whole nexus of hypocrisy by turning the entire issue into one of power and counterpower. Then the question is no more one of respect, but of taking sides, of solidarity. But this is hardly a satisfactory solution, because in taking sides they miss the driving force of this kind of politics, which is precisely the search for recognition and respect." Taylor, "The Politics of Recognition," 70. In the same breath, Taylor is happy to place conditions on who gets the presumption of worth. Conditions include "that cultures that have provided the horizon of meaning for large numbers of human beings, of diverse characters and temperaments, over a long period of time—that have, in other words, articulated their sense of the good, the holy, the admirable—are almost certain to have something that deserves our admiration and respect, even if it is accompanied by much that we have to abhor and reject." Taylor, "The Politics of Recognition," 70.

20 *Mabo and Others v. the State of Queensland (No. 2)*, [1992] HCA 23; (1992) 175 CLR 1.

21 Brennan, *Mabo v. Queensland (No. 2)*, §29.

22 Scambary, *My Country, My Mine*; Coulthard, *Red Skin, White Masks*.

23 Anand, *Hydraulic City*, 7.

CHAPTER ONE. THE FOUR AXIOMS OF EXISTENCE

1 What Sylvia Wynter has argued is a "descriptive statement of the human, in whose logic the non-Western, nonwhite peoples can only, at best, be assimilated as honorary human." Wynter, "Unsettling the Coloniality," 329. See also da Silva, *Toward a Global Idea of Race*.

2 Anand, *Hydraulic City*, 7.

3 Barad, *Meeting the Universe Halfway*, ix.

4 Haraway, *When Species Meet*, 32. Haraway makes the political stakes clear, "If we appreciate the foolishness of human exceptionalism then we know that becoming is always becoming with, in a contact zone where the outcome, where who is in the world, is at stake." Haraway, *When Species Meet*, 244. Haraway's

recent conversations with Isabelle Stengers show the potential power and difference of their two approaches to science. Haraway, "SF with Stengers."

5   Nicholson, "More Than $600,000 Spent."

6   MacKenzie, "What Is a Political Event?"

7   Badiou, *Saint Paul*.

8   Deleuze and Guattari, *A Thousand Plateaus*.

9   Deleuze, *The Logic of Sense*.

10 For multiple ways people have approached this form of violence, see slow violence in Nixon, *Slow Violence*; slow death in Berlant, *Cruel Optimism*; infrastructures of the dominated in Scott, *Domination and the Arts of Resistance*; and politics of a lower frequency in Gilroy, *The Black Atlantic*.

11 For instance, consider Nicholas Shapiro's study of FEMA trailers handed out after Hurricane Katrina in New Orleans. Shapiro, *Where Have All the Trailers Gone?*

12 Deleuze, *Difference and Repetition*.

13 Arendt, *The Human Condition*, 190.

14 Hartman, *Scenes of Subjection*, 61.

15 Fanon, *Black Skin, White Masks*, 21, 35, and 109.

16 Da Silva has argued that because Western philosophical and governmental concepts such as the citizen, subject, democracy, and so on were developed in and are a justification-legitimation of racialized colonialism—that is, a racial imaginary is irreducibly part and parcel of them—their remobilization in radical political work merely extends this racial logic. Da Silva, *Toward a Global Idea of Race*.

17 Stengers, *Another Science Is Possible*, 100.

18 Glowczewski, *Indigenising Anthropology*.

19 For the potentials of this move, see Ferreira, "Symbiotic Bodies and Evolutionary Tropes."

20 Dosse, *Gilles Deleuze and Félix Guattari*.

21 Allar notes that Glissant was developing his concept of Relation in his poetry long before the fateful 1980 meeting. Allar, "Rhizomatic Influence," 2.

22 Nesbitt, "The Postcolonial Event."

23 Barad, *Meeting the Universe Halfway*.

24 Deleuze and Guattari, *A Thousand Plateaus*, 19.

25 Glissant, *Poetics of Relation*, 12.

26 Glissant, *Poetics of Relation*, 12.

27 Glissant, *Poetics of Relation*, 14.

28 Yountae, "Beginning in the Middle."

29 Yountae, "Beginning in the Middle," 287.

30 Drabinski, "Sites of Relation and 'Tout-Monde.'"

31 Sharpe, *In the Wake*.

32 Glissant, *Poetics of Relation*, 5–6.

33 Glissant, *Poetics of Relation*, 6.

34 Glissant, *Poetics of Relation*, 6.

35 Allar, "Rhizomatic Influence," 2.

36 Anand, *Hydraulic City*, 7. See also von Schnitzler, *Democracy's Infrastructure*.

37 Anand, *Hydraulic City*, 13.

38 Gaber, "Blue Lines and Blues Infrastructure."

39 Anand, *Hydraulic City*, 225.

40 Muehlebach, "A Vital Politics."

41 For a general background, see Highsmith, *Demolition Means Progress*.

42 The following summary is adapted from Kennedy, "Lead-Laced Water in Flint."

43 Personal communication, February 19, 2018.

44 Douglas, "Without Black Lives Matter."

45 Atkinson and Davey, "Five Charged."

46 Highsmith, "Op-Ed."

47 See the City of Flint's declaration of the state of emergency at https://www
.cityofflint.com/state-of-emergency/, accessed November 24, 2020.

48 Gaber, "Mobilizing Health Metrics," 180.

49 Lakhani, "Millions in US at Risk."

50 Hird, "The Phenomenon of Waste-World-Making."

51 For a history of race poverty and infrastructural toxicity, see Sellers, "The
Flint Water Crisis." For forms of citizen science emerging from this toxic dis-
tribution, see Shapiro, Zakariya, and Roberts, "A Wary Alliance"; and Lea,
"This Is Not a Pipe."

52 Sharpe, *In the Wake*, 35.

53 For instance, see Hird, "Waste, Environmental Politics"; and MacBride, *Recycling Reconsidered*.

54 Hird, "Waste, Environmental Politics."

CHAPTER TWO. TOXIC LATE LIBERALISM

1 Derrida, "Plato's Pharmacy."

2 Bagnato, "Microscopic Colonialism."

3 Little argues that this work reconstitutes rather than critically engages the
sacrosanct veneer of democracy. Little, "Democratic Melancholy," 971. See Laclau, *On Populist Reason*; Mouffe, *Agonistics*; and Brown, *Undoing the Demos*.

4 Butler, *Frames of War*.

5 Nussbaum enumerates several capabilities: life, bodily health, bodily integrity,
senses, imagination, thought, emotions, practical reason, affiliation, other species, play, and control over one's environment. Nussbaum, *Frontiers of Justice*,
76–77.

6 Habermas, "A Review," 217.

7 Hegel, *The Philosophy of History*, 33.

8 Parkinson, "Hegel, Marx and the Cunning of Reason," 289.

9 See Povinelli, *The Cunning of Recognition*, 1–34.

10 Povinelli, "After the Last Man."

11 Trouillot, "Abortive Rituals."

12 *Mabo and Others v. the State of Queensland (No. 2)*, [1992] HCA 23; (1992), para. 39.

13 I make a similar but more elaborated argument in Povinelli, *The Cunning of Recognition.*

14 Trouillot, "Abortive Rituals."

15 See Ureta, "Chemical Rubble."

16 Gilmore, "Abolition Geography."

17 For instance, see Reible et al., "Toxic and Contaminant Concerns."

18 Chen, *Animacies*, 167.

19 Ureta and Flores, "Don't Wake Up the Dragon," 1064.

20 Demos, "To Save a World."

21 Wynter, "Unsettling the Coloniality."

22 Max Liboiron has compiled an excellent reading list in toxicity and sociality relative to discard studies. Liboiron, "Bibliography on Critical Approaches to Toxics and Toxicity."

23 Silva, "Mining the Deep Sea."

24 Mintz, *Sweetness and Power.*

25 Quoted in Raoul Peck, dir., *I Am Not Your Negro* (Magnolia Pictures, 2016).

26 Lewis, *W. E. B. Du Bois*, 394–95.

27 Benjamin, *The Arcades Project*, 94.

28 "Belgium," *History of Sanitary Sewers*, accessed November 24, 2020, http:/www
    .sewerhistory.org/photosgraphics/belgium/.

29 Hochschild, *Kind Leopold's Ghost.*

30 Benjamin, *The Arcades Project*, 31.

31 César, "Meteorisations."

32 Césaire, *Discourse on Colonialism*, 35–36.

33 See Murphy, *Sick Building Syndrome*; and Mitman, Murphy, and Sellers, *Landscapes of Exposure.*

34 Liu, Probst, and Liao, "Metal Contamination."

35 For instance, see Inskeep and Burdette, "Assessing the Contamination"; and Wong, "Ecological Restoration."

36 Vince, "The Heat Is On over the Climate Crisis."

37 Hernández, "Climate Change May Be Intensifying."

38 Livni, "Radioactive Wild Boars."

39 Kim, "Invasive Others and Significant Others."

40 Helmenstine, "Chernobyl's Animal Mutations." See also Wood and Beresford, "The Wildlife of Chernobyl."

41 Hobart and Kneese, "Radical Care," 2. See also John, *Sovereign Bodies.*

42 The use of *extimate* here repurposes Jacques Lacan's use of the term, which he reserved for human psychic formations, to describe how all substance is, in its most intimate internality, composed of a variety of external forces and materials. Lacan, *The Ethics of Psychoanalysis.*

43 Nixon, *Slow Violence*.

44 Césaire, *Discourse on Colonialism*, 43.

45 Makhuby, "The Poetics of Entanglement."

46 See Vizenor, *Manifest Manners* and *Survivance*.

47 See Simpson, *Mohawk Interruptus*, on Indigenous refusal.

48 Povinelli and Edmunds, "A Conversation."

49 Glowczewski discusses this problem more broadly in "Resisting Disaster."

50 Agard-Jones, "Spray."

51 Callison and Manfredi, *Mutant Neoliberalism*.

52 Hanley, "Eastman Kodak Admits Violations."

53 Hanley, "Eastman Kodak Admits Violations."

54 Pine, "Economy of Speed."

55 Shapiro, "Attuning to the Chemosphere."

56 Feser, "'It Was a Family.'"

57 Povinelli, *Geontologies*.

CHAPTER THREE. ATOMIC ENDS

1 Here and elsewhere, I use Karrabing kinship logics.

2 For instance, see Stephenson, "Learning to Live in the Dark"; Malm, *After the Storm*; Davison, "'Not to Escape the World but to Join It.'"

3 See Foxwell-Norton, "What Would Hannah Arendt Have Seen?"

4 Stephenson, "Learning to Live in the Dark."

5 Sloan Morgan, "Moving from Rights to Responsibilities." See also Strakosch, "Beyond Colonial Completion"; and Honig, "What Kind of Thing Is Land?" Markell notes Arendt's specific use of culture in Markell, "Arendt's Work," 32.

6 Davies, "Nothing to Say Sorry For."

7 Chakrabarty, "The Human Condition in the Anthropocene."

8 Chakrabarty, "The Human Condition in the Anthropocene," 183.

9 Chakrabarty, "The Human Condition in the Anthropocene," 183.

10 Freeman, introduction.

11 Brian Simbirski notes that while long suspicious of automation, by the late 1950s Arendt "came to associate nuclear violence with automation and cybernetics." Simbirski, "Cybernetic Muse."

12 Arendt, *The Human Condition*, 2.

13 See Giroux, *University in Chains*.

14 Arendt, *The Human Condition*, 7.

15 Arendt, *The Human Condition*, 91.

16 See Vatter, "Natality and Biopolitics"; and Bowen-Moore, *Hannah Arendt's Philosophy of Natality*.

17 Arendt, *The Human Condition*, 150–51.

18 Arendt, *The Human Condition*, 7.

19 Arendt, *The Human Condition*, 178.

20 Arendt, *The Human Condition*, 190.
21 Arendt, *The Human Condition*, 190.
22 Markell, "Arendt's Work."
23 Arendt, *The Human Condition*, x.
24 Arendt, *The Human Condition*, 7.
25 Arendt, *The Human Condition*, 177.
26 Arendt, *The Human Condition*, 177.
27 Benjamin, "Theses on the Philosophy of History," 249.
28 Arendt, *The Origins of Totalitarianism*, 186.
29 Arendt, *On Revolution*, 23.
30 Arendt, *On Revolution*, 11.
31 Esposito, *The Origin of the Political*, 44.
32 See Moten, "The New International." See also Mbembe, "Necropolitics"; and Owens, "Racism in the Theory Canon."
33 See Gines, *Hannah Arendt and the Negro Question*.
34 See Jurkevics's reading of Arendt's understanding of revolution from the perspective of the marginalia she wrote on her copy of Schmitt's *Nomos of the Earth*. Jurkevics, "Hannah Arendt Reads."
35 Spillers, "Mama's Baby, Papa's Maybe," 65.
36 Peck, *I Am Not Your Negro*.
37 Villa, "Arendt and Totalitarianism," 290.
38 Villa, "Arendt and Totalitarianism," 289.
39 Villa, "Arendt and Totalitarianism," 291.
40 Kelley, "Classic Texts: #15."
41 Du Bois, *The World and Africa*, 15.
42 Arendt, "Reflections on Little Rock"; Penn, *Who Speaks for the Negro?*
43 Nesbitt argues that Césaire and other proponents of the departmentalization of Martinique, Guadeloupe, French Guiana, and Réunion aimed the "objective juridical equality of the vieilles colonies" squarely "against the domination of the white béké elites." See Nesbitt, "Departmentalization."
44 Wilder, *Freedom Time*, 2.
45 Gilroy, "Lecture I," 24.
46 See National Museum of Australia, "Warburton Ranges Controversy."
47 McGrath and Brooks, "Their Darkest Hour," 118.
48 Grayden, *Report of the Select Committee*, 18.
49 Quoted in Berndt, "The 'Warburton Range' Controversy."
50 Berndt, "The 'Warburton Range' Controversy."
51 Murdoch, "Sick, Starving Natives."
52 Murdoch, "Sick, Starving Natives."
53 Murdoch, "Sick, Starving Natives."
54 Berndt, "The 'Warburton Range' Controversy."
55 Berndt, "The 'Warburton Range' Controversy," 36.
56 Berndt, "The 'Warburton Range' Controversy," 37.

57 Marcia Langton has defended the methodology of the Berndts in the shadow of what she describes as contemporary essentialist and communal modes of Aboriginal activism. See Langton, "Anthropology, Politics."

58 For a history of the tests, see Arnold, *Britain, Australia, and the Bomb.*

59 McGrath and Brooks, "Their Darkest Hour," 132.

60 Halverson and Greenberg, *Islamists of the Maghreb*, 41.

61 Halverson and Greenberg, *Islamists of the Maghreb*, 41.

62 See Wolfe, *Traces of History*; and Immerwahr, *How to Hide an Empire.*

63 Luttrell, "Alienation and Global Poverty."

64 Arendt, *The Human Condition*, 7.

65 Melsan, "The Liberating Power of Words," 5.

66 Melsan, "The Liberating Power of Words," 5.

67 Grosfoguel, "Decolonizing Western Uni-versalisms," 95.

68 Hiddleston, "Aimé Césaire," 88 and 90. See also Garraway, "'What Is Mine.'"

69 Gilroy, "Lecture I," 22.

70 Gilroy, "Lecture I," 23.

71 Gilroy, "Lecture I," 32.

72 Gilroy, "Lecture I," 23.

73 Gilroy, "Lecture I," 36.

74 Gilroy, "Lecture I," 37.

75 Gilroy, "Lecture I," 36–37.

76 Moreton-Robinson, *The White Possessive.*

77 Coulthard, *Red Skin, White Masks*, 60.

78 Coulthard, "The Colonialism of the Present."

79 Glowczewski, *Indigenising Anthropology.*

CHAPTER FOUR. TOXIC ENDS

1 Carson, *Silent Spring*. See also McWilliams, *American Pests.*

2 See Zierler, *The Invention of Ecocide*; and Martin, "Defoliating the World."

3 Todd, "An Indigenous Feminist's Take on the Ontological Turn."

4 Berger, *Northern Frontier, Northern Homeland.*

5 Keeling and Sandlos, "Environmental Justice Goes Underground?," 117.

6 Keeling and Sandlos, "Environmental Justice Goes Underground?," 117. Keeling and Sandlos note, "Despite the relatively small number and wide geographic dispersal of development sites, industrial mining activity had a transformative impact on the region." Mining and other extraction in the 1950s "accounted for over 80 percent of territorial economic output." Keeling and Sandlos, "Environmental Justice Goes Underground?," 119.

7 See Cole and Foster, *From the Ground Up*; Taylor, *Toxic Communities*; Grinde and Johansen, *Ecocide of Native America*; Keeling and Sandlos, "Environmental Justice Goes Underground?"; Clark, "The Indigenous Environmental Movement"; Brugge and Goble, "The History of Uranium Mining"; Brugge, Be-

nally, and Yazzie-Lewis, *The Navajo People and Uranium Mining*; Mogren, *Warm Sands*; Peach and Hovdebo, *The Case for a Federal Role*; and Stanley, "Citizenship and the Production of Landscape and Knowledge."

8 Kristjansson, *Wages of Care*. For a similar logic of health and welfare in the Australian context, see Lea, *Bureaucrats and Bleeding Hearts*.

9 The residential school system was part of the policy of Canada's Department of Indian Affairs to sever an entire generation of First Nations children from their ancestral knowledge and lands. The atrocious social practices at these schools led to the establishment of a truth and reconciliation commission and ultimately an apology by Prime Minister Stephen Harper. See Goforth, "Aboriginal Healing Methods for Residential School Abuse and Intergenerational Effects." By 1970, some of these children started the Indian Brotherhood of the Northwest Territories, which historian Paul Sabin notes was modeled "after the Manitoba Indian Brotherhood that some young leaders visited in 1968." Sabin, "Voices from the Hydrocarbon Frontier," 26.

10 Sabin, "Voices from the Hydrocarbon Frontier," 28.

11 James, *Pragmatism*, 28.

12 Moreton-Robinson, *The White Possessive*.

13 Hartman, *Scenes of Subjection*, 6.

14 Deloria, *God Is Red*, 65.

15 Deloria, *God Is Red*, 65.

16 Deloria, *God Is Red*, 66.

17 Todd, "Fish, Kin and Hope," 139. For an understanding of the politics of the human and more-than-human world among Kānaka Maoli, see Fujikane, *Mapping Abundance for a Planetary Future*.

18 Coulthard, "From Wards of the State," 69–70.

19 Coulthard, "From Wards of the State," 69–70.

20 Coulthard, "Place against Empire," 80.

21 Nadasdy, "'Property' and Aboriginal Land Claims," 247.

22 Deloria, *God Is Red*, 65.

23 For the different histories of the application of the concept of terra nullius in the Americas and Australia, see Banner, "Why Terra Nullius?"

24 For a brief overview of the history of uranium mining in Australia, see Phillips, "The Long and Controversial History of Uranium Mining in Australia."

25 See Williams, *The Yolngu and Their Land*.

26 Aboriginal Land Rights Commission, 1973 report (Canberra: Australian Government Publishing Service, 1973), iii.

27 Aboriginal Land Rights Commission, 1974 report (Canberra: Australian Government Publishing Service, 1974), 5–6.

28 Aboriginal Land Rights Commission, 1974 report, 6.

29 Aboriginal Land Rights Commission, 1973 report, 2.

30 Aboriginal Land Rights Commission, 1973 report, 5.

31 Aboriginal Land Rights Commission, 1973 report, 5; emphasis added. See also Schaap, "The Absurd Logic of Aboriginal Sovereignty."

32 Aboriginal Land Rights Commission, 1974 report, 142. Woodward marks an anthropological debate about the relationship between the clan and the horde, exemplified by A. P. Elkin's understanding of the dynamic ancestral relationship that Karrabing ancestors had to their ancestral lands as opposed to strict social descent. See Elkin, "The Complexity of Social Organization" and "Ngirawat." See also Hiatt's summary of debates in "Local Organization."

33 See Povinelli, *Belyuen Traditional Aboriginal Owners*; Brandl, Haritos, and Walsh, *Kenbi Land Claim*.

34 For a robust discussion of this see "Poetics of Ghosts" in Povinelli, *The Cunning of Recognition*.

35 Karrabing Film Collective, *The Riot*.

36 Conversation with author, January 21, 2021.

37 See Aboriginal Land Rights (Northern Territory) Act (1976), part 1, section 3.

38 The legislation that came after the ALRA learned some tricks from this founding instrument, too: under subsequent and nationally available native title, the right to veto became a simpler right to negotiate. Even the ALRA was severely curtailed: traditional Aboriginal owners lost their right to veto mining in 1984 and then the space for lodging any new claims under this more generous original legislation was closed altogether, though traditional owner consent to exploration still matters. Under native title, a brief six-month window for consultation is all that's guaranteed. Lea, *Wild Policy*. See also Schaap, "The Absurd Logic."

39 Povinelli and Edmunds, "A Conversation."

40 Karrabing Film Collective. "Roan-Roan and Connected."

41 Povinelli, *Geontologies*, esp. 58–60.

42 Barbara Glowczewski sees a similar dynamic among the peoples of Yuendumu, demonstrating simultaneously how Indigenous ontologies map on to Guattari's ecosophy and how his ecosophy was influenced by these Indigenous analytics. See Glowczewski, *Indigenising Anthropology* and *Totemic Becomings*.

43 Karrabing Film Collective, "Australian Babel."

44 Shaw, "Bringing Deleuze and Guattari."

45 See Hayles, *How We Became Posthuman*; Kline, *The Cybernetics Moment*; and Chaney, *Runaway*.

46 Bateson, *Naven*, 175.

47 Bateson, *Naven*, 176.

48 Bateson, *Naven*, 176–77.

49 Price, "Gregory Bateson and the OSS."

50 Price, "Gregory Bateson and the OSS."

51 See Pias, *The Macy Conferences*.

52 We have several excellent histories of the rise of cybernetics showing its original deployment as a means of better targeting German missiles during World

War II to the intense interpersonal, institutional, and political disagreements as the field expanded and diversified across disciplines. For instance, see Kline, *The Cybernetics Moment;* and Rid, *The Rise of the Machines.*

53 Kline, *The Cybernetics Moment,* 7.

54 Pias, *The Macy Conferences.*

55 Rid, *Rise of the Machines,* 53–69.

56 Simbirski, "Cybernetic Muse," 529.

57 Arendt, "Lecture on Cybernetics."

58 Arendt, "Lecture on Cybernetics."

59 Bateson, *Mind and Nature,* 228.

60 Peirce, "Evolutionary Love."

61 For continued scientific interest in metapatterns, see Volk, Bloom, and Richards, "Towards a Science of Metapatterns."

62 Bateson, *Mind and Nature,* 131. The tautology of this initial mind was not just acknowledged by Bateson but was fundamental to his understanding of self, mind, and life. See also Wright, "Epistemology, Language, Play."

63 "The interaction between parts of mind is triggered by difference, and difference is a non-substantial phenomenon not located in space or time; difference is related to neg-entropy and entropy rather than energy." Bateson, *Mind and Nature,* 102.

64 Bateson, *Mind and Nature,* 132.

65 Bateson, *Mind and Nature,* 133.

66 Bateson, *Steps to an Ecology of Mind,* 460.

67 Leon Marvell has observed Michel Serres's "extreme amplification of Bateson's ideas (although he makes no reference to Bateson's work)" in such works as *The Parasite.* See Marvell, *Transfigured Light;* and Serres, *The Parasite.*

68 Bateson uses the terms *tautology* and *explanation.* Bateson, *Mind and Nature,* 81.

69 Bateson, *Steps to an Ecology of Mind,* 467. See also Kohn, *How Forests Think;* and Hoffmeyer, *A Legacy for Living Systems.*

70 "A mind is the aggregate of interacting parts of components." Bateson, *Mind and Nature,* 102.

71 For the origins of the term *biosphere,* see Roosth, *The Quick and the Dead;* Guillaume, "Vernadsky's Philosophical Legacy"; and Piqueras, "Meeting the Biospheres."

72 Bateson, *Mind and Nature,* 240.

73 Bateson, *Steps to an Ecology of Mind,* 488.

74 Bateson, *Steps to an Ecology of Mind,* 483–84. See Bahr, Jokiel, and Toonen, "The Unnatural History of Kāneʻohe Bay," for background on the anthropogenic stresses Bateson refers to.

75 Bateson, *Mind and Nature,* 88.

76 Césaire, *Discourse on Colonialism,* 33.

77 Césaire, *Discourse on Colonialism,* 33.

78 Halpern, "Schizophrenic Techniques."

79 For instance, Bateson's criterion 6 states: "The description and classification of these processes of transformation disclose a hierarchy of logical types immanent in the phenomena." Bateson, *Mind and Nature*, 92.

80 Bateson, *Steps to an Ecology of Mind*, 483.

81 Bateson, *Mind and Nature*, 94.

82 Bateson, *Mind and Nature*, 103.

83 Estes, "Freedom Is a Place."

CHAPTER FIVE. CONCEPTUAL ENDS

1 Taylor, *Rise of the American Conservation Movement*. See also Whyte, "Settler Colonialism"; and Bacon, "Settler Colonialism."

2 Quoted in Purdy, "Environmentalism's Racist History."

3 Bernstein, "A Growing Problem after Wildfires."

4 See Dunst and Schlensag, *World According to Philip K. Dick*; and Gibson, "Machinic Interagency and Co-evolution."

5 Coulthard argues that, while the closure of the European common produced the proletariat, in the Native-colonial relation, there was only land dispossession with no parallel process of proletarianization. See Coulthard, *Red Skin, White Masks*.

6 As Timothy S. Murphy notes, Mario Tronti's focus on worker subjectivity "as an active but historically variable phenomenon immediately set workerism apart from both the abstract, transhistorical humanism of Erich Fromm and Georg Lukács then dominant among western Marxists and the anti-subjectivism of the other important strands of theoretical Marxism to emerge from the postwar period, the Frankfurt School's negative dialectics and Louis Althusser's structuralism, which effectively stripped working-class subjectivity of all possible agency for social/political transformation. Max Horkheimer and T. W. Adorno's analysis of 'administered life' in works like *Dialectic of Enlightenment* (1944) emphasized the extent to which the formation of subjectivity under advanced capitalism was pre-programmed and controlled." Murphy, "The Workerist Matrix," 331.

7 It famously put the movement at odds with trade unionism and capitalists in the 1960s and 1970s. Thus, Berardi worries, like Deleuze and Guattari, that schizoanalysis will be quickly collapsed into a Marxist-Leninist framework. See Hardt, *Gilles Deleuze*.

8 "Here, as in every subsequent classic product of economic thought, everything that happens within the working class presents itself as happening within capital." Tronti, *Workers and Capital*, 283.

9 Berardi, *The Soul at Work*, 176.

10 Berardi, *The Soul at Work*, 186.

11 For the language of the doctrine, see Pierrat, *Antimanuel de droit*, 192.

12 Berardi, *Félix Guattari*.

13 Berardi, *After the Future*, 100. See also Berardi, "Cognitarian Subjectivation."
14 Berardi, *The Soul at Work*, 88.
15 Berardi, *The Soul at Work*, 93.
16 Hardt and Negri, *Empire*.
17 Baudrillard, *Simulacra and Simulation*, 153.
18 Berardi, *The Soul at Work*, 88–90.
19 For instance, see Rose, *The Politics of Life Itself*; Sunder Rajan, *Biocapital*; and Cooper, *Life as Surplus*.
20 For instance, see Carruth, "The Digital Cloud"; Starosielski, "'Warning: Do Not Dig'"; and Günel, *Spaceship in the Desert*.
21 Hugill and Thorburn, "Interview with 'Bifo,'" 213.
22 Simpson, *Mohawk Interruptus*.
23 Aboriginal Land Right (Northern Territory) Act, Part I, Section 3.
24 For instance, see Povinelli, *The Cunning of Recognition*.
25 Deloria, *God Is Red*, 66.
26 Serres, *The Parasite*.
27 Ureta and Flores, "Don't Wake Up the Dragon!"
28 Yusoff, "Epochal Aesthetics."
29 See Teaiwa, *Consuming Ocean Island*.
30 Yusoff, "Epochal Aesthetics." For the vertical dimensions of aquatic existence, see Ballestero, "Aquifers."
31 See James, *Principles of Psychology*, esp. 170–94.

POSTSCRIPT

1 Loichot, *Water Graves*, 43.
2 Loichot, *Water Graves*, 43.

GLOSSARY

1 Parkinson, "Hegel, Marx and the Cunning of Reason," 291.
2 Bergson, *Creative Evolution*, 4.
3 Povinelli, *Empire of Love*, 77.
4 Povinelli, *The Cunning of Late Liberalism*, 6.

BIBLIOGRAPHY

Agard-Jones, Vanessa. "Spray." *Somatosphere*, May 27, 2014. http://somatosphere.net/2014/spray.html/.

Allar, Neal A. "Rhizomatic Influence: The Antigenealogy of Glissant and Deleuze." *Cambridge Journal of Postcolonial Literary Inquiry* 6, no. 1 (2019): 1–13.

Anand, Nikhil. *Hydraulic City: Water and the Infrastructures of Citizenship in Mumbai.* Durham, NC: Duke University Press, 2017.

Arendt, Hannah. "Lecture on Cybernetics." Hannah Arendt Papers, Library of Congress, 1964. Accessed December 3, 2020, http://memory.loc.gov/cgi-bin/ampage?collId=mharendt_pub&fileName=05/051170/051170page.db&recNum=1&itemLink=/ammem/arendthtml/mharendtFolderP05.html&linkText=7.

Arendt, Hannah. *The Human Condition.* Chicago: University of Chicago Press, 1958.

Arendt, Hannah. *On Revolution.* New York: Penguin, 1963.

Arendt, Hannah. *The Origins of Totalitarianism.* London: Harcourt, Brace, Jovanovich, 1973.

Arendt, Hannah. "Reflections on Little Rock." *Dissent* 6 (1959): 45–56.

Arnold, Lorna. *Britain, Australia, and the Bomb: The Nuclear Tests and Their Aftermath.* Basingstoke, UK: Palgrave Macmillan, 2006.

Atkinson, Scott, and Monica Davey. "Five Charged with Involuntary Manslaughter in Flint Water Crisis." *New York Times*, June 14, 2017. https://www.nytimes.com/2017/06/14/us/flint-water-crisis-manslaughter.html.

Bacon, J. M. "Settler Colonialism as Eco-Social Structure and the Production of Colonial Ecological Violence." *Environmental Sociology* 5, no. 1 (2019): 59–69.

Badiou, Alain. *Saint Paul: The Foundation of Universalism.* Translated by Ray Brassier. Stanford, CA: Stanford University Press, 2003.

Bagnato, Andrea. "Microscopic Colonialism." *e-flux architecture*, 2017. https://www.e-flux.com/architecture/positions/153900/microscopic-colonialism/.

Bahr, Keisha D., Paul L. Jokiel, and Robert J. Toonen. "The Unnatural History of Kāneʻohe Bay: Coral Reef Resilience in the Face of Centuries of Anthropogenic Impacts." *PeerJ* 3:e950 (May 12, 2015). https://doi.org/10.7717/peerj.950.

Ballestero, Andrea. "Aquifers (or, Hydrolithic Elemental Choreographies)." Theorizing the Contemporary, Fieldsights, June 27, 2019. https://culanth.org /fieldsights/aquifers-or-hydrolithic-elemental-choreographies.

Banner, Stuart. "Why Terra Nullius? Anthropology and Property Law in Early Australia." *Law and History Review* 23, no. 1 (2005): 95–131.

Barad, Karen. *Meeting the Universe Halfway: Quantum Physics and the Entanglement of Matter and Meaning.* Durham, NC: Duke University Press, 2007.

Bateson, Gregory. *Mind and Nature: A Necessary Union.* New York: E. P. Dutton, 1979.

Bateson, Gregory. *Naven: A Survey of the Problems Suggested by a Composite Picture of the Culture of a New Guinea Tribe Drawn from Three Points of View.* 1936; Stanford, CA: Stanford University Press, 1958.

Bateson, Gregory. *Steps to an Ecology of Mind: A Revolutionary Approach to Man's Understanding of Himself.* San Francisco: Chandler, 1972.

Baudrillard, Jean. *Simulacra and Simulation.* Translated by Sheila Faria Glaser. Ann Arbor: University of Michigan Press, 1994.

Benjamin, Walter. *The Arcades Project.* Translated by Howard Eiland and Kevin McLaughlin. Cambridge, MA: Belknap Press of Harvard University Press, 1999.

Benjamin, Walter. "Theses on the Philosophy of History." In *Illuminations*, translated by Harry Zohn, 196–209. Boston: First Mariner Books, 2019.

Berardi, Franco "Bifo." *After the Future.* Edited by Gary Genosko and Nicholas Thoburn. Chico, CA: AK Press, 2011.

Berardi, Franco "Bifo." "Cognitarian Subjectivation." *e-flux journal* 20, no. 11 (2010). http://www.e-flux.com/journal/cognitarian-subjectivation/.

Berardi, Franco "Bifo." *Félix Guattari: Thought, Friendship, and Visionary Cartography.* New York: Palgrave Macmillan, 2008.

Berardi, Franco "Bifo." *The Soul at Work: From Alienation to Autonomy.* Cambridge, MA: MIT Press, 2009.

Berger, Thomas R. *Northern Frontier, Northern Homeland: The Report of the Mackenzie Valley Pipeline Inquiry.* Ottawa: Minister of Supply and Services, 1977.

Bergson, Henri. *Creative Evolution.* 1911; Mineola, NY: Dover, 1998.

Berlant, Lauren. *Cruel Optimism.* Durham, NC: Duke University Press, 2011.

Berlant, Lauren, and Elizabeth A. Povinelli. "Holding Up the World, Part III: In the Event of Precarity . . . A Conversation." *e-flux journal*, no. 58 (2014). https://www.e-flux.com/journal/58/61149/holding-up-the-world-part-iii-in -the-event-of-precarity-a-conversation/.

Berndt, Ronald. "The 'Warburton Range' Controversy." *Australian Quarterly* 29, no. 2 (1957): 29–44.

Bernstein, Sharon. "A Growing Problem after Wildfires: Toxic Chemicals." *Washington Post*, April 9, 2019. https://www.washingtonpost.com/national

/health-science/a-growing-problem-after-wildfires-toxic-chemicals/2019
/04/05/7243d6b4-45bb-11e9-90f0-0ccfeec87a61_story.html.

Bowen-Moore, Patricia. *Hannah Arendt's Philosophy of Natality*. London: Macmillan, 1989.

Brandl, Maria, Adrienne Haritos, and Michael Walsh. *Kenbi Land Claim*. Darwin, NT: Northern Land Council, 1979.

Brown, Wendy. *Undoing the Demos: Neoliberalism's Stealth Revolution*. Cambridge, MA: MIT Press, 2015.

Brugge, Doug, Timothy Benally, and Esther Yazzie-Lewis. *The Navajo People and Uranium Mining*. Albuquerque: University of New Mexico Press, 2006.

Brugge, Doug, and Rob Goble. "The History of Uranium Mining and the Navajo People." *American Journal of Public Health* 92, no. 9 (2002): 1410–19.

Butler, Judith. *Frames of War: When Is Life Grievable?* London: Verso, 2016.

Callison, William, and Zachary Manfredi, eds. *Mutant Neoliberalism: Market Rule and Political Rupture*. New York: Fordham University Press, 2019.

Carruth, Allison. "The Digital Cloud and the Micropolitics of Energy." *Public Culture* 26, no. 2 (2014): 339–64.

Carson, Rachel. *Silent Spring*. New York: Houghton Mifflin, 1962.

Césaire, Aimé. *Discourse on Colonialism*. Translated by Joan Pinkham. New York: Monthly Review Press, 2000.

César, Filipa. "Meteorisations: Reading Amílcar Cabral's *Agronomy of Liberation*." *Third Text* 32, nos. 2–3 (2018): 254–72.

Chakrabarty, Dipesh. "The Human Condition in the Anthropocene." The Tanner Lectures in Human Values. Yale University, February 18–19, 2015. https://tannerlectures.utah.edu/Chakrabarty%20manuscript.pdf.

Chaney, Anthony. *Runaway: Gregory Bateson, the Double Bind, and the Rise of the Ecological Consciousness*. Chapel Hill: University of North Carolina Press, 2017.

Chen, Mel Y. *Animacies: Biopolitics, Racial Mattering, and Queer Affect*. Durham, NC: Duke University Press, 2012.

Clark, Brett. "The Indigenous Environmental Movement in the United States." *Organization and Environment* 15, no. 4 (2002): 410–42.

Cole, Luke W., and Sheila R. Foster. *From the Ground Up: Environmental Racism and the Rise of the Environmental Justice Movement*. New York: New York University Press, 2001.

Cooper, Melinda. *Life as Surplus: Biotechnology and Capitalism in the Neoliberal Era*. Seattle: University of Washington Press, 2008.

Coulthard, Glen. "The Colonialism of the Present: An Interview with Glen Coulthard." By Andrew Bard Epstein. *Jacobin*, no. 1 (2015). https://www.jacobinmag.com/2015/01/indigenous-left-glen-coulthard-interview/.

Coulthard, Glen. "From Wards of the State to Subjects of Recognition? Marx, Indigenous Peoples, and the Politics of Dispossession in Denendeh." In *Theorizing Native Studies*, edited by Audra Simpson and Andrea Smith, 59–98. Durham, NC: Duke University Press, 2014.

Coulthard, Glen. "Place against Empire: Understanding Anti-colonialism." *Affinities: A Journal of Radical Theory, Culture, and Action* 4, no. 2 (2010): 79-83.

Coulthard, Glen. *Red Skin, White Masks: Rejecting the Colonial Politics of Recognition*. Minneapolis: University of Minnesota Press, 2014.

Das, Veena, and Didier Fassin, eds. *Words and Worlds: A Lexicon for Dark Times*. Durham, NC: Duke University Press, 2021.

da Silva, Denise Ferreira. *Toward a Global Idea of Race*. Minneapolis: University of Minnesota Press, 2007.

Davies, Anne. "Nothing to Say Sorry For: Howard." *Sydney Morning Herald*, March 12, 2008. http://www.smh.com.au/news/national/nothing-to-say-sorry-for-howard/2008/03/11/1205125911444.html.

Davison, Andrew. "'Not to Escape the World but to Join It': Responding to Climate Change with Imagination Not Fantasy." *Philosophical Transactions of the Royal Society A* 375, no. 2095 (2017). https://doi.org/10.1098/rsta.2016.0365.

Deleuze, Gilles. *Difference and Repetition*. Translated by Paul Patton. New York: Columbia University Press, 1995.

Deleuze, Gilles. *The Logic of Sense*. Translated by Mark Lester with Charles Stivale. New York: Columbia University Press, 1990.

Deleuze, Gilles, and Félix Guattari. *A Thousand Plateaus: Capitalism and Schizophrenia*. Translated by Brian Massumi. Minneapolis: University of Minnesota Press, 1987.

Deleuze, Gilles, and Félix Guattari. *What Is Philosophy?* Translated by Graham Burchell and Hugh Tomlinson. New York: Columbia University Press, 1994.

Deloria, Vine, Jr. *God Is Red: A Native View of Religion*. Golden, CO: Fulcrum, 2003.

Demos, T. J. "To Save a World: Geoengineering, Conflictual Futurisms, and the Unthinkable." *e-flux Journal*, no. 94 (2018). https://www.e-flux.com/journal/94/221148/to-save-a-world-geoengineering-conflictual-futurisms-and-the-unthinkable/.

Derrida, Jacques. "Plato's Pharmacy." In *Dissemination*, translated by Barbara Johnson, 63-171. Chicago: University of Chicago Press, 1981.

Descola, Philippe. *Beyond Nature and Culture*. Chicago: University of Chicago Press, 2013.

Diawara, Manitha, dir. *Édouard Glissant: One World in Relation*. Paris: K'a Yéléma Productions, 2010.

DiFruscia, Kim Turcot. "Shapes of Freedom: A Conversation with Elizabeth A. Povinelli." *e-flux journal*, no. 53 (2014). https://www.e-flux.com/journal/53/59889/shapes-of-freedom-a-conversation-with-elizabeth-a-povinelli/.

Dosse, François. *Gilles Deleuze and Félix Guattari: Intersecting Lives*. New York: Columbia University Press, 2010.

Douglas, Susan J. "Without Black Lives Matter, Would Flint's Water Crisis Have Made Headlines?" *In These Times*, February 10, 2016. https://inthesetimes.com

/article/18843/without-black-lives-matter-would-flints-water-crisis-have
-made-headlines.

Drabinski, John E. "Sites of Relation and '*Tout-Monde*': Reflections of Glissant's Late Work." *Angelaki: Journal of the Theoretical Humanities* 24, no. 3 (2019): 157–72.

Du Bois, W. E. B. *The World and Africa and Color and Democracy.* Oxford: Oxford University Press, 2014.

Dunst, Alexander, and Stefan Schlensag. *The World According to Philip K. Dick.* New York: Palgrave Macmillan, 2015.

Elkin, A. P. "The Complexity of Social Organization in Arnhem Land." *Southwestern Journal of Anthropology* 6, no. 1 (1950): 1–20.

Elkin, A. P. "Ngirawat, or the Sharing of Names in the Wagaitj Tribe, Northern Australia." In *Beiträge zur Gesellungs- und Völkerwissenschaft*, 67–81. Berlin: Gebr. Mann, 1950.

Esposito, Roberto. *The Origin of the Political: Hannah Arendt or Simone Weil?* Translated by Vincenzo Binetti and Gareth Williams. New York: Fordham University Press, 2017.

Estes, Nick. "'Freedom Is a Place': Long Traditions of Anti-colonial Resistance in Turtle Island." *Funambulist* 20 (November–December 2018). https://thefunambulist.net/articles/freedom-place-long-traditions-anti-colonial-resistance-turtle-island-nick-estes.

Fanon, Frantz. *Black Skin, White Masks.* 1952; Boston: Grove, 1994.

Ferreira, Maria Aline. "Symbiotic Bodies and Evolutionary Tropes in the Work of Octavia Butler." *Science Fiction Studies* 37, no. 3 (2010): 401–15.

Feser, Ali. "'It Was a Family': Picturing Corporate Kinship in Eastman-Kodak." Drawing Together: Solidarities, Pictures and Politics, Tenth Visual and Cultural Studies Graduate Conference. April 17, 2015.

Foxwell-Norton, Kerrie. "What Would Hannah Arendt Have Seen on a Beach Covered in Plastic Bottles?" *Climate Home News*, December 5, 2017. https://www.climatechangenews.com/2017/12/05/hannah-arendt-seen-beach-covered-plastic-bottles/.

Freeman, Elizabeth. Introduction to "Queer Temporalities" (special issue). *GLQ: A Journal of Lesbian and Gay Studies* 13, nos. 2–3 (2007): 159–76.

Fujikane, Candace. *Mapping Abundance for a Planetary Future: Kanaka Maoli and Critical Settler Cartographies in Hawai'i.* Durham, NC: Duke University Press, 2021.

Gaber, Nadia. "Blue Lines and Blues Infrastructure: Notes on Water, Race, and Space." Unpublished manuscript.

Gaber, Nadia. "Mobilizing Health Metrics for the Human Right to Water in Flint and Detroit, Michigan." *Health and Human Rights Journal* 21, no. 1 (2019): 179–89.

Gaonkar, Dilip Parameshwar, and Elizabeth A. Povinelli. "Technologies of Public Persuasion: Circulation, Translation, Recognition." *Public Culture* 15, no. 3 (2003): 385–97.

Garraway, Doris L. "'What Is Mine': Césairean Negritude between the Particular and the Universal." *Research in African Literatures* 41, no. 1 (2010): 71–86.

Gibson, Prue. "Machinic Interagency and Co-evolution." *M/C Journal* 16, no. 6 (2013). http://journal.media-culture.org.au/index.php/mcjournal/article/view/719.

Gilmore, Ruth Wilson. "Abolition Geography and the Problem of Innocence." *Tabula Rasa*, no. 28 (2018): 57–77.

Gilroy, Paul. *The Black Atlantic: Modernity and Double Consciousness.* Cambridge, MA: Harvard University Press, 1993.

Gilroy, Paul. "Lecture I: Suffering and Infrahumanity." The Tanner Lectures in Human Values. Yale University, February 21, 2014. https://tannerlectures.utah.edu/Gilroy%20manuscript%20PDF.pdf.

Gines, Kathryn T. *Hannah Arendt and the Negro Question.* Bloomington: Indiana University Press, 2014.

Giroux, Henry A. *The University in Chains: Confronting the Military-Industrial-Academic Complex.* Boulder, CO: Paradigm, 2007.

Glissant, Édouard. *Poetics of Relation.* Translated by Betsy Wing. Ann Arbor: University of Michigan Press, 1997.

Glissant, Édouard. *Treatise on the Whole-World.* Translated by Celia Britton. Liverpool: Liverpool University Press, 2020.

Glowczewski, Barbara. *Indigenising Anthropology with Guattari and Deleuze.* Edinburgh: Edinburgh University Press, 2019.

Glowczewski, Barbara. "Resisting Disaster: Between Exhaustion and Creation." *Spheres: Journal for Digital Cultures* (December 2015). http://spheres-journal.org/resisting-the-disaster-between-exhaustion-and-creation/.

Glowczewski, Barbara. *Totemic Becomings: Cosmopolitics of the Dreaming.* Edinburgh: Edinburgh University Press, 2015.

Goforth, Shelley. "Aboriginal Healing Methods for Residential School Abuse and Intergenerational Effects: A Review of the Literature." *Native Social Work Journal* 6 (2007): 11–32.

Goodeve, Thyrza Nichols. "In Conversation: Donna Haraway with Thyrza Nichols Goodeve." *Brooklyn Rail*, December 13, 2017. https://brooklynrail.org/2017/12/.

Grayden, W. L. *Report of the Select Committee Appointed to Inquire into Native Welfare Conditions in the Laverton-Warburton Range Area.* December 12, 1956. Perth: William H. Wyatt, Government Printer, 1956.

Grealy, Liam, and Kirsty Howie. "Securing Supply: Governing Drinking Water in the Northern Territory." *Australian Geographer* 51, no. 3 (2020): 341–60.

Grinde, Donald A., and Bruce E. Johansen. *Ecocide of Native America: Environmental Destruction of Indian Lands and People.* Santa Fe, NM: Clear Light, 1995.

Grosfoguel, Ramón. "Decolonizing Western Uni-versalisms: Decolonial Pluri-versalism from Aimé Césaire to the Zapatistas." *Transmodernity: A Journal of Peripheral Cultural Production of the Luso-Hispanic World* 1, no. 3 (2012): 88–104.

Guillaume, Bertrand. "Vernadsky's Philosophical Legacy: A Perspective from the Anthropocene." *Anthropocene Review* 1, no. 2 (2014): 137–46.

Günel, Gökçe. *Spaceship in the Desert: Energy, Climate Change, and Urban Design in Abu Dhabi*. Durham, NC: Duke University Press, 2019.

Habermas, Jürgen. "A Review of Gadamer's *Truth and Method.*" In *The Hermeneutic Tradition: From Ast to Ricoeur*, edited by Gayle L. Ormiston and Alan D. Schrift, 213–44. Albany, NY: SUNY Press, 1990.

Halpern, Orit. "Schizophrenic Techniques: Cybernetics, the Human Sciences, and the Double Bind." *S&F Online* 10, no. 3 (2012). http://sfonline.barnard.edu/feminist-media-theory/schizophrenic-techniques-cybernetics-the-human-sciences-and-the-double-bind/0/.

Halverson, Jeffry R., and Nathaniel Greenberg. *Islamists of the Maghreb*. London: Routledge, 2017.

Hanley, Robert. "Eastman Kodak Admits Violations of Anti-pollution Laws." *New York Times*, April 6, 1990.

Haraway, Donna J. *The Companion Species Manifesto: Dogs, People and Significant Otherness*. Chicago: University of Chicago Press, 2003.

Haraway, Donna J. "SF with Stengers: Asked For or Not, the Pattern Is Now in Your Hands." *SubStance* 47, no. 1 (2018): 60–63.

Haraway, Donna J. *When Species Meet*. Minneapolis: University of Minnesota Press, 2008.

Hardt, Michael. *Gilles Deleuze: An Apprenticeship in Philosophy*. Minneapolis: University of Minnesota Press, 1993.

Hardt, Michael, and Antonio Negri. *Empire*. Cambridge, MA: Harvard University Press, 2000.

Hartman, Saidiya V. *Scenes of Subjection: Terror, Slavery, and Self-Making in Nineteenth-Century America*. Oxford: Oxford University Press, 1997.

Hayles, N. Katherine. *How We Became Posthuman: Virtual Bodies in Cybernetics, Literature, and Informatics*. Chicago: University of Chicago Press, 1999.

Hegel, G. W. F. *The Philosophy of History*. London: Dover, 2004.

Helmenstine, Anne Marie. "Chernobyl's Animal Mutations Shed Light on the Impact of Nuclear Releases." *ThoughtCo*, December 20, 2017. https://www.thoughtco.com/chernobyl-animal-mutations-4155348.

Hernández, Javier C. "Climate Change May Be Intensifying China's Smog Crisis." *New York Times*, March 24, 2017. https://www.nytimes.com/2017/03/24/world/asia/china-air-pollution-smog-climate-change.html.

Hiatt, L. R. "Local Organization among the Australian Aborigines." *Oceania* 32, no. 4 (1962): 267–86.

Hiddleston, Jane. "Aimé Césaire and Postcolonial Humanism." *Modern Language Review* 105, no. 1 (January 2010): 87–102.

Highsmith, Andrew R. *Demolition Means Progress: Flint, Michigan, and the Fate of the American Metropolis*. Chicago: University of Chicago Press, 2015.

Highsmith, Andrew R. "Op-Ed: Flint's Toxic Water Crisis Was 50 Years in the

Making." *Los Angeles Times*, January 29, 2016. https://www.latimes.com/opinion /op-ed/la-oe-0131-highsmith-flint-water-crisis-20160131-story.html.

Hird, Myra J. "The Phenomenon of Waste-World-Making," *Rhizomes: Cultural Studies in Emerging Knowledge* 30 (2016). http://www.rhizomes.net/issue30/hird .html.

Hird, Myra J. "Waste, Environmental Politics and Dis/Engaged Publics." *Theory, Culture, and Society* 34, nos. 2–3 (2017): 187–209.

Hobart, Hiʻilei Julia Kawehipuaakahaopulani, and Tamara Kneese. "Radical Care: Survival Strategies for Uncertain Times." *Social Text* 142, no. 1 (2020): 1–16.

Hochschild, Adam. *Kind Leopold's Ghost: A Story of Greed, Terror, and Heroism in Colonial Africa*. Boston: Mariner, 1999.

Hoffmeyer, Jesper. *A Legacy for Living Systems: Gregory Bateson as Precursor to Biosemiotics*. Amsterdam: Springer, 2008.

Honig, Bonnie. "What Kind of Thing Is Land? Hannah Arendt's Object Relations, or: The Jewish Unconscious of Arendt's Most 'Greek' Text." *Political Theory* 44, no. 3 (2016): 307–36.

Hugill, David, and Elise Thorburn. "Interview with 'Bifo': Reactivating the Social Body in Insurrectionary Times." *Berkeley Planning Journal* 25 (2012): 210–20.

Immerwahr, Daniel. *How to Hide an Empire: A History of the Greater United States*. New York: Farrar, Straus and Giroux, 2019.

Inskeep, Steve, and Kemp Burdette. "Assessing the Contamination Brought by Flooding." *Morning Edition*, NPR, September 20, 2018. https://www.npr.org /2018/09/20/649779303/assessing-the-contamination-brought-by-flooding.

James, William. *Pragmatism and Other Writings*. New York: Penguin Classics, 2000.

James, William. *Principles of Psychology, Volume 1*. New York: Dover, 1950.

John, Maria. "Sovereign Bodies: Urban Indigenous Health and the Politics of Self-Determination in Seattle and Sydney, 1950–1980." PhD diss., Columbia University, 2016.

Jurkevics, Anna. "Hannah Arendt Reads Carl Schmitt's *The Nomos of the Earth*: A Dialogue on Law and Geopolitics from the Margins." *European Journal of Political Theory* 16, no. 3 (2017): 345–66.

Karrabing Film Collective. "Australian Babel: A Conversation with the Karrabing." *Specimen: The Babel Review of Translations*, October 31, 2017. http://www .specimen.press/writers/karrabing/.

Karrabing Film Collective. *Day in the Life*. Karrabing Indigenous Corporation, 2020.

Karrabing Film Collective. *Mermaids, Mirror Worlds*. Karrabing Indigenous Corporation, 2018.

Karrabing Film Collective. *The Mermaids, or Aiden in Wonderland*. Karrabing Indigenous Corporation, 2018.

Karrabing Film Collective. *The Riot*. Karrabing Indigenous Corporation, 2017

Karrabing Film Collective. "Roan-Roan and Connected, That's How We Make

Karrabing." Middle Earth, Art Gallery of New South Wales. Accessed December 4, 2020, https://togetherinart.org/karrabing-in-medium-earth/.

Karrabing Film Collective. *Windjarrameru, The Stealing C*nt$*. Karrabing Indigenous Corporation, 2015.

Karrabing Film Collective. *Wutharr, Saltwater Dreams*. Karrabing Indigenous Corporation, 2016.

Keeling, Arn, and John Sandlos. "Environmental Justice Goes Underground? Historical Notes from Canada's Northern Mining Frontier." *Environmental Justice* 2, no. 3 (2009): 117–25.

Kelley, Robin D. G. "Classic Texts: #15." *Community Development Journal* 47, no. 1 (2012): 150–55.

Kennedy, Merrit. "Lead-Laced Water in Flint: A Step-by-Step Look at the Makings of a Crisis." *The Two-Way*, NPR, April 20, 2016. https://www.npr.org/sections /thetwo-way/2016/04/20/465545378/lead-laced-water-in-flint-a-step-by-step -look-at-the-makings-of-a-crisis.

Kenton, Luke. "South Dakota ER Nurse Says Some COVID-19 Patients Insist the Virus Isn't Real Even as They're Dying from It." *Daily Mail*, November 24, 2020. https://www.dailymail.co.uk/news/article-8955047/South-Dakota-nurse-says-COVID-19-patients-insist-virus-isnt-real-theyre-dying-it.html.

Kim, Eleana. "Invasive Others and Significant Others: Strange Kinship and Interspecies Ethics near the Korean Demilitarized Zone." *Social Research: An International Quarterly* 84, no. 1 (2017): 203–20.

Kline, Ronald R. *The Cybernetics Moment: Or Why We Call Our Age the Information Age*. Baltimore: Johns Hopkins University Press, 2017.

Kohn, Eduardo. *How Forests Think: Toward an Anthropology beyond the Human*. Berkeley: University of California Press, 2013.

Kristjansson, Margaux L. "The Wages of Care in Anishinaabe Aki." PhD diss., Columbia University, 2020.

Lacan, Jacques. *The Ethics of Psychoanalysis, 1959–1960*. Translated by Dennis Porter. London: Routledge, 1992.

Laclau, Ernesto. *On Populist Reason*. London: Verso, 2005.

Lakhani, Nina. "Millions in US at Risk of 'Water Shut Offs' amid Layoffs Triggered by Pandemic." *Guardian*, April 6, 2020. https://www.theguardian.com /environment/2020/apr/06/millions-us-at-risk-losing-running-water-amid -layoffs-triggered-coronavirus-pandemic.

Langton, Marcia. "Anthropology, Politics and the Changing World of Aboriginal Australians." *Anthropological Forum: A Journal of Social Anthropology and Comparative Sociology* 21, no. 1 (2011): 1–22.

Lapoujade, David. *William James: Empiricism and Pragmatism*. Translated by Thomas Lamarre. Durham, NC: Duke University Press, 2019.

Lea, Tess. *Bureaucrats and Bleeding Hearts: Indigenous Health in Northern Australia*. Sydney: University of New South Wales Press, 2008.

Lea, Tess. "This Is Not a Pipe: The Treacheries of Indigenous Housing." *Public Culture* 22, no. 1 (2010): 187–209.

Lea, Tess. *Wild Policy: Indigeneity and the Unruly Logics of Intervention.* Stanford, CA: Stanford University Press, 2020.

Lewis, David Levering. *W. E. B. Du Bois: The Fight for Equality and the American Century, 1919–1963.* New York: Henry Holt, 2001.

Liboiron, Max. "Bibliography on Critical Approaches to Toxics and Toxicity." *Discard Studies,* July 10, 2017. https://discardstudies.com/2017/07/10/bibliography-on-critical-approaches-to-toxics-and-toxicity/.

Little, Adrian. "Democratic Melancholy: On the Sacrosanct Place of Democracy in Radical Democratic Theory." *Political Studies* 58, no. 5 (2010): 971–87.

Liu, Hongyu, Anne Probst, and Bohan Liao. "Metal Contamination of Soils and Crops Affected by the Chenzhou Lead/Zinc Mine Spill (Hunan, China)." *Science of the Total Environment* 339, nos. 1–3 (2005): 153–66.

Livni, Ephrat. "Radioactive Wild Boars in Sweden Are Eating Nuclear Mushrooms." *Quartz,* October 11, 2017. https://qz.com/1099248/radioactive-wild-boars-in-sweden-are-eating-nuclear-mushrooms/.

Loichot, Valérie. *Water Graves: The Art of the Unritual in the Greater Caribbean.* Charlottesville: University of Virginia Press, 2020.

Luttrell, Johanna C. "Alienation and Global Poverty: Arendt on the Loss of the World." *Philosophy and Social Criticism* 41, no. 9 (2015): 869–84.

MacBride, Samantha. *Recycling Reconsidered: The Present Failure and Future Promise of Environmental Action in the United States.* Cambridge, MA: MIT Press, 2013.

MacKenzie, Iain. "What Is a Political Event?" *Theory and Event* 11, no. 3 (2008). https://doi.org/10.1353/tae.0.0020.

Makhubu, Nomusa. "The Poetics of Entanglement in Zina Saro-Wiwa's Food Interventions." *Third Text* 32, nos. 2–3 (2018): 176–99.

Malm, Andreas. *After the Storm: Nature and Society in a Warming World.* London: Verso, 2018.

Markell, Patchen. "Arendt's Work: On the Architecture of *The Human Condition.*" *College Literature* 38, no. 1 (2011): 15–44.

Martin, Hannah Meszaros. "'Defoliating the World': Ecocide, Visual Evidence and 'Earth Memory.'" *Third Text* 32, nos. 2–3 (2018): 230–53.

Marvell, Leon. *Transfigured Light: Philosophy, Cybernetics and the Hermetic Imaginary.* Washington, DC: Academic Press, 2007.

Massumi, Brian. "Such as It Is: A Short Essay in Extreme Realism." *Body and Society* 22, no. 1 (2016): 115–27.

Mbembe, Achille. "Necropolitics." Translated by Libby Meintjes. *Public Culture* 15, no. 1 (2003): 11–40.

McGrath, Pamela Faye, and David Brooks. "Their Darkest Hour: The Films and Photographs of William Grayden and the History of the 'Warburton Ranges Controversy' of 1957." *Aboriginal History* 24 (2010): 115–41.

McWilliams, James E. *American Pests: The Losing War on Insects from Colonial Times to DDT*. New York: Columbia University Press, 2008.

Melsan, Annick Thebia. "The Liberating Power of Words: An Interview with Poet Aimé Césaire." *Journal of Pan African Studies* 2, no. 4 (2008). http://www.jpanafrican.org/docs/vol2no4/2.4_The_Liberating_Power_of_Words.pdf.

Mintz, Sidney W. *Sweetness and Power: The Place of Sugar in Modern History*. London: Penguin, 1986.

Mitman, Greg, Michelle Murphy, and Christopher Sellers, eds. *Landscapes of Exposure: Knowledge and Illness in Modern Environments*. Chicago: University of Chicago Press, 2004.

Mogren, Eric W. *Warm Sands: Uranium Mill Tailings Policy in the Atomic West*. Albuquerque: University of New Mexico Press, 2002.

Moreton-Robertson, Aileen. *The White Possessive: Property, Power, and Indigenous Sovereignty*. Minneapolis: University of Minnesota Press, 2015.

Moten, Fred. "The New International of Insurgent Feeling." Palestinian Campaign for the Academic and Cultural Boycott of Israel, November 7, 2009. http://www.pacbi.org/etemplate.php?id=1130.

Mouffe, Chantal. *Agonistics: Thinking the World Politically*. London: Verso, 2013.

Muehlebach, Andrea. "A Vital Politics: Water Insurgencies in Europe." Unpublished manuscript.

Murdoch, Rupert. "Sick, Starving Natives: Report Is Exaggeration." *News* (Adelaide), February 1, 1957. Accessed December 2, 2020, https://www.nma.gov.au/__data/assets/pdf_file/0004/692383/warburton-ranges-report-an-exaggeration.pdf.

Murphy, Michelle. *Sick Building Syndrome and the Problem of Uncertainty: Environmental Politics, Technoscience, and Women Workers*. Durham, NC: Duke University Press, 2006.

Murphy, Timothy S. "The Workerist Matrix: Introduction to Mario Tronti's *Worker and Capital* and Massimo Cacciari's 'Confrontation with Heidegger.'" *Genre* 43, nos. 3–4 (2010): 327–36.

Musu, Costanza. "War Metaphors Used for COVID-19 Useful but also Dangerous." *Conversation*, April 8, 2020. https://theconversation.com/war-metaphors-used-for-covid-19-are-compelling-but-also-dangerous-135406.

Nadasdy, Paul. "'Property' and Aboriginal Land Claims in the Canadian Subarctic: Some Theoretical Considerations." *American Anthropologist* 104, no. 1 (2002): 247–61.

National Museum of Australia. "Warburton Ranges Controversy, 1957." Accessed January 7, 2021, https://www.nma.gov.au/explore/features/indigenous-rights/civil-rights/warburton-ranges.

Nesbitt, Nick. "Departmentalization and the Logic of Decolonization." *L'Esprit Créateur* 47, no. 1 (2007): 32–43.

Nesbitt, Nick. "The Postcolonial Event: Deleuze, Glissant and the Problem of the

Political." In *Deleuze and the Postcolonial*, edited by Paul Patton and Simone Bignall, 103–18. Edinburgh: University of Edinburgh Press, 2010.

Nicholson, Blake. "More Than $600,000 Spent by North Dakota on Police Gear for Pipeline Protest." *Star Tribune/Associated Press*, December 16, 2017.

Nixon, Rob. *Slow Violence and the Environmentalism of the Poor*. Cambridge, MA: Harvard University Press, 2011.

Nussbaum, Martha C. *Frontiers of Justice: Disability, Nationality, Species Membership*. Cambridge, MA: Belknap Press at Harvard University Press, 2006.

Owens, Patricia. "Racism in the Theory Canon: Hannah Arendt and 'The One Great Crime in Which America Was Never Involved.'" *Millennium: Journal of International Studies* 45, no. 3 (2017): 403–24.

Parkinson, G. H. R. "Hegel, Marx and the Cunning of Reason." *Philosophy* 64, no. 249 (1989): 287–302.

Peach, Ian, and Don Hovdebo. *The Case for a Federal Role in Decommissioning and Reclaiming Abandoned Uranium Mines in Northern Saskatchewan*. Regina: Saskatchewan Institute of Public Policy, 2003.

Peck, Raoul, dir. *I Am Not Your Negro*. New York: Magnolia Pictures, 2016.

Peirce, Charles Sanders. "The Doctrine of Necessity." *Monist* 2 (1892): 321–37.

Peirce, Charles Sanders. "Evolutionary Love." *Monist* 3 (1893): 176–200.

Phillips, Keri. "The Long and Controversial History of Uranium Mining in Australia." *Rear Vision*, July 14, 2015. https://www.abc.net.au/radionational /programs/rearvision/history-of-uranium-mining-in-australia/6607212.

Pias, Claus, ed. *The Macy Conferences, 1946–1953: The Complete Transcripts*. Chicago: University of Chicago Press, 2016.

Pierrat, Emmanuel. *Antimanuel de droit*. Rome: Bréal, 2007.

Pine, Jason. "Economy of Speed: The New Narco-capitalism." *Public Culture* 19, no. 2 (2007): 357–66.

Piqueras, M. "Meeting the Biospheres: On the Translations of Vernadsky's Work." *International Microbiology: The Official Journal of the Spanish Society for Microbiology* 1, no. 2 (1998): 165–70.

Povinelli, Elizabeth A. "After the Last Man: Images and Ethics of Becoming Otherwise." *e-flux journal*, no. 35 (2012). https://www.e-flux.com/journal/35/68380 /after-the-last-man-images-and-ethics-of-becoming-otherwise/.

Povinelli, Elizabeth A. *Belyuen Traditional Aboriginal Owners (Kenbi Land Claim)*. Darwin, NT: Northern Land Council, 1996.

Povinelli, Elizabeth A. *The Cunning of Recognition: Indigenous Alterity and the Making of Australian Multiculturalism*. Durham, NC: Duke University Press, 2002.

Povinelli, Elizabeth A. *Economies of Abandonment: Social Belonging and Abandonment in Late Liberalism*. Durham, NC: Duke University Press, 2011.

Povinelli, Elizabeth A. *The Empire of Love: Toward a Theory of Intimacy, Genealogy, and Carnality*. Durham, NC: Duke University Press, 2006.

Povinelli, Elizabeth A. *Geontologies: A Requiem to Late Liberalism*. Durham, NC: Duke University Press, 2016.

Povinelli, Elizabeth A. "Radical Worlds: The Anthropology of Incommensurability and Inconceivability." *Annual Review of Anthropology* 30, no. 1 (2001): 319–34.

Povinelli, Elizabeth A. "The Urban Intensions of Geontopower." *e-flux architecture*, May 3, 2019. https://www.e-flux.com/architecture/liquid-utility/259667 /the-urban-intensions-of-geontopower/.

Povinelli, Elizabeth A. "The Will to Be Otherwise/The Effort of Endurance." *South Atlantic Quarterly* 111, no. 3 (2012): 453–75.

Povinelli, Elizabeth A., and Rex Edmunds. "A Conversation at Bamayak and Mabaluk, Part of the Coastal Lands of the Emmiyengal People." *L'internationale online*, October 2, 2019. https://www.internationaleonline.org/people /elizabeth_a_povinelli_and_rex_edmunds/.

Price, David. "Gregory Bateson and the OSS: World War II and Bateson's Assessment of Applied Anthropology." *Human Organization* 57, no. 4 (1998): 379–84.

Purdy, Jedediah. "Environmentalism's Racist History." *New Yorker*, August 13, 2015. https://www.newyorker.com/news/news-desk/environmentalisms -racist-history.

Reible, Danny D., Charles N. Haas, John H. Pardue, and William J. Walsh. "Toxic and Contaminant Concerns Generated by Hurricane Katrina." *National Academy of Engineering* 36, no. 1 (2006). https://www.nae.edu/7623 /ToxicandContaminantConcernsGeneratedbyHurricaneKatrina.

Rid, Thomas. *Rise of the Machines: A Cybernetic History*. New York: Norton, 2016.

Roosth, Sophia. "The Quick and the Dead: Life, Latency and the Limits of the Biological." Lecture, American Academy in Berlin, April 11, 2016. https://vimeo .com/162412284.

Rose, Nikolas. *The Politics of Life Itself: Biomedicine, Power, and Subjectivity in the Twenty-First Century*. Princeton, NJ: Princeton University Press, 2006.

Russell, Edmund. *War and Nature: Fighting Humans and Insects with Chemicals from World War I to "Silent Spring."* Cambridge: Cambridge University Press, 2001.

Sabin, Paul. "Voices from the Hydrocarbon Frontier: Canada's Mackenzie Valley Pipeline (1974–1977)." *Environmental History Review* 19, no. 1 (1995): 17–48.

Scambary, Benedict. *My Country, My Mine: Indigenous People, Mining and Development Contestation in Remote Australia*. Canberra: ANU Press, 2013.

Schaap, Andrew. "The Absurd Logic of Aboriginal Sovereignty." In *Law and Agonistic Politics*, edited by Andrew Schaap, 209–25. Farnham, UK: Ashgate, 2009.

Scott, James. *Domination and the Arts of Resistance*. New Haven, CT: Yale University Press, 1990.

Sellers, Christopher. "The Flint Water Crisis: A Special Edition Environment and Health Roundtable." Edge Effects, February 24, 2016. http://edgeeffects.net /flint-water-crisis/.

Serres, Michel. *The Parasite*. Translated by Lawrence R. Schehr. Minneapolis: University of Minnesota Press, 2007.

Shapiro, Nicholas. "Attuning to the Chemosphere: Domestic Formaldehyde,

Bodily Reasoning, and the Chemical Sublime." *Cultural Anthropology* 30, no. 3 (2015): 368–93.

Shapiro, Nicholas. *Where Have All the Trailers Gone?* Science History Institute, You-Tube, August 27, 2015. http://www.youtube.com/watch?v=-XzWrCe2F2E.

Shapiro, Nicholas, Nasser Zakariya, and Jody A. Roberts. "A Wary Alliance: From Enumerating the Environment to Inviting Apprehension." *Engaging Science, Technology, and Society* 3 (2017): 575–602.

Sharpe, Christina. *In the Wake: On Blackness and Being.* Durham, NC: Duke University Press, 2016.

Shaw, Robert. "Bringing Deleuze and Guattari down to Earth through Gregory Bateson: Plateaus, Rhizomes and Ecosophical Subjectivity." *Theory, Culture, and Society* 32, nos. 7–8 (2015): 151–71.

Silva, Mariana. "Mining the Deep Sea." *e-flux journal* 104 (2020). https://www.e-flux.com/journal/109/331369/mining-the-deep-sea/.

Simbirski, Brian. "Cybernetic Muse: Hannah Arendt on Automation, 1951–1958." *Journal of the History of Ideas* 77, no. 4 (2016): 589–613.

Simpson, Audra. *Mohawk Interruptus: Political Life at the Border of Settler States.* Durham, NC: Duke University Press, 2016.

Sloan Morgan, Vanessa. "Moving from Rights to Responsibilities: Extending Hannah Arendt's Critique of Collective Responsibility to the Settler Colonial Context of Canada." *Settler Colonial Studies* 8, no. 3 (2018): 332–48.

Spillers, Hortense J. "Mama's Baby, Papa's Maybe: An American Grammar Book." *Diacritics* 17, no. 2 (1987): 64–81.

Stanley, Anna. "Citizenship and the Production of Landscape and Knowledge in Contemporary Canadian Nuclear Fuel Waste Management." *Canadian Geographer* 52 (2008): 64–82.

Starosielski, Nicole. "'Warning: Do Not Dig': Negotiating the Visibility of Critical Infrastructures." *Journal of Visual Culture* 11, no. 1 (2012): 38–57.

Stengers, Isabelle. *Another Science Is Possible: A Manifesto for Slow Science.* Cambridge: Polity, 2018.

Stephenson, Wen. "Learning to Live in the Dark: Reading Arendt in the Time of Climate Change." *Los Angeles Review of Books*, September 22, 2017. https://lareviewofbooks.org/article/learning-to-live-in-the-dark-reading-arendt-in-the-time-of-climate-change/.

Strakosch, Elizabeth. "Beyond Colonial Completion: Arendt, Settler Colonialism, and the End of Politics." In *The Limits of Settler Colonial Reconciliation: Non-Indigenous People and the Responsibility to Engage*, edited by Sarah Maddison, Tom Clark, and Ravi de Costa, 15–33. Singapore: Springer Books, 2016.

Sunder Rajan, Kaushik. *Biocapital: The Constitution of Postgenomic Life.* Durham, NC: Duke University Press, 2006.

Taylor, Charles. "The Politics of Recognition." In *Multiculturalism*, edited by Amy Gutmann, 25–73. Princeton, NJ: Princeton University Press, 1994.

Taylor, Dorceta E. *The Rise of the American Conservation Movement: Power, Privilege and Environmental Protection*. Durham, NC: Duke University Press, 2015.

Taylor, Dorceta E. *Toxic Communities: Environmental Racism, Industrial Pollution, and Residential Mobility*. New York: New York University Press, 2014.

Teaiwa, Katerina Martina. *Consuming Ocean Island: Stories of People and Phosphate from Banaba*. Bloomington: Indiana University Press, 2014.

Todd, Zoe. "An Indigenous Feminist's Take on the Ontological Turn: 'Ontology' Is Just Another Word for Colonialism." *Journal of Historical Sociology* 29, no. 1 (2016): 4–22.

Todd, Zoe. "Fish, Kin and Hope: Tending to Water Violations in *amiskwaciwâskahikan* and Treaty Six Territory." *Afterall: A Journal of Art, Context and Enquiry* 43 (2017): 102–7.

Tronti, Mario. *Workers and Capital*. Translated by David Broder. London: Verso, 2019.

Trouillot, Michel-Rolph. "Abortive Rituals: Historical Apologies in the Global Era." *Interventions: International Journal of Postcolonial Studies* 2, no. 2 (2000): 171–86.

Ureta, Sebastián. "Chemical Rubble: Historicizing Toxic Waste in a Former Mining Town in Northern Chile." *Environment and Society Portal, Arcadia* 20 (2016). https://doi.org/10.5282/rcc/7704.

Ureta, Sebastián, and Patricio Flores. "Don't Wake Up the Dragon! Monstrous Geontologies in a Mining Waste Impoundment." *Environment and Planning D: Society and Space* 36, no. 6 (2018): 1064–80.

Vatter, Miguel. "Natality and Biopolitics in Hannah Arendt." *Revista de Cienca Política* 26, no. 2 (2006): 137–59. https://doi.org/10.4067/S0718-090X2006000200008.

Villa, Dana. "Arendt and Totalitarianism: Context of Interpretation." *European Journal of Political Theory* 10, no. 2 (2011): 287–96.

Vince, Gaia. "The Heat Is On over the Climate Crisis: Only Radical Measures Will Work." *Guardian*, May 18, 2019.

Vizenor, Gerald. *Manifest Manners: Narratives on Postindian Survivance*. Lincoln: University of Nebraska Press, 1999.

Vizenor, Gerald, ed. *Survivance: Narratives of Native Presence*. Lincoln: University of Nebraska Press, 2008.

Volk, Tylor, Jeffrey Bloom, and John Richards. "Towards a Science of Metapatterns: Building upon Bateson's Foundation." *Kybernetes* 36, nos. 7–8 (2007): 1070–80. http://metapatterns.wdfiles.com/local--files/members:tylervolk/Volk.Bateson.27Jul07.pdf.

von Schnitzler, Antina. *Democracy's Infrastructure: Techno-Politics and Protest after Apartheid*. Princeton, NJ: Princeton University Press, 2016.

Warren, Robert Penn. *Who Speaks for the Negro?* New York: Random House, 1965.

Whyte, Kyle Powys. "Settler Colonialism, Ecology, and Environmental Injustice." *Environment and Society* 9 (2018): 125–44.

Wilder, Gary. *Freedom Time: Negritude, Decolonization, and the Future of the World*. Durham, NC: Duke University Press, 2015.

Williams, Nancy M. *The Yolngu and Their Land: A System of Land Tenure and a Fight for Its Recognition*. Canberra : AIAS, 1986.

Wolfe, Patrick. *Traces of History: Elementary Structures of Race*. London: Verso, 2016.

Wong, M. H. "Ecological Restoration of Mine Degraded Souls, with Emphasis on Metal Contaminated Soils." *Chemosphere* 50, no. 6 (2003): 775–80.

Wood, Mike, and Nick Beresford. "The Wildlife of Chernobyl: 30 Years without Man." *Biologist* 63, no. 2 (2016): 16–19.

Wright, Edmond. "Epistemology, Language, Play and the Double Bind." *Anthropoetics: The Journal of Generative Anthropology* 14, no. 1 (2008). http://anthropoetics .ucla.edu/ap1401/1401wright/.

Wynter, Sylvia. "Unsettling the Coloniality of Being/Power/Truth/Freedom: Towards the Human, after Man, Its Overrepresentation—An Argument." *CR: The New Centennial Review* 3, no. 3 (2003): 257–337.

Yountae, An. "Beginning in the Middle: Deleuze, Glissant, and Colonial Difference." *Culture, Theory, and Critique* 55, no. 3 (2014): 286–301.

Yusoff, Kathryn. "Epochal Aesthetics: Affectual Infrastructures of the Anthropocene." *e-flux architecture*, March 29, 2017. https://www.e-flux.com /architecture/accumulation/121847/epochal-aesthetics-affectual -infrastructures-of-the-anthropocene/.

Zierler, David. *The Invention of Ecocide: Agent Orange, Vietnam, and the Scientists Who Changed the Way We Think about the Environment*. Athens: University of Georgia Press, 2011.

INDEX

abduction, 108

abolitionist geography, 45

Aboriginal Areas and Protection Authority, 121

Aboriginal Lands and Sacred Sites Bill, 121

Aboriginal tradition, 122

abstraction: axiomatic, 18; celestial, 72;
critical, 35; formal, 3; of labor power, 117;
planetary, 12; political, 32; social, 102; of
surplus labor, 50

accumulation: capital, 43, 50, 56, 114, 119;
colonial, 48, 56; originary, 48; personal,
69; postcolonial, 56; primitive, 48; toxic,
16, 46

action, 2, 9, 34, 48; Arendt's understanding
of, 21, 69, 70–73, 75, 82; collective, 118;
colonial, 73, 81; conceptual, 1; discursive,
42; economic, 65; ethical, 32; imperial,
73; liberal, 42, 44, 90; liberal capitalism,
89; militant, 5; political, 32, 65, 74, 114,
116; political thought and, 1; revolutionary, 73; spooky at a distance, 16, 32, 44;
unpredictability of, 75

aesthetic patterning, 108

affect(s), 6, 7, 32, 33, 35, 43, 112, 114, 127, 132;
Indigenous, 8; liberal, 8

Agamben, Giorgio, 19

Agard-Jones, Vanessa, 57

Agent Orange, 87

alienation: from earth, 69; human, 69, 72;
from nature, 68; Western, 84, 93; world,
82; from world, 68

Allar, Neal A., 23, 26, 145n21

ancestral: beings, 96, 99, 119; belonging,
55, 80; catastrophe, i, xii, xiii, 2–3, 10–11,
27, 37, 46, 49, 54–55, 77, 88, 108, 114,
131–32, 142; countries, 63; desire, 95; interactions, 96; knowledge, 56; past, 80;
presence, 48; present, 16, 21, 54, 65, 80,
95–96, 100, 121, 125–26, 130, 134; spirit, 57;
totems, 99

animal, 84; becoming, 84–85; hierarchy, 84,
86; life, 128; needs, 70; political, 69

animal laborans, 69

animist, 134–35, 141; figure of, xii; materialities, 64

antagonism(s), 115, 116, 117, 118

anthropogenic: climate, 67, 115, 125, 153n74

anthropos, 46–47

anticapitalist: movements, 8; perspectives,
17

anticolonial: activists, 144n16; Amílcar
Cabral, 51; critique, xiii, 108; movements,
8, 65, 136, 139; struggles, 1, 8–9

antipolitical, 2

apology, 41; Michel-Rolph Trouillot, 41;
state, 151n9

a priori, 4; Kantian, 4

Arendt, Hannah, 9–10, 21, 31, 51, 64–76, 78, 81–82, 84–86, 87, 103–4, 109, 131, 148n11, 149n34
Aristotle, 128
art, xiii, 53, 126; and affects, 6; and percepts, 6; practice of, 15
artistic creation, 54
Ashby, William Ross, 103
Asia, 50, 73
Asimov, Isaac, 104
Athens, 74
atomic: annihilation, 10, 65–66, 73, 86; bomb, 76, 116; catastrophe, 10; crisis, 78; event, 8; explosions, 81; half-legacies, 82; lives, 82; storm, 65, 69; technologies, 81; test sites, 80
attention, 31, 92, 101; critical, 18; effort of, 5, 6, 109, 129; semiocapitalism, 119
attitude, 69, 87
Atwood, Margaret, 53
Australia, xiii, 9, 10, 28, 37, 41, 43, 50, 53, 55, 65–66, 73–74, 78–84, 93–94, 101, 121, 126; colonial administration, 101; settler colonialism, 41; sovereignty, 39
autological subject, 135, 137, 141
automation, 103–4, 120, 148n11
autonomism, 117, 120; Italian, 116
autonomist movement, 115
autonomist refusal, 118
autonomist struggle, 117–18
autonomy, 11, 96, 114. *See also* nonautonomy

Badiou, Alain, 19
Bagnato, Andrea, 37
Baldwin, James, 48
Barad, Karen, 17, 24
Bateson, Gregory, 9, 86–87, 100–102, 104–11, 129, 131, 153n62, 153n63, 153n70
Baudrillard, Jean, 119
being: ancestral, 90–91, 119; emergent, 4, 110, 116; geontological, 84; human, 70, 82; location of, 7; modes of, 7, 117; perseverance of, 140; problem of, 16; ontological, 25, 27, 137–38; substance of, 7; in the wake, 25; in the world, 65, 74
belief, 3–4, 31, 43, 64, 108

Benjamin, Walter, 69
Berardi, Franco, 116–20, 123–24, 154n7
Berger, Thomas, 88–90, 92–93, 100
Berndt, Catherine, 78
Berndt, Ronald, 78–80
Bernstein, Sharon, 114
biocide, 87, 107
biology, 69, 105, 137; evolutionary, 17
biological: concept, 135, 137; condition, 69, 72; entities, 68; families, 69; forms, 52; function, 36, 46; life, 70; natality, 70; necessity, 69–70; process, 69; reduction, 123; sciences, 17; survival, 23; world, 72
bionormativity, 57
biopower, xii, 138; four figures of, xii
bios, 68, 82, 86, 106, 111. See also *zoe*
bios nullius, 68
biosphere, 3, 8, 9, 87, 105, 106, 108, 153n71
biospheric: Gaia, 105; mind, 100, 105–7, 109
Black Atlantic, 10, 65, 73, 82–83, 145n10
Blackburn, Justice Richard, 94, 99
Black Lives Matter, 30, 33–34; protests, xi
Bolsonaro, Jair, 57, 112
Brown, Wendy, 38
Bureau of Indian Affairs, 94
Butler, Judith, 38, 124
Butler, Octavia, 23

Cabral, Amílcar, 51
Callison, William, 57
camouflage, 44, 135–36
Canada, 9, 41, 50, 55, 58, 91, 93–94, 116
capital: accumulation, 43, 48; chemo-, 59; cognitive, 120; and consumption, 59, 87; contradictions of, 19; dialectic of, 117, 120; extractive, 5, 32, 36, 43, 47, 87, 89; geontological underpinnings of, 37, 47; history of, 117, 120; industrial, 36, 126; and labor power, 117–18, 120; pesti-, 57; and production, 59; and property, 99, 136; Silicon Valley, 47; strategies of, 117; teleology of, 117; transport, 89
capitalism: agricultural, 93; and colonialism, xi, 2, 8, 27, 48, 50, 54–55, 73, 77, 99, 108; democracy and, 135; of desire, 116, 118; corporate, 117; digital, 118; ex-

Gaber, Nadia, 27
Gaia, 105
Galston, Arthur, 52, 64, 68, 87
genealogical: approach, 23; society, 135, 137, 141; source, 39
genealogy, 9, 64, 122
geoengineering, 47
geography: abolitionist, 45
geological: engineers, 125; forces, 125; forms, 52, 68; knowledge, 67; noise, 111; processes, 67; systems, 115; world, 85
geontological: endurance, 27; entanglements, 84; frameworks, 110–11; imaginaries, 45, 85; orders of life and nonlife, 67–68, 131; underpinnings, 37, 65
geontologies: liberal, 65; of life and nonlife, 140; Western, 123
geontopower, xii, 1–2, 11, 15–16, 45, 47, 59, 84, 114, 116, 134, 136–38, 141
ghoul health, xiii–xiv, 138
Gilmore, Ruth Wilson, 45
Gilroy, Paul, 77, 83–84, 145n10
Gines, Kathryn, 10, 65, 74–75
Glissant, Édouard, 3, 6–7, 9, 23–27, 33, 132, 145n21
globalization, 67, 69
Global South, 28, 32, 50, 113
Glowczewski, Barbara, 84, 101, 152n42
governance of the prior, 136, 138–41
Grayden, William, 78–79, 82
Greece, pre-Socratic, 64, 72, 76, 104
grievability, 11, 18, 38, 114
Grosfoguel, Ramón, 82
Guadeloupe, 57, 149n43
Guattari, Félix, 3, 5–7, 9, 23–24, 109, 118, 152n42, 154n7

Habermas, Jürgen, 39, 42
habit(s): of existence, 3, 59; of mind, 3, 142
habituation, 104
Haddon, A. C., 101
Haiti, 43
Halpern, Orit, 109
Harari, Yuval Noah, 46
Haraway, Donna, 17, 144n4
Hartman, Saidiya, 21, 90

Hegel, G. W. F., 42, 56; cunning of reason, 39, 136; post-Hegelians, 39
hermeneutic, 16, 75
Hobart, Hi'ilei Julia Kawehipuaakahaopulani, 53
Holocene, 116
Homo faber, 69, 71, 82
hope, 3, 8, 9, 67, 112, 132
horizon, xi, 20, 26, 37, 44, 49–50, 54, 59, 65, 68, 78, 113, 131, 144n19; of anthropogenic climate collapse, 10, 38, 43, 125; frontier and, 38, 42, 47–48; of human extinction, 87; liberal figures of, 47; of liberal justice, 42; of liberal progress, 3, 38, 39–42, 46; lunar, 11, 86; of mutual recognition, 132; toxic, 51. *See also* frontier
Horkheimer, Max, 5
hot zones, 52
Howard, John, 66
Howey, Kirsty, 28
human condition, 65–70, 72–78, 81–87, 103; exclusion zone, 53; more-than-, 84, 90–91, 96, 99, 120, 123, 142; species, 67, 70
humanism, 47, 50, 82–83, 124, 131, 133, 144n16, 154n6. *See also* transhumanism
Hungary, 57
Huntington, Samuel, 128
hydraulic: capitalization, 18; citizenship, 10, 16, 27–28, 32

Iatmul, 101, 108–9
immanence, 6–7
immanent, 4, 86, 105–6, 118, 139–40, 154n79
immortality, 72, 75, 82
imperialism, 73–75, 77, 84
inanimate, 45, 68, 137
India, 81, 121, 133
Indigenous, xi, xiii, 7–11, 19, 24, 28, 32, 34–35, 39, 41, 48, 53–56, 63–67, 74, 78–80, 82, 84, 86, 89–95, 97, 99, 101, 108, 113, 116, 121–26, 134, 138–40, 142
industrial chemistry, 81
Industrial Revolution, 103–4
inert, 45, 68, 84, 111, 128, 137, 138, 141
infidelity, 19

pesticides, 57, 86
Philippines, 49
philosophy, 5–6, 16, 23, 35, 45, 75, 78, 106, 117, 132
planet, 38, 64, 67–69, 108, 112, 117, 125, 132
planetary evolution, 104
plateau: Deleuze and Guattari's concept of, 6, 19, 101, 106
plurality, 69–71, 74, 82–84
pluriversalism, 83
political action, 32, 65, 70–72, 74, 114; concept(s), 8, 11, 114–15; event, 18–19, 54; eventfulness, 19; imaginary, 74, 82; life, 70; plurality, 74; solidarity, 16; theory, 18–19, 39, 74
politics: agonistic, 10, 75; of citation, 109; of inclusion, 113; of orientation, 109; prefigurative, 66
poor, xiii, 5, 19, 20, 46, 54, 82, 113, 132, 142
possessive: disruption, 88; of liberalism and capitalism, 136, 139; logic, 47; white, 90
postcolonial, 56, 83, 101, 126, 139
postcybernetics, 118. *See also* cybernetics
posthuman: feminist, 17; worlds, 140
posthumanism, 16, 83
postpragmatism, 130
potentiality, 34
pragmatism, 4, 5
precariousness, 130
precarity, 11, 114, 124
production, 16, 49, 59, 71–72, 118–19, 123
progress, 40, 137; liberal, 3; spiritual, 50
proletarianization, 116, 154n5
property, 90, 94, 95, 97, 99, 123

quantum entanglements, 16, 24; physics, 17, 24
quasi event, 20, 140

racism, xii–xiii, 3, 28, 32, 74–75, 81, 83, 113, 142
racist attitudes, 74
radioactive, 55, 89
Rancière, Jacques, 19
reason, 6, 15–16, 23, 39, 42, 113, 136, 138–39
recognition: cultural, 8; late liberal, 8–9;

135; liberal, 9; settler law of, 123; universal mutual, 132
reconciliation: national, 55. *See also* Truth and Reconciliation Commission of Canada
recycling, 32, 34
redemption: liberal, 37
referendum (1967), 80, 122
refusal, 8, 9, 11, 27, 31, 55, 92, 108, 118, 122, 132, 137
relation: and Glissant, 6, 23–24, 26–27, 33, 106
repetition: compulsion of late liberalism, 16; of Geist, 130
resistance, 3, 19, 21, 77, 89, 113, 114, 128, 145n10
reterritorialization, 51; rooting, 25
revolution: American, 74; French, 74; Green, 129; Haitian, 43
rhizomatic: amnesia, 25; frontier, 24, 45; movement, 24, 44; power, 23; rooting, 24
rhizome, 23, 24, 25, 43, 101
ritual, 55, 79, 95, 97, 123
Rorty, Richard, 5
Rose, Deborah Bird, 101

sacred site, 97, 121, 122, 123, 124
Salvini, Matteo, 57
Saro-Wiwa, Ken, 34, 54, 120
Saro-Wiwa, Zina, 54
Sartre, Jean-Paul, 76
Scambary, Benedict, 9
schismogenesis, 101, 106; complementary, 101, 106; symmetrical, 101, 102
schizoanalysis, 101, 154n7
Schmitt, Carl, 39
science: and the arts, 6; citizen, 30; of climate, 47; cybernetic, 87; and epistemology, 108; and logic, 6; of symbiogenesis, 23; and techne, 46
science fiction, 56, 115
self-correction, 41
self-determination, 9, 55, 135
self-reflection, 41, 42, 88
semantic: equivalence, 33; hierarchies, 16; meaning, 110; perspectives, 18
semiocapitalism, 118–20